BEST
FOOD
WRITING
2002

Best
FOOD
WRITING
2002

EDITED BY

Holly Hughes

Marlowe & Company
New York

Best Food Writing 2002

Compilation and introductions copyright © 2002 by Holly Hughes
and Avalon Publishing Group Incorporated

Published by
Marlowe & Company
A Division of Avalon Publishing Group Incorporated
161 William Street
16th floor
New York, NY 10038

Book Design: Michael Walters and Susan Canavan

Photography: © Judd Pilossof/Foodpix

Library of Congress Cataloging-in-Publication Data is available.

ISBN: 1-56924-524-X

9 8 7 6 5 4 3 2

Printed in the United States of America

Distributed by Publishers Group West

Contents

Home Cooking

Someone's in the Kitchen

Dining Around

Personal Tastes

Introduction

by Holly Hughes

Which are you—a cook, or an eater?

In one sense, of course, we are all of us eaters; all humans need to eat to support our bodies' daily activities. But if you've picked up this book, then food probably means more to you than mere fuel.

The spectrum from Eater to Cook is wide indeed, all the way from the world-class omnivore who never sets foot in a kitchen to the reed-thin master chef who barely bothers to taste his own cuisine. There are Eaters who cook discontentedly, never quite capturing the taste of their cravings, and accomplished Cooks who lick the stirring spoon so voluptuously they betray their identity as Eaters. There are Cooks more interested in the art of cooking than in consuming what they've cooked, as well as Cooks for whom the pleasure of feeding others is paramount. There are Eaters who rarely eat but constantly think about food (from anorexics to wistful diabetics), and there are Cooks who spend more time reading cookbooks than actually cooking out of them.

And the contributors to this year's *Best Food Writing* collection range everywhere along this vast Cook-Eater spectrum.

Eaters, of course, are the sorts of folks who obsessively recall spectacular meals, who keep a mental file of restaurants to try out, who pay rapt and total attention to what their fellow diners order in a restaurant (even those at neighboring tables). They're like my all-time favorite dining companion, who always insists that everybody in our party orders different dishes, and that we all taste what the others are having—even when he's not being paid to write about it. This year's book includes a strong contingent of Eaters: among them, *Vogue* columnist Jeffrey Steingarten (author of the aptly named *The Man Who Ate Everything*); chowhound.com's Jim Leff, scourer of outer-borough ethnic storefronts; and the peripatetic Calvin Trillin. There's Lydia Itoi, the self-described "hungry traveler" who plans vacations based on what sort of food she'll find at the other end. In these pages you'll sit down to table with veteran dining critics such as Mimi Sheraton, James Villas, and John Mariani, as well as a newer generation of reviewers including Brett Anderson and Robb Walsh, who intently deconstruct whatever they're eating until we can practically taste it ourselves.

Cooks approach things a bit differently. Leafing through a magazine in the dentist's office, they ponder the ethics of whether or not to tear out an intriguing recipe. Walking past a produce stand, they're arrested by the sight of a gloriously ripe pile of plum tomatoes and immediately plot a meal built around them. In a restaurant, they interrogate the waiter on how the chef cooked this marvelous dish, or talk their way into the kitchen to get the details straight from the source. In the ranks of the Cooks in this year's edition are professional chefs such as Patric Kuh, Gabrielle Hamilton, Greg Atkinson, and the mediagenic Anthony Bourdain, all of whom moonlight as gifted writers. (Or are they professional writers who moonlight as chefs? Your call.) It's no surprise, if a trifle discouraging, to discover that a cluster of full-time food writers with killer prose styles—John Kessler, Megan Wetherall, Amanda Hesser—have classical culinary training as well. Then there's that subset of enthusiastic Eaters including Elliot Kaplan, Jonathan Hayes, and Steven Shaw who mine their own misadventures as Cooks to wonderful comic effect.

For a Cook, is a recipe a sacrosanct text or a mere jumping-off point? In a special section called "The Recipe File," we watch food writers such as John Thorne, Regina Schrambling, and Lisa Yokelson putter about in the kitchen, recipes in hand: for some, the joy of cooking lies in jazzlike improvisation, for others the beatific bliss of following instructions. Or is it that a recipe's value lies in how well it recreates a souvenir dish from your past? That's the sort of question to turn over to our band of culinary historians, like Laura Shapiro, Barbara Haber, and Betty Fussell.

We're all somewhere along that great Cook-Eater spectrum. And food writing is vital for us all. It's food writing, in the form of restaurant reviews and travel essays, that tells an Eater what to eat and where to get it; an exceptional piece of prose can by itself deliver ninety percent of the eating experience. And it's food writing, in the form of cookbooks and recipe articles, that gets a Cook going (how faithfully the Cook chooses to follow the recipes is another question altogether). When required, food writing becomes "food pornography," standing in for actual food like sexual pornography takes the place of actual sex.

It's been my pleasure this year to pore through many sources of food writing—daily newspapers, glossy magazines, newsletters, websites, radio shows, culinary, memoirs, and a whole range of cookbooks, from the spiral-bound community recipe collection to a color-laden tome fit for a coffee table—to cull the best from what has been a very rich crop indeed. Several of the writers whose work is included here were represented in one or both of our two previous annual collections; others are fresh to these pages. Some are what I think of as "accidental" food writers: novelists, nonfiction writers, journalists, poets who happen to tackle a food topic. Being professional writers gave them a head start on putting the words together, but it was their avocation as Eaters or Cooks that made their pieces truly sing.

To all of you food writers across the country who sent me your most memorable pieces, even if I couldn't use them all in the end: Keep on submitting, please! I'm already collecting for next year's edition.

I feel compelled to recommend some excellent recent food books that didn't quite lend themselves to this collection: Alice Water's elegant *Chez Panisse Fruit;* Cheryl Alters Jamison and Bill Jamison's definitive cookbook *A Real American Breakfast;* Gray Kunz and Peter Kaminsky's *The Elements of Taste;* Gary Paul Nabhan's fascinating account of living off his local foodways, *Coming Home to Eat;* and two absorbing memoirs, Patricia Volk's *Stuffed* and Sharon Boorstin's *Let Them Eat Cake.* Some books need to be read whole to be appreciated; excerpts from them didn't quite work, but I hugely enjoyed them cover to cover and I think you would too.

The historical events that have clouded this past year had their impact on food writing as well. A score of essays I read referred directly to the events of September 11, and a perceptibly elegaic tone tinged so many other pieces. I'm sure it was no coincidence that much of this year's food writing focused on the dishes our mothers cooked (indeed, on the very look and smells of our ancestral kitchens); dining out became a mode of soul-searching. A year ago, a piece in this anthology ridiculed the notion of "comfort food," but in late 2001 and early 2002, there's no doubt that the comfort of food sustained many of us, Cooks and Eaters alike.

We're still here. We're still eating. We're still cooking. And we're still reading about it. May we continue to do so.

Stocking the Larder

Let Us Now Praise Bacon

by Scott Raab

from *Esquire*

> What other magazine but *Esquire* would devote an entire special food section to bacon, the ultimate guy food? Frequent *Esquire* contributor Scott Raab kicked it off with this effusive essay.

A traveling salesman is driving through the countryside when he sees a pig with a wooden foreleg hobbling near a barn. Curious, the salesman stops and knocks on the farmer's door.

"What's up with that pig?" he asks.

" 'Tain't no regular pig, mister," says the farmer. "One night last year, the house catches fire and that pig come a-runnin', busts right through the door, up the stairs, and drags me and the missus outta bed. Saved both our lives, that pig."

"Amazing," the salesman says. "But that doesn't explain the wooden leg."

"Well, hell, buddy," says the farmer, "you don't eat a pig like that all at once."

THAT'S NOT JUST A CUTE JOKE. It's deep, too; you've got the skewed nature of human gratitude, the marrow-deep bigotry our species inflicts upon the rest of the animal kingdom, and the predatory but sadly displaced hostility the farmer obviously fears to direct at his wife, a feckless harridan who forgot to turn off the oven. Mainly, though, you've got this: Pigs taste great, and nothing else about them truly matters. They may be smart, yes, and they may be peaceable (absent the most severe provocation, they will not assault Homo sapiens), yet nobody gives an oink. Even the pig to whom you owe your life is absolutely delicious, too good not to eat. I've eaten my share, plus maybe some of yours. Hocks, chops, and ribs; chitterlings, knuckles, and jowls; hams, shoulders, and shanks: Oh, I've tasted me some pig. And in a class all by its lonesome, indisputably the most savory part of a pig, bacon.

Goddamn, how I do love the taste of bacon, the yin of flesh and fat, the yang of salt and smoke, the downright sinful joy of it. But it isn't just the taste, buddy—you and I know that. Proust can keep his tea pastries; I smell bacon and swoon. Life's clock stops. I see my father at the stove. I hear him singing "Show Me the Way to Go Home." It's 4:00 a.m., our fishing rods are in the backseat of the Hudson, I'm sitting in my pajamas in the kitchen, rubbing my eyes, smelling bacon—that smell uncurled me from sleep—listening to the hiss and pop of it above my old man's warbling, and when that first still-sizzling strip of swine meets my lips and teeth and tongue, I feel more free of care, more at home in this world, than I ever will feel again. That's bacon to me.

I love bacon so much that I no longer order it at restaurants, because what, really, is the point of eating two, three, or four paltry strips of bacon? That's not even foreplay. But Saturday mornings I have a standing breakfast date with a pal who always gets an order, and he'll usually toss a strip or two my way. That's a double gift: the gift of his friendship, plus the gift of the pig.

That's bacon to me.

I prefer to feast on bacon at home. I get me some soft bread. Soft. Then I panfry up a pound of bacon. Not crisp, chewy. The whole damn slab, yeah, because it cooks down pretty good. Then I lay out a couple of sandwiches. I put a dabbing of pho sauce on 'em—hottish Vietnamese red. Then I press the bread down and let it soak up the grease and sauce. Then I eat. That's not just bacon to me; that's heaven.

Guilt? Health? Look, I've got a few years behind me and plenty of regret for the hurts I've put on this world; a pound or two of bacon down my craw doesn't add up to much remorse. Health-wise, I don't know. I wouldn't recommend a steady diet of bacon to anyone, but that's mainly because it wouldn't taste so special if you ate it all the time.

It broils down to this: We're alive, right now, our hearts beating strong, and we're living in a golden age of pig. Specialty houses are selling boutique bacon, thick-cut bacon, ten-simoleons-per-pound bacon. There is a Bacon of the Month Club, and there are raging debates about the arcana of curing and smoking and what to feed the hog before the slaughter. Hot chefs now crumble bacon into their confit and emulsify its fat to sauce their soft-shell crabs. I'd say bacon is back, but bacon never went anywhere. You name it, bacon survived it: Deuteronomy, Oprah, the tech bubble bursting. Bacon abideth.

So join the party. Celebrate the belly of the beast. And pay no heed when the National Pork Producers Council prints drivel like "Two slices of cooked bacon contain just 73 calories and 6 grams of fat" and "just two slices of bacon can add volumes of flavor, turning an average meal into a taste sensation."

Two slices? You don't eat a pig like that all at once, buddy, but that ain't eating pig at all.

Elegance

by Megan Wetherall
from *Saveur*

One of a series of marvelous *Saveur* essays celebrating various herbs, staff editor Megan Wetherall's homage to tarragon focuses on one oft-used ingredient that is anything but common.

It was one of my first mornings as chef's assistant and translator at the Ritz-Escoffier cooking school, in the basement of the Hôtel Ritz in Paris, and I had descended to the *chambre froide* to bring up the provisions for that day. I stood in the steely chambers of a cavernous fridge, gazing at produce that would have made Cézanne moan with pleasure, and tried to find, among trays of herbs, the four needed for the classic French mixture called fines herbes, used to flavor salads, omelettes, and sauces: tarragon, chervil, parsley, and chives. I was familiar with the last two, of course, and having seen gauzy little sprigs of chervil as garnish on French fish dishes, I picked that out. But I had only the dimmest recollection of what tarragon was supposed to look like. I took a guess, though, plucking a cool, bottle green leaf from a willowy stem and rubbing it between my fingers—and I recognized it at once. A tremulous waft of anise was released—so French, I thought happily, picturing a cloudy tumbler of pastis in a dusty corner of Provence.

In the months that followed, I became imbued with a fresh reverence for all herbs but in particular for tarragon. It seemed to have an aristocratic bearing, an innate elegance, and an enigmatic quality I failed to find in other herbs. And, in the hands of the school's devoted chefs, it flavored perfect mouthfuls of summer: in mayonnaise spooned over waxy new potatoes or in tangy vinaigrette drizzled over warm, sweet baby carrots or succulent, bursting tomatoes. Such flavors could transport me directly from that sprawling air-conditioned underworld of rigorous training and worker-ant activity to a meadow with foxgloves, buzzing bees, and a bottomless picnic hamper.

But tarragon also helped teach me the discipline essential to Escoffier-style cuisine. Without that to temper its use—as we discovered one lunchtime, when a student got carried away stuffing sprigs beneath the skin of a chicken—the herb could turn nasty and unruly, leaving an unpleasant bitterness, even a numbness, in the mouth.

The Arabs, who may have introduced tarragon into Europe from Asia in the Middle Ages (it is the only important herb unknown to the ancient Greeks and Romans), used it medicinally—among other things taking advantage of its numbing qualities by offering sprigs of it to patients to chew, to deaden their tongues before they quaffed some foul-tasting draft or other. The Arabs called the herb *tarkhon,* the sound of which—perhaps combined with tarragon's use in treating snakebites or its coiled, serpentine roots—led Europeans to associate the herb with dragons (the Dutch call it *dragon* and the Italians, *dragoncello,* for instance). Arabs used tarragon in the kitchen as well as the doctor's office, and by the late medieval period the herb had begun to appear in French and Italian cookery. It reached England in the 16th century, and, in 1597, the botanist Gerard mentioned it in his *Herball.* "Tarragon is not to be eaten alone in sallades," he advised, "but joyned with other herbes, as Lettuce, Purslain, and such like, that it may also temper the coldnesse of them. . . ."

True tarragon, *Artemisia dracunculus* 'Sativa', known in culinary circles as French tarragon, is sometimes usurped in the nursery trade by its rank relative, plain old *Artemisia dracunculus,* or Russian tarragon, an ornamental plant too pungent and bitter to be agreeable. You can generally spot this imposter by its lack of anise scent and its narrower, paler leaves. Calling the good stuff French is appropriate, considering that it is in France that tarragon has been immortalized so brilliantly—in things like the great sauce béarnaise, a reduction of white wine and vinegar flavored with tarragon and shallots, then whisked to a velvety smoothness with egg yolks and butter; poulet á l'estragon, chicken sautéed with tarragon and coated with a tarragon-infused demi-glace; and all manner of mustards, vinegars, and pickles (most notably the cornichons that so often accompany pâté on the French table) and as a warm, swelling note in the harmony of the fines herbes quartet.

Despite its large personality, tarragon has a fleeting life once it is picked and is too delicate to survive freezing or drying unscathed, but I plant it in my New York City window box in June so that I'll have it at my fingertips for months. A handful of its leaves is all I need to remind me of France, meadows of foxgloves, and my summer with Escoffier.

Poulet à l'Estragon (Tarragon Chicken)

Serves 4

1 tbsp. extra-virgin olive oil
3 tbsp. butter
1 3 ½-lb. chicken, cut into 8 pieces
Salt and freshly ground black pepper
8 stems fresh tarragon
¼ cup white wine
1 cup rich veal, beef, or chicken stock

1. Heat oil and 2 tbsp. of the butter in a large skillet over medium-high heat. Season chicken with salt and pepper and cook, skin side down, until well browned, about 5 minutes. Turn chicken and add 4 stems of the tarragon. Cover, reduce heat to medium, and cook until juices run clear when pierced with a knife, 10–15 minutes.

2. Meanwhile, blanch 2 stems of the tarragon in a pot of boiling water over high heat for 5 seconds; drain and set aside. Chop leaves (discard stalks) from remaining 2 stems of the tarragon and set aside.

3. Transfer chicken to a platter, discarding tarragon, and keep warm in oven set on lowest temperature. Pour off fat, then return skillet to medium-high heat. Add wine and cook, scraping browned bits stuck to bottom of skillet, for 1 minute. Add stock and reduce by half, about 5 minutes. Strain sauce into a small bowl, then return sauce to skillet over medium heat. Stir in remaining 1 tbsp. butter and reserved chopped tarragon.

4. Add chicken and any accumulated juices to skillet and baste with sauce. Serve garnished with blanched tarragon.

Tomato Lust

by Gerri Hirshey
from *Food & Wine*

Author of *We Gotta Get Out of This Place: The True, Tough Story of Women in Rock*, Gerri Hirshey here unleashes her hyperbolic prose style on a garden-variety food obsession.

The tomato vines—seven-footers that suckled round Italian Romas and thick clusters of yellow and red pear tomatoes—are a twisted black heap at the back of our field. The season's last tomato was sliced, laid gently on a slice of semolina bread, dotted with black olive tapenade and then—gone!

Already I am pining. Get clinical and call it a fruit-specific eating disorder; go highbrow and call it an epicurean quest. What my obsession boils down to is Tomato Lust—in my case, long-standing and incurable. TL's closest parallel is love itself. As anyone who adores real in-season tomatoes can tell you, unspeakable effort goes into the seeking out, the courtship of sources, the obsessive hunt for perfection. But the rewards are sweet. The first touch of flesh to lips brings bliss. Joy, wantonness and overindulgence may follow. (I have been known to get what my family called "tomato rash" between my fingers.) And finally, as the first gassed-pink winter strumpets commandeer the market shelves, desolation—the end of the affair.

The romance analogy is nearly as old as the fruit itself: The tomato has long been called "the love apple" and "the amorous apple." We have had a tempestuous relationship with it since the 1500s, when the Spanish conquistadors first brought this divine food back to Europe from Mexico. As members of the occasionally deadly nightshade family, tomatoes also suffered periodic slur campaigns, with some seventeenth-century herbalists declaring them corrupt, non-nourishing and poisonous—like certain forms of love.

I can see how tomatoes might have gotten what girl groups used to call "a bad repu-*tay*-shun." Tomato Lust has sometimes driven me to extreme behavior. A longtime apartment dweller without even a windowsill for growing, I decided that I had to have my own tomatoes at my island beach house. Undeterred by the swampy, sandy strips of yard surrounding the place, I piled a load of lumber onto a freight ferry and hammered together odd but workable planters for the deck. Cockeyed lath trellises tied with string contained vine sprawl. When deer discovered the joys of patio dining, I installed pricey gates; anyone calculating the cost per tomato would certify me as crazy indeed. I carried on this way for a decade. The harvests were bountiful, and some of the rewards were unexpected. It was during one season's fall tomatothon, when the house was being closed and the last ferry beckoned, that my future husband and I first stumbled toward each other amid the intoxicating aromas from two steaming pots of sauce—and a pitcher of throbbingly fresh Bloody Marys.

From such Tomato Lust children eventually resulted. We sold the beach house, and I girded myself for the ultimate combat. Manhattanites at my West Side farmers' market lined up feistily for just-picked tomatoes much the way Muscovites were kneecapping one another for butter. Startled farmers, pinned behind their ruby-red bunkers, pleaded for calm. Then they got wise and jacked up the prices: $2, $3, $4 a pound. They knew we had to have it. The market was in a schoolyard once known for serious drug dealing, a history not lost on me as I struggled from the stand with my booty one day and leaned against the chain-link fence for a quick hit. As I sucked rapturously on an heirloom Brandywine, the farmer's teenage daughter—a sylph in a Metallica T-shirt—elbowed her dad. He walked over and dumped a basket of glistening yellow pear tomatoes into my bag. "There," he said, "just so you make it home with some." I thanked him as best I could with seeds on my chin.

I caught TL early on from my father, a beefsteak devotee who fussed, sprayed and staked a patch in our small suburban yard. It consumed him almost year-round. In winter he collected plastic coffee-creamer containers at the diner and fashioned them into snug collars to shield seedlings from murderous cutworms. Come spring, he'd head to a place a few towns away he called the Polish flower farm, a misbegotten set of greenhouses surrounded by propane tanks and old sinks. There, in spirited Polish, he'd exchange growing tips and creative insults with the broad-cheeked woman who oversaw the Early Girls, the Better Boys, the utilitarian Romas. He always planted them on or about Mother's Day. Mom got the Whitman Sampler; the seedlings got fish emulsion.

Sixty to eighty days later, this was his just dessert: Into a soup bowl, cut your best tomato. Add a pinch of salt, a grinding of pepper, slivered basil and a scant teaspoon of transparent-sliced red onion. Drizzle with olive oil; add a splash of red-wine vinegar. Let the mixture steep through the rest of the meal. Savor the tomatoes last, then scoop up their basil-scented elixir with a soupspoon. Better still, sop it up with bread. I can still see my dad under the kitchen light, eyes closed, bowl empty. "Oh yeah," he'd breathe, "this year is *good*."

Sometimes it was not. Perfect love gone bad—holes torn by the ugly maws of slugs and hornworms, too much rain, heartbreaking late-season blight—would find my dad inconsolable after that first taste. "Too watery. Aw, jeez . . . mealy." These disappointments were slid contemptuously into hamburger buns, mashed into sauce. Dad ranted; he grieved. He blamed himself.

A good harvest requires artful presentation. One of the most luscious showcases is a recipe attributed to a most passionate pair of hobo voluptuaries. Salvador and Gala Dalí dressed for dinner as though it were the apocalypse, and they cooked with no less abandon, publishing their own richly illustrated surrealist cookbook, *Les Dîners de Gala.* As adapted by Deborah Madison in her classic *Greens Cookbook,* Dalí's Provençal gratin—a gorgeous composition of potatoes, red onions, olives, herbs and tomatoes—has reduced the wittiest dinner companion to whimpering.

How mad is my love? I now cosset homegrowns on a rocky Connecticut hillside. And I confess I grew barking mad during the '96-to-'98 Chipmunk Wars, when those rats with racing stripes gnawed my darlings at the first blush of pink. Taking a tip from my husband's grandma, a no-nonsense woman plagued with raccoons in her corn patch, I strapped a plastic-wrapped transistor radio to a tomato stake and set the dial to a megawatt rap station. Coolio and Dr. Dre shook up the cukes, but the varmints chomped on. Frantic, I found myself cruising the Predator Urine aisle at Agway. Forking over $14 for some repellent eau de coyote, I finally admitted to myself: Honey, you've wandered out where the buses don't run.

The madness continues undiminished. Our neighbors averted their eyes this past summer at the undignified sight of me hopping into the garden using a walker with a colander wired to the front. No broken leg was going to make me neglect the vines. My husband twitched visibly as I described the combination composter/tomato trellis I want to build this spring. But knowing full well the inexorable tug of Tomato Lust, he bought me the most romantic Christmas gifts he could think of: a book on garden pests and a big celadon bowl just perfect for . . . you know.

Cheeses for All Seasons

by Patricia Michelson
from *The Cheese Room*

Presiding over the much-admired La fromagerie cheese shop in north London, Michelson has ridden (and no doubt helped to fuel) cheese's remarkable recent surge in popularity. Her writing is graceful, authoritative—and infectiously enthusiastic.

THE FIRST TASTE OF AUTUMN

The first true taste of autumn for me comes when the cheese table in my shop displays Vacherin Mont d'Or. Not for me the bland taste of early September cheeses: I prefer to wait until the end of October—or the weekend when we turn back the clocks in Britain—until the most seductive and sensual of cheeses is available.

To set the scene, understand the cheese . . . The milk is rich and buttery, from the Montbéliarde cattle—hardy creatures used to roaming mountain pastures in the Haut Doubs region of France. In summer they move to high-mountain grazing to enjoy the lush herb- and flower-strewn pastures and fresh clean mountain air. Next time you go skiing look out for the weathered faces of the lift operators: they are, more often than not, the herdsmen who look after the cattle in summer; in the winter months they make money 'herding' ski-mad tourists on to the lifts.

At the end of August the cattle are led down to the lower valleys, which are still warm and lush from the summer. They are in good humour, relaxed and producing an abundance of fine rich milk, which is transformed into voluptuous thick curds and placed in wooden moulds to settle. Then a strip of bark encircles each cheese to keep it intact and impart to it a sappy alpine flavour. When the cheeses arrive at the shop we enhance the flavour by lightly washing the crust with a Jura or an Arbois white wine, mixed with boiled and cooled water, then leaving the cheeses to ripen in our cool cellars with high humidity. One of the reasons I called my business La Fromagerie was because I wanted to run it on the lines of the French cheese shops where *affinage* is an integral part of the service. We treat British, Italian, Irish, Spanish and Portuguese cheeses with the same care and attention to bring out their unique flavours. Sometimes we go a little too far—after all, we are dealing with a natural, living product—and the tastes go a bit wild but no matter: they are still interesting, if somewhat explosive, and we turn what many would consider simple yellow stuff into a full-flavoured complex confection.

The peachy crust on top of the Vacherin has a downy fluff, making it look like the folds of a satin peignoir, and the taste is a soft, silky, melting sensation. The velvet texture and sappy earthy taste is an experience to be shared, and keeps my spirits up during the cold dark months of winter.

With the smaller individually boxed cheeses, you can make a fondue.

WINTER CHEESES—WHEN BEAUFORT MET PATRICIA

I came to skiing rather late, but after the initial shock of constantly losing my balance and coming down the mountain on my backside rather than upright, I grew to love it. Especially when I was following ski instructors with their easy, cheeky style of shimmying down the runs. You use every muscle in your body and a tremendous amount of energy so by the end of the day you're really hungry. It was on a particular late afternoon after a strenuous pounding of the slopes that I was dragging myself through the village of Méribel back to the chalet and I was starving. I dropped into the local cheese shop and bought a small piece of Beaufort, the local cheese, to nibble on my way. The taste was so satisfying that I expect it was then I decided my life had to change: I wanted *everyone* to be able to enjoy this cheese. So, when it comes to cold winter days I think of Beaufort, with its rich, savoury fruitiness and grainy chewy texture. Just a small piece fills you up and makes you feel happy. I have fond memories of finding my original cheesemaker, Monsieur Jules Roux-Daigue, at the Moutiers Farmers' Market and lugging my first 35-kilo cheese home in the back of the car, both daughters wedged beside it and complaining about its pong. What struck me about Monsieur Roux-Daigue's cheeses was that they tasted like new season's hazelnuts—milky and nutty—with a sweet floral tang. He explained that his farm in Aiguebelle was in a sheltered part of the valley and the Tarentaise cows had quite an easy journey up to the *alpage*, high herb farm- and flower-strewn pastures, in the summer, so they were contented, well fed and not put under undue stress. His cheeses, all hand-made from scratch, developed their own identity, some with small cracks appearing in the cheese where the salt had dipersed, and some with maybe one or two tiny holes that gave character and charm to the finished cheese. Sadly he is no longer with us, but his reputation lingers on with each cheese I open just before Christmas—we save the special two-year forms for the end of the year.

In cold weather we need fuel food to keep us going, but it doesn't have to be boring. A plate of cheese at this time of the year serves as a restorative, and think of all the vitamins and proteins in it that ensure your body keeps healthy and strong.

Whether you use cheese in toasted snacks, or layered with potatoes and ham, or melted into fondue, it is essentially a complete food, a primary source of nourishment. Try to keep it separate from other foods: make cheese the main rather than the auxiliary part of what you are eating.

When children come home from school, have ready cubes of mild or medium-strong cheese with slices of apple for instant hunger relief. At breakfast, instead of a fry-up, thinly slice Mimolette Vieux, an orange-coloured hard cheese from Flanders with a taste not dissimilar to Gouda, and pile it on toasted buttered sourdough bread. A mild Gouda-type cheese is nourishing first thing in the morning or as an early lunch. If you look at one of Monet's paintings, *The Luncheon* (1868), you will see a table set for his meal—which was always timed for 11:30 a.m.—with a plate of sliced cheese, cold meats and soft-boiled eggs in the English style: he was very fond of English cheeses and especially the ritual of breakfast.

CHEESES FOR SPRING

First we have to decide when spring actually starts. Is it the beginning, middle or end of March? For me it's when the Vacherin Mont d'Or season finishes, towards the end of the month. By then I'm ready for refreshing goat's cheeses: sharp and tangy from the newly sprouted fresh grass and young stinging nettles topped with their pretty mauve flowers—a natural coagulant for the milk—that the animals are chewing. I have a theory about the character of milk: cows chew all day long, slowly digesting their food and producing a rich and buttery-textured milk. Sheep, with their small scissor-shaped teeth, neatly graze the top of the fleshy grass, leaving a wedge to shoot up new blades quickly; the animals are nervous but easily herded together, prefer comfort and routine, and their translucent milk tastes sweet and floral. Goats devour the grass right down to soil level; they are highly strung with a prickly temperament, searching out food high and low, and using up a lot of energy in the process. Their milk tastes sharp and sometimes aggressive, especially if they have been allowed to roam in hilly, rocky terrain. If a dairy keeps its goats indoors under controlled conditions, the milk tastes uniform and rather bland.

A tray of fresh goat's cheeses in all their different shapes and sizes—some with plain white bloomy moulds, some with a charcoal-ash coat, some covered with chestnut leaves—is a truly beautiful sight to behold. And the taste is a welcome respite from the heavier winter cheeses: it is a cheerful, lively herald of, hopefully, sunnier days and warm, balmy evenings. Tiny spring artichokes can be deep-fried in a light oil until golden and crisp, then served piping hot with a cold fresh moist goat's cheese crumbled over the top.

CHEESES FOR SUMMER

Can we ever rely on summer weather in England? Probably not . . . but there again I think it would be pretty boring if every day we could say, 'Well, it's another fabulous morning, isn't it?' Handsome is as handsome does, and I prefer my days to be unpredictable. Whether I'm picnicking with the warm breeze fluttering my hair, or cowering under a tree as the rain pelts down, as long as my basket of favourite food is safe, I'm happy.

Now you may think that cheeses for summer would be an oozing Brie, or a salad with mozzarella and tomatoes, but that is not always the case. In England we can enjoy the simple pleasure of a Guernsey milk cheese called Waterloo, with a rich buttery density and nutty taste, from cheesemakers Andy and Ann Wigmore, based in Riseley, Berkshire. I mature their cheeses for a few weeks until the thin white mould on the rind has wrinkled a little and turned a dusty biscuit grey. As you cut through the crust the interior is soft and melting, the centre slightly crumbly. The taste is rounded, nutty and interesting, and most agreeable with a tray of squeaky fresh baby carrots, celery, radishes and crisp home-baked Scottish oatcakes. The Salers Cantal cheese from the

Auvergne is in complete contrast: like a Cheddar but with more fruit and nut flavours and, as it warms in the mouth, a definite tingle on the tongue. Served with a slightly chilled Beaujolais and crusty bread it's a great way to end the day and watch the sun set.

Cheese really comes into its own at this time of year, and it's so easy to prepare a feast based around it with bread, salad, fruit and wine or cider. Before you feel confident enough to mix and match, stick to a theme of, say, seven French, Italian or English varieties, with light to medium to strong flavours. When you are ready to experiment, start with an Explorateur, which is a rich, triple-cream cheese, a creamy white mould rind, such as Brie de Meaux or Brie de Melun, or Coulommiers, a supple-textured cheese, not too aged, in the style of St Nectaire, with its farmyard rustic aroma but smooth chewy texture. Include a goat's milk cheese with a coat of ash that somehow evens out the acidity, then turn your attention to something like a young, rich, creamy Gorgonzola *dolce cremificato,* and end with a mellow hard sheep's milk cheese, such as Berkswell from Coventry in the West Midlands, and a fresh, crumbly farmhouse Lancashire or Wensleydale, tasting of newly cut sweetly savoury meadow grass. Have a big basket of assorted bread, a dish of sea-salt crystals to sprinkle over the cheese, a salad dressed with walnut oil and walnut vinegar (or lemon juice), olives, baby gherkins and roasted shallots in balsamic vinaigrette.

To go with the very rich triple-cream cheeses, have ready a bowl of cherries and strawberries and use the fruit to scoop up the cheese. Or have a selection of fresh goat's cheeses, especially those from Provence, such as Banon, Pebre d'Ase and Sariette, to serve with hot, peppery salad leaves dressed with walnut or hazelnut oil. Whether you are putting together a selection for two or two hundred, this is a trouble-free, easy way of entertaining.

Light, salty cheeses, such as a real Greek feta made with goat's and sheep's milk, are refreshing in hot weather. Served cubed and tossed with roughly torn crunchy lettuce and sorrel leaves, chopped cucumber, stoned Kalamata olives, snipped chives and chervil, then dressed with a fruity olive oil and lemon juice, it is a treat to savour with its bright, perky, effervescent tastes. (Sorrel is really easy to grow, either in a pot or among the roses in your flower-bed. Prized for its sharp lemon tangy leaves, it works a treat with fresh creamy cheeses or chopped into *fromage frais* as a dip.)

At this time of year, experiment with cheeses you would normally eat matured: it opens up a whole new taste experience. Take a plump ripe fig or plum, split it (and stone a plum) then crumble over it the freshest possible Richard III Wensleydale—difficult to get, I know, but tell your cheesemonger that it is sensational eaten like this: the sweetness of the fruit and the salty *crème fraiche* tang of the cheese is memorable.

War Fare

by Patricia Sharpe
from *Texas Monthly*

With the news full of military doings in Afghanistan in late 2001, Patricia Sharpe reacted as you might expect a food editor to do—by wondering what the troops would be eating overseas.

T he Editor of this magazine is trying to kill me.

Oh, I know what you're thinking: "Come on, that can't be right. Why, Evan Smith seems so nice, a family man and all. Whatever could make you think he has it in for you?"

But I swear it's true. How else am I to interpret his twisted response to the story idea I suggested a few weeks ago, not long after I saw a mention in the newspaper that a Texas business—the Wornick Company, of McAllen—is one of three companies in the country that assemble and package portable meals for soldiers in places like Afghanistan?

"I've read that story before," Evan said.

"You've read about the *humanitarian* food," I told him, a bit testily. "The military meals are different. They aren't just made for the armed services. Ordinary people can get them at military-surplus stores and over the Internet. Our readers could get them to take on camping trips; they could stock them in their basement survival bunkers; they could . . ."

Suddenly a wicked little smile began to play about Evan's lips. "Okay, Pat," he said. "You can do this story, but I want you to eat nothing but MRE's for forty-eight hours. Review them like you would a restaurant and write them up." And that is how I found myself sitting on the floor of a military-surplus store in front of a bin of "meals ready to eat" (MRE's, as they're generally called), trying to decide whether I wanted to shuffle off this mortal coil with menu number 2 (boneless pork chop) or menu number 17 (beef teriyaki).

Meal 1, dinner. I have snipped open the 8- by 12.5-inch, tan, heavy-duty plastic pouch containing menu number 9 and arranged the contents on my kitchen counter: a packet of beef stew (moist, not freeze-dried); two large crackers (equal to eight saltines); jalapeño-cheese spread; an airline-size packet of dry-roasted salted peanuts; presweetened, lemon-flavored instant-tea mix; powdered cocoa mix; a tiny bottle of Tabasco sauce; a package of M&M's; salt; an MRE heater pouch (more about this later); a tan plastic spoon (but no fork or knife); two pieces of green Chiclet-type gum; a book of matches; a moist towelette; and a packet of toilet paper (22 sheets).

I heat up the beef stew, which looks like less-chunky Dinty Moore and—guess what—tastes like it too. Actually it's not bad but awfully bland. What this baby needs is Tabasco. Ah, yes— perfect. Along with crumbled crackers, that makes it absolutely, uh, inoffensive. For a side dish, I squeeze some of the cheese spread, which is practically identical to Cheez Whiz, onto the bland, nearly salt-free cracker. I don't feel like having two beverages, so I just mix up the cocoa with hot water, and it's great. The peanuts and M&M's are the reward for cleaning my plate. One meal down, six to go.

Personally, I would have preferred more stew and fewer side dishes, but I'm not the target audience. "These meals are geared for the nineteen-year-old soldier running around all day carrying an eighty-pound pack and a rifle," says Jim Lecollier, a contracting officer with the Defense Supply Center, in Philadelphia, part of the Department of Defense. "They're nutritionally balanced and have about 1,300 calories per meal." The moist components of the meal, like the stew, are precooked; sealed in a pouch—sort of a flat bag—made of bonded layers of plastic, nylon, and aluminum foil; and heat-sterilized the same way canned goods are. This explains why most of the MRE entrées I tried tasted canned. Stored at 70 degrees, they can last for more than eight years (frightening thought), although the DOD keeps them for only three.

Meal 2, breakfast. The military does not offer breakfast-type MRE's. Soldiers need protein and a lot of calories three times a day, but the thought of something like pork chow mein at seven in the morning is making me bilious. Luckily, my lunch package contains two Nature's Valley peanut-butter granola bars, crumbly and good. Yesterday's instant-tea mix is great hot; it doesn't even taste like instant. Somehow I feel guilty for enjoying this meager repast; maybe I should put on camouflage to eat this and dig a fox-hole in the back yard.

Even though breakfast isn't offered, there is variety in the selection of regular entrées—24 choices, including 4 vegetarian ones. For a reality check, the Department of Defense conducts focus groups and taste tests. "We'll take some new entrées to, say, a base in Texas and ask the troops what they like," says Frank Johnson, a spokesman for the Defense Supply Center. Each year, the two least-popular meals are dropped and two new ones are added.

Meal 3, lunch. Bunch of wimps, that's what they are. Nobody in the *Texas Monthly* editorial department will so much as take a bite of my MRE. "Oh, no, that's fine," they say. "Er, I think I hear my mother calling." Are they clairvoyant? The cheese tortellini with tomato sauce is a dead ringer for something out of a Chef Boyardee can. Happily, a fresh bottle of Tabasco is at hand. The sauce manufacturer, the McElhinny Company of Louisiana, should get a medal of honor from the DOD. As for the rest, the apple-sauce is fine, the peanut butter isn't salty enough. By the way, the toilet paper comes in handy for blowing your nose when it's running like a faucet after eating a meal drenched in Tabasco.

As I've opened each new pouch over the past day and a half, I've been struck by how reassured I feel when I pull out a brand-name product and how dubious I feel about the generic foods. Lecollier explains that the military makes a point of including major labels: "If you were a soldier out in the middle of nowhere, wouldn't it make you feel better to open up a package and find something that reminded you of home?"

Meal 4, dinner. I've conned my friend Robert into having supper with me. We'll see whether he's still speaking to me after tonight. We are splurging and having the "grilled reconstituted chopped and formed" beefsteak and the cooked ham slice with "natural juices" and "smoke flavoring." Robert decides that they're actually edible sponges. I think they're more like a better class of Spam. The beef comes, oddly, with canned-tasting Mexican rice. The side dish for the ham is innocuous noodles in butter-flavored sauce. We split his hot cocoa and my lemon pound cake. He skips his two Tootsie Rolls. The cake isn't homemade quality, but relatively speaking, it's quite good. For once, I'm not tempted to add Tabasco.

The Wornick Company, the private business that makes and packages meal components under contract with the Department of Defense, has been turning out MRE's for about twenty years (it also make microwaveable entrées for 7-Eleven). At its branches in McAllen and Cincinnati, Wornick produced approximately 780,000 cases of MRE's—twelve meals to a case—for the military last year, a fourth of the 3.1 million cases made nationwide. (The rest are made by companies in Indiana and South Carolina.) The DOD expects to buy 3.1 million cases of MRE's again this year.

Meal 5, breakfast. Oh, groan. I guess it's presweetened tea and a granola bar again. I would kill for a latte.

Meal 6, lunch. Today is the day I attempt to heat my meal—chicken and cavatelli (shell pasta)—with the chemical heater included in every pack. Since I nearly failed high school chemistry, the prospect of accidentally setting the office on fire is filling me with angst. After reading the instructions five times, I pour water into the special heater pouch, slip in the chicken with cavatelli (still in its package), fold the top over and wait while—miracle of miracles—the promised water-activated chemical reaction occurs (don't ask me to explain it). The now-warm chicken patty looks like pressed meat but tastes okay. And the pasta with its tomatolike sauce is considerably better than yesterday's cheese tortellini; only half a tiny bottle of Tabasco is required to make it palatable. Today's drink is a cherry Kool-Aid-type beverage (a little weird with the tomato sauce, but my standards are eroding fast). Dessert is more pound cake, topped with good blackberry jam squeezed from a plastic pouch. My après-dinner beverage is Taster's Choice instant coffee. Skittles fruit-flavored candies stand in for chocolate truffles.

Meal 7, dinner. Oh happy day! *The West Wing* is on, and I'm having my last MRE, chili and macaroni, in front of the TV. The chili—which contains soy protein as well as ground meat—is not as bad as the ham slice but not as good as the beef stew (did I actually say the beef stew was good?). I've started measuring quality in TS units—the amount of the Tabasco sauce that's required to render a meal pleasantly palatable. The chili mac gets a 1—a whole bottle. Dessert is—please, not pound cake again. I know there are other desserts out there—fudge brownies and fig bars, to name two—but I didn't happen to get them.

What's my final take on surviving for 48 hours on MRE's? I'm still alive (take that, Evan Smith). I didn't get indigestion. I gained half a pound. And I realized how much I take for granted certain things that are missing from these hardy combat-food packets, like a variety of vegetables and fruits. I also developed a profound appreciation for what our soldiers in the field endure, culinarily speaking. To them I raise a glass of presweetened, lemon-flavored instant tea and say "God Bless America."

Hidden Charms

by Patric Kuh

from *Gourmet*

A true double-threat—working chef and gifted writer—Patric Kuh, author of the culinary history *The Last Days of Haute Cuisine*, knows his way around a kitchen. Working as a private chef for a wealthy couple in San Francisco gave him a fresh perspective on how to cook for others.

The engraved invitations had gone out and been eagerly accepted. Tonight was the dinner party. Outside, the parking valets were lined up on a stretch of outer Broadway, in the Pacific Heights neighborhood of San Francisco. Inside, the seating charts were on the marble table by the front door. Maria, the maid, used a wick inside a long brass holder to light the beeswax candles of the antique chandeliers. Trevor, the butler, gave the staff last-minute instructions. I was the cook for one of the grandest families in the city, and I stood at the kitchen window in what would be my last moment of calm for many hours. In the evening light, the Golden Gate Bridge, with a lick of fog passing under it, was of a beauty that I would not have imagined before I saw it. Another thing I would not have imagined was that I would get myself talked into making, for more than 50 guests, a first course of fried baby artichokes.

We'd come a long way since my first day on the job, four weeks previously. I'd been accompanying Trevor as he took Wallis, the pug, on her morning walk when—with undeniable pleasure and with a wave of his hand that encompassed all the surrounding mansions—he said, "These people aren't millionaires, they're billionaires." Perhaps they were. They'd certainly had household staffs for so long that the graciousness they showed us never would have been bestowed on the latest parvenu attempting to scale the Parnassian heights of their social standing. Maria was invariably complimented on her needlework. There was always a moment to talk with Trevor about dear old England. I was punctiliously thanked for each one of my meals. But I soon learned to differentiate between various levels of gratitude. My cooking was pleasing, but it wasn't wowing.

I knew I had to start doing the shopping. In that house, everything just materialized: the ironed sheets, shirts, and tablecloths from the Peninou French Laundry & Cleaners, on Sacramento Street. The orchids from the gardeners' greenhouses. The groceries were no different, and I had allowed myself to be seduced by the ease of picking up the phone and having a deliveryman ring the doorbell a few hours later. I had been cooking as if from a script. I needed to stop planning and start reacting, to feel a vegetable in my hand and let a recipe come to me. On my next day off, I headed to Monterey Market, in Berkeley, and wandered the produce aisles. Soon I was eyeing the baby artichokes. I didn't so much visualize the end result as remember from somewhere the shade that an artichoke leaf turns when fried—deep brown at the tip, a lighter shade at the base. I knew I wanted to fry them. Coming back on the BART train, I had ten pounds of them in a paper bag on my lap. The next night, my employers were hosting a bridge supper, and I'd serve them as finger food between rubbers.

I did as little to those artichokes as possible. I tore off the hard outer leaves, shortened the stems and peeled them with a paring knife, then cut the heads in half and cleaned out the fur. When Trevor signaled that the players would soon be ready for something to nibble on, I dropped the artichokes in oil I'd heated in a skillet and fried them. After draining, I squeezed a lemon over them, added a pinch of kosher salt, and crowned them with fried whole parsley sprigs. The results were spectacular. I was summoned. What was this divine dish? "A fritto that isn't very misto," I mumbled. Oh, divine, just like the one several of them had shared on that driving tour of Italy in 1954, when half the roads weren't even paved. Indeed, and wasn't that the same trip . . . Backing out of the room, I realized that my employers considered a dish noteworthy if it contributed to the conversation. The next morning I was informed that the artichokes simply had to be the first course for the upcoming dinner party.

That day, I thought I was ready. I'd ordered sufficient artichokes from Monterey Market and had them peeled and put in lemony baths. I'd bought eight woks from one of the hardware stores on Grant Avenue in Chinatown. With all the burners of the Wolf range blasting and sufficient paper towels for draining, I felt I might just pull it off.

The thing about socialites is that one never knows when a gaffe will be forgiven. The thing about billionaires is that one never knows when someone's private plane will touch down. I'll never know the reason, but three hours before the meal was to start I was told that an additional 14 guests were coming. Lengthening the tables wasn't a problem—there were still many, many polished mahogany leaves left to add before that could happen. A shortage of crystal or silver? Hardly. There were basement rooms in which shelves sagged with the stuff. The problem was in the kitchen. I could slice the meat thin and plate less garnish for the main course, but I couldn't stretch the artichokes. And with the clock ticking, I wasn't about to go looking for more.

With the same daring resolve that his ancestors had shown when they headed west in Conestoga wagons, my employer announced that he himself would go to Berkeley. A map was drawn. "Gilman exit," I said. "Gilman exit," he repeated, managing to give it an exotic frisson. And off he went—a man who lunched daily at "the P.U." (the ultraselect Pacific Union Club, on Nob Hill), a man in a Huntsman tweed jacket, a man at the wheel of a Bentley convertible speeding across the Bay Bridge in search of baby artichokes. I still have that image seared into my brain. And it flashes before me whenever I hear that California is no longer a place of endless self-discovery.

He was back in time to drop the artichokes on the kitchen counter and run upstairs to change into his dinner clothes. Maria and I prepped them while Wallis, sensing the tension that a large party creates in a house, barked incessantly. When the guests were finally seated, Trevor gave me the go-ahead. Then there was a blur of action as the fritto not-very-misto was fried, drained, salted, sprinkled with lemon juice, topped with fried parsley, and sent out—surely a first—on Limoges plates. I peered out from the kitchen to look at my employer. On either side of him were ladies in evening dress. "Wherever did you get these fantastic arti-chokes?" one enthused. "In Berkeley," he answered. "I went to get them myself." And under the table his monogrammed Lobb slip-pers did a little dance of delight because he knew that, in his circle, this could never be topped.

The Recipe File

The Reviewer and the Recipe

by John Thorne
from *Simple Cooking* newsletter

Up-and-coming food writers often name John Thorne as their model, both for his engaging writing style and his unpretentious approach. These are the mellow musings of an Outlaw Cook who doesn't take himself (or gastronomy) overly seriously.

No one has ever stepped twice into the same river. But did anyone ever step twice into the same cookbook?
—with apologies to Marina Tsvetaeva

Sometime in early 1997 I got an e-mail from Russ Parsons, food editor of the *Los Angeles Times*, inviting me to participate with him in two panel discussions at a food and wine exposition being organized by Giuliano Bugialli that summer in Stowe, Vermont. I had never done this sort of thing before and initially had no intention of doing it then. But Russ was persuasive, there were going to be a lot of food people attending whom I had never met, and I was brought up to believe that you ought to try something once before ruling it out of your life.

In other words, I have no excuse whatsoever for saying yes. But I did, and a few months later I was unpacking my bags in the complimentary room provided me at a Swiss-chalet-like inn. I was already feeling that I might have made a big mistake—and not only because I had been given a tiny room directly across from the checkout desk (i.e., noisy and not very private), with no air conditioning (i.e., claustral and hot) and a single high casement window that opened onto the rubbish bins under the outside stairs (did I say "noisy, not very private, claustral, and hot"?).

No, it was because tomorrow and the day after I would be appearing in front of an audience of other food professionals (the paying participants, mostly physicians, would understandably be heading for the wine- and food-tasting events) in two discussions—one on the state of home cooking and the other on the art of cookbook reviewing—two subjects about which my opinions were, at best, very mixed.

Even though cooking is an integral part of my life, I've never felt that it ought to be treated as a defining characteristic of a happy home. In fact, I won't be in the least surprised if in the next decade the rising prices of gas and electricity and the ever-appreciating value of free time will see preparing the family meal go the same way as sewing its clothing or hammering together its furniture. Certainly, there's nothing creepier than those obviously unused showcase kitchens in upscale houses that have all the marble—and all the warmth—of a mausoleum.

As to the art of cookbook reviewing, I already knew the score. Russ and I had had a preliminary meeting to discuss topics that this panel might cover. The first thing he said to me was that in his view, before anything else, the most important part of cookbook reviewing was *testing the recipes*. He probably thought that this was a point on which he and I would certainly agree, thus establishing a collegial bond from the very beginning. Sure, we might quarrel about the value of this or that cookbook, but certainly not about the ethical foundation from which we issued our judgments.

A moment of awkward silence. Then: "Russ," I said. "I *never* test recipes." Furthermore, although I didn't say this, the very idea fills me with something close to revulsion. There are countless cookbooks from which I have never made a single dish but for which

I have the highest regard and which I would recommend unreservedly to anyone. In fact, I would be hard put, if asked, to point to almost *any* cookbook—apart from Fannie Farmer—whose recipes I have faithfully followed. They exist, but they're the exception that proves the rule.

It's hard for a conversation to recover once it has begun by running full tilt into a stone wall. Even so, the panel discussion, as I remember it, was a success. Much of it had to do with the difficulties of getting good but quiet cookbooks noticed in a world where trendiness and celebrity rules. However, when the panel opened up its discussion to the audience, the first person to stand up was Mimi Sheraton, author of several commendable cookbooks and, of course, the former *New York Times* restaurant reviewer, as formidable now as she was when restaurateurs trembled at the mention of her name. "I just want to say," she said, "that I think it is *essential* for a reviewer to test at least *six* or *seven* recipes if they're going to give an honest evaluation of a cookbook."

Beside me, I felt Russ quiver slightly, like a terrier who knows a rat is about to get a good shaking by the neck. He cast a glance in my direction but, bless him, spoke not a word, letting me—and to this day I feel no embarrassment about this (apart from having gotten myself into the situation in the first place)—just sit there with my mouth shut. No one but Russ even noticed, because no one in the tent expected any disagreement. Sage nods all around, and the discussion continued. Like a Unitarian caught up in a gathering of Evangelicals, I felt argument was simply beside the point. They were coming from one place, and I from another, a universe away.

Of course, it's not in the least surprising to me that people believe that recipes ought to work and that if they don't something is wrong with them. As a writer of recipes myself, I lay out their workings as clearly and completely as Matt can make me. (She's the one with the logical mind and the eye for the fine detail.) And it pleases us both very much when someone writes to tell us that one of our recipes has become a favorite of their own. But this is the decent, caring, parental side of my personality, not the part of me that cooks.

I have written before—most specifically when recounting my wood-fired bread oven adventures—that I do not take instruction gladly. Push a book in my hand and tell me I just *have* to read it and chances are it will be a decade before I can bear to pick it up. If someone tells me that *this* is the way something must be done, I take no pleasure in doing it unless I can somehow prove them wrong. As a student, I sat at the back of the classroom writhing in the self-inflicted agony of bad attitude. Facts only interest me when they are pieces to a puzzle I have already decided to assemble, and then I would rather find them after hours of rooting around in a junk yard than have them handed to me on a plate.

Of course, there are many things I had to learn by being taught them—it's just that the more that teaching was required the less likely I was to learn. I took to reading like a fish to water; I learned the niceties of spelling and grammar—so far as I have—only by unconsciously absorbing the way they work. The things that I had to learn by concentrated application were mastered at first just sufficiently to get by—multiplication—and later not at all. My final grade in a required freshman college course that combined physics and calculus was 11 out of a possible 100; my physics professor told me that I didn't even belong in college. Probably that's why I went on to graduate *magna cum laude*: just to piss him off.

Cooking, though, was never like that, maybe because I grew up observing a practiced cook at work, day after day. Although she has always liked to eat, my mother's idea of a truly enjoyable meal is one made for her at a good restaurant. Apart from baking, she rarely takes an interest in cooking for its own sake; she treats it as what it always was—a major household chore.

However, she is also a person who gets pleasure from doing chores well. She likes her sheets ironed and the bed she makes them with to have tight corners. (A bed isn't made right, she taught me, until the bedclothes are pulled taut enough to bounce a quarter.) She cooks in the same spirit; she feels genuine satisfaction when she sits down to a meal that has turned out the way it ought.

I was not an observant boy nor one who hung out much in the kitchen. It was my mother's spirit that I absorbed, not her expertise. When I moved into my first apartment, in a Lower East Side slum, I spent the first night on my hands and knees rubbing paste wax into the worn wood parquet floor and buffing it with one of my undershirts. I did it because that was what you did when you moved into a new place. That I didn't have a clue about how to do it properly was of no real matter. If the result was, well, idiosyncratic, that was okay with me. I had no notion of turning the apartment into a showplace; I just wanted to make it feel like mine.

Cooking, like many other things in life, can be a matter of confidence leading to competence, not the other way around. The first time I boiled an egg, sautéed an onion, broiled a piece of meat, I drew on nothing but the experience of my mother's rigorous self-assurance. It didn't even occur to me to think that I might be tackling something difficult. These were things a person just rolled up their sleeves and *did*.

Sum all this up and what you have is a very ambivalent relationship with cookbooks. As records of how somebody else does their cooking, I find them fascinating and rewarding of study. But the moment that I sense them turning into an instructional lecture on how I ought to do things in the kitchen, I slam the door in their face.

One of the biggest sources of miscommunication between Matt and myself occurs when I suddenly fall in love with a recipe. This is because Matt takes the recipe as being instructions for making a dish, where, as often as not, its nuts-and-bolts aspect (which some might say is its *only* aspect) rarely holds my attention. Instead, I see a dish wildly signalling to me on the other side, begging to be let out. If there's a problem here, it's that I sincerely believe that I *have* read and understood the recipe. And I couldn't be more wrong.

Let me give you a simple example. A few years ago I was captivated by the following recipe, which appeared on the back of a box of De Cecco fusilli.

Fusilli with Tomato and Green Olive Sauce

[SERVES 4 TO 6]

pot of salted pasta-cooking water
4 tablespoons extra-virgin olive oil
2 cloves garlic, minced
4 anchovy fillets
1 pound puréed tomatoes
1 tablespoon chopped capers
½ cup green olives, pitted and finely chopped
4 or 5 chopped fresh basil leaves
salt and pepper
1 pound De Cecco fusilli
pinch of dried oregano

• Turn on the flame under the pot of salted pasta water. Meanwhile, heat the olive oil in a skillet. Add the minced garlic and sauté to a golden brown. Crush the anchovies with a fork and add them to the skillet. Then stir in the tomato purée and the olives, capers, and basil. Taste to check the seasoning.

• When the pasta water comes to a brisk boil, add the fusilli and cook until al dente, about 12 minutes. Drain. Add the sauce and sprinkle with oregano. Toss and serve.

I haven't looked at this recipe since I tucked it away in my recipe file. Now that I do, I almost have to laugh. What was it that had called out to me? I have never liked cooked tomatoes; the recipe requires a whole pound of them. I had then only just begun to tolerate green olives; the recipe calls for a solid half-cup of them. But this didn't matter to me, because I simply ignored these things, whisking them away like gaudy tissue paper concealing a present I was eager to open. Here, approximately,* is how the dish came out. Let's call it . . .

Gemelli with Red Onion, Yellow Bell Pepper, Black Olives, & Tuna

[SERVES 2 OR 3]

4 quarts salted pasta-cooking water
½ pound gemelli or similar short pasta
olive oil reserved from draining the tuna can (see notes)
½ teaspoon powdered hot red chile
½ teaspoon kosher (coarse-grained) salt
½ teaspoon crumbled dried oregano leaf (see notes)
1 or 2 garlic cloves, finely minced
2 tablespoons decent-quality balsamic vinegar
2 hefty stalks celery, cut into bite-size pieces, with any
  attached leaves finely minced
1 large red salad onion, cut into bite-size pieces
1 yellow bell pepper, cored, seeded, and cut into bite-
  size pieces
12 or so Niçoise olives, pitted and shredded
½ tablespoon salted capers, coarsely chopped
1 6-ounce can olive-oil-packed tuna, drained (see notes)
½ dozen fresh basil leaves, torn to bits (see notes)
extra-virgin olive oil
freshly milled black pepper to taste

---

* I say "approximately" because at the time I first made this we ate it on plain boiled rice rather than with any sort of pasta. These days, however, I'm going through a gemelli phase (see, for example, the zucchini recipes in *Simple Cooking* #73), and for this sort of dish—right now—nothing else will do.

• Heat the pasta water over a high flame. When it reaches a rolling boil, add the gemelli. Let the water come back to a boil and then stir the pasta to make sure the pieces aren't sticking to each other or to the bottom of the pot. Adjust the flame to maintain a steady boil.

• Heat the olive oil drained from the tuna can in a skillet. Add the powdered chile, salt, crumbled oregano (if using), and minced garlic. Let this cook over medium-low heat until the garlic turns translucent, about 2 minutes. Then stir in the balsamic vinegar.

• I cut up the vegetables while the pasta water is heating and add them to the skillet in the order in which they appear in the ingredient list. If you have everything prepped ahead of time, start about 10 minutes after the pasta water has been turned on. Let the celery cook alone for 3 or 4 minutes before adding the onion; then let this mixture cook for 3 or 4 more minutes before adding the bell pepper, giving everything a thorough stir each time a new ingredient is added.

• Continue cooking, occasionally tasting the vegetables for doneness. Each of them should be tender, but still crisp and succulent. At this point, turn the heat down to low and stir in the remaining ingredients, breaking the tuna apart with a fork. Cook, stirring gently, until everything is heated through. Finally, stir ½ cup of the pasta water into the sauce, drain the gemelli, toss it thoroughly into the sauce, and serve in warmed bowls.

• **Cook's Notes: Tuna.** As far as I'm concerned, water-packed canned tuna tastes like laundered tuna, with all the flavor washed away. Most oil-packed canned tuna, on the other hand, is too mushy. We stick to an Italian-style olive-oil-packed solid light tuna—like Chicken of the Sea's Genova Tonno—which is firm in texture and full of flavor. Even better, if you can find (and afford) it, is the genuine article, imported from Italy and usually packed in jars. **Oil.** Until recently, we drained off the rather vapid-tasting olive oil used for packing the tuna and replaced it with our own extra-virgin. But then I discovered that in discarding the oil we were also tossing out much of the tuna's oil-soluble fatty acids. So now I cook the dish in the oil from the can and drizzle in a little extra-virgin oil at the same time that I add the olives and capers. **Oregano/Basil.** If I have lots of fresh basil at hand, I add a generous amount of it and omit the oregano entirely. Otherwise, I use a combination of both herbs or just the oregano by itself.

In some ways, it's not hard to see what happened when I appropriated this recipe: the red pepper replaced the abhorred tomatoes; the tuna subbed for the anchovies (where's the meat?!). However, to me, the most interesting factor is that, not so long before, I had done some extended experimenting with caponata, the Sicilian sweet-and-sour vegetable appetizer. This not only explains where the extra ingredients—celery, onion, balsamic vinegar—came from, but it also points to why the De Cecco recipe drew me in the first place. We had, in fact, often used our caponata as a pasta sauce. But caponata is a little on the heavy side and it takes time to make; this dish was lighter and it could be prepared while the pasta cooked.

In other words, one recipe had functioned as a sort of fulcrum to shift my thinking about another one. The result was a dish that retained some connections with both but fell more directly in line with our taste. We're still eating it several years later and still finding it delicious.

Surely, an important aspect of any recipe is its use as a tool for understanding other recipes. The most familiar example of this, perhaps, is when one recipe is compared to another in a search for the "perfect" version of a dish. Ours is a competitive society, and in competition ranking is everything. Who would buy *The Place-and-Show Cookbook: Recipes That Almost Won a Blue Ribbon*? But to ask the question is to show the sterility of the approach: the greatest value recipes offer is their strange and wonderful display of diversity. *Iron Chef* to the contrary, cooking is not, at its best, a competitive sport. Some recipes are surely better than others—and without doubt some are more clearly explained than others—but beyond that what makes for perfection gets increasingly difficult to say.

For example, Russ, in his new book, *How to Read a French Fry* (Houghton Mifflin, 2001), says in the section on cooking eggs: "Even fried eggs should be cooked gently. Use medium heat rather than high to keep them from forming that tough, brown, frizzled bottom." But there are those for whom that brown, frizzled bottom is the whole point of a fried egg. "Place [the eggs] one by one in smoking hot oil," writes Robert Courtine in *La Vraie Cuisine Française* (1968). "Put a pinch of salt on each yolk and fold in the white, as it sets, with a spoon. Brown lightly, drain away the fat, and serve." Kitchen science may explain why eggs fried the one way or the other end up the way they do, but it takes no position on which we should prefer. In fact, knowing both schools of thought gives us a richer conception of what a fried egg *is*.

Recipe collectors tend to fall into two groups: those who save recipes for every dish that catches their fancy and those who essentially save the same recipe over and over again. Before I carted the bulk of my recipe clippings to the dump, you would have found a single file folder containing, say, twenty or thirty recipes for French onion soup. I didn't collect these because I thought that one day I'd hold a cook-off to discover which one was best. No, like a teenage boy who covers his bedroom wall with photographs of Christina Aguilera, I just couldn't have too many glimpses of the same desirable object.

A fundamental idea behind *Simple Cooking* is that one of the best ways to learn more about a dish is to get a bunch of recipes arguing with each other. But until I started wondering why I review cookbooks the way I do, I hadn't given any thought at all to how recipes for entirely *different* dishes might have something to say to each other, let alone profoundly influence my reaction to one I happened to spot on the back of a fusilli box.

If this is the case, and—especially after a lifetime of looking through cookbooks—I think that it surely is, it is likely that the new recipe that will interest me the most will be the one that I can use to give shape to some nebulous longing that is already alive and stirring within me. This might mean that the true test of a recipe lies somewhere else than in its making.

Back in the late eighties, I wrote a cookbook review column for *Book World*, the Sunday book review supplement of *The Washington Post*. They would ship me box after box packed with cookbooks, and I found less and less to say about any of them ... except, "Hold! Enough!" They didn't require that I test recipes, but they emphatically wanted me to focus my reviews on those cookbooks for which recipe testing was the only possible response—at least if the response was to be positive. So, instead, I decided to quit.

By then, however, I could usually learn everything there was to know about that sort of book by looking at its dust jacket. I knew it would be full of delicious recipes, because all cookbooks are full of delicious recipes these days. I knew almost all the recipes would work, because cookbook publishers spend lots of money to ensure that they *do* work, after their fashion. But the reason I didn't have to even open the book was because I knew that the recipes in these books were—in any meaningful way—pretty much all the same. "Wilted Mustard Greens with Shallots and Sherry Vinegar." "Chard Stalks Sautéed with Garlic, Parsley, Chives, and Thyme." Deborah

Madison? Alice Waters? Molly O'Neill? Diane Shaw? Georgeanne Brennan? Sarah Schlesinger? Susan Sontag? Who cared?

Well, to be honest, a lot of cookbook buyers. These books sweep us off to a world where page-long ingredient lists have no connection to grocery bills, where what we make turns out just right and, most wondrously, makes everybody at the table happy. In this world, in other words, good food is what dinner is all about —whereas in real life, more often than not, it is little more than a fueling stop or the family jousting field. Like romance novels, cookbooks are powered by the fantasy of happy endings.

If you think I sound a little sour here, you're right. In fact, I used to believe the world conveyed in these books was all a sham. But that conviction has been beaten down by the sheer weight of the opposing view. Nowadays, I take a more conciliatory position. One definition of a pessimist is someone forced to spend too much time in the company of optimists. In the same way, I feel better the more I keep away from such books . . . and so that's just what I do.

Finding cookbooks that truly seize hold of my imagination is hard enough, but explaining *why* they do so is even harder, since each succeeds at this in its own individual and not always easily explicable way. Consequently, if I've never felt a whit of guilt recommending cookbooks without first testing their recipes, I'm wracked with it regarding those to which I haven't been able to find the time or inspiration to give their due . . . for instance, Ken Hom's *Easy Family Recipes from a Chinese-American Childhood*, Arthur Schwartz's *Naples at Table*, David Lebovitz's *Room for Dessert*—as well as such more deeply buried treasures as Richard Hosking's *A Dictionary of Japanese Food*, Larry Zuckerman's *The Potato*, and Irving Davis's *A Catalan Cookery Book*.

How to Read a French Fry is a case in point. It contains plenty of recipes, but for the most part I found myself skipping over them, appealing though they were, because I was so engrossed in the text itself. Time after time, Russ dives into the esoteric ocean of kitchen science and pops back up to the surface with another fascinating food fact alive and wriggling in his mouth: how the seasoning of cast-iron skillets works; why food doesn't fry as well in fresh oil as it does once the oil has been used a few times; why brining makes the best (and possibly the only really effective) tenderizing marinade; why custard sauces are made on top of the stove while custards themselves are baked in the oven. It's hard to imagine anyone spending time with this book and not making at least a few radical departures from the way they ordinarily cook.

My own by the revelation that braising tough cuts of meat over high heat, if done properly, produces buttery tender chunks rather than the shreds associated with low-heat braising. Here is about as clear an example as you could want of a good food writer getting you interested in trying a recipe—even propelling you straight to the stove. And I went to mine, for once, sincerely expecting to stick to Russ's recipe. The method was new to me, the ingredients all appealed to me . . . what was to change? But as soon as I got down to his specific instructions, a familiar hand seized hold of the tiller and headed the ship off on a different course. Here is the recipe, with my divergences spelled out in italics.

Mushroom Pot Roast
(from *How To Read a French Fry*, by Russ Parsons)

(SERVES 6 TO 8)

1 (3 ½-to-4-pound) chuck roast
salt
1 (750-milliliter) bottle dry red wine
3 tablespoons olive oil
1 pound yellow onions, sliced
½ pound carrots, sliced
6 garlic cloves, smashed
1 stalk celery

1 bay leaf
Stems from 1 bunch parsley, plus ¼ cup finely chopped
    fresh parsley
1 whole clove
½ cup red wine vinegar
2 tablespoons butter
1 pound button mushrooms, cleaned and quartered
Freshly ground black pepper

When we went to the supermarket to buy the chuck roast,
we found whole Australian leg of lamb on sale. Russ has a
recipe for whole leg of lamb, too, but for various reasons it was
more than I wanted to tackle. So I boned our leg of lamb and
cut three slabs of it—total weight 3 ½ pounds—to substitute
for the beef, reserving the rest for other uses.

• Sprinkle the roast with salt on both sides and place in
a 1-gallon zipperlock plastic bag. Add the wine, seal the
bag, and refrigerate for 8 hours, or overnight, turning
occasionally to make sure all the meat is covered with
wine.

I started marinating the meat as soon as I had cut it up, which
meant it was in the wine for about 24 hours instead of 8. I
also drank a glass of it (quality check) before pouring the rest
of the bottle over the meat.

• Preheat the oven to 450°F. Heat the oil in a Dutch
oven over medium-high heat. Remove the roast from
the bag, reserving the wine, and pat it dry with paper
towels. Place the roast in the Dutch oven and brown
well on both sides, 5 to 10 minutes per side.

Instead of a cast-iron Dutch oven, I went with a Calphalon
nonstick 5-quart casserole, since I knew that anything in

which meat was cooked for hours at high heat was going to be no joke to clean.

• Transfer the roast to a plate. Pour off all but 1 tablespoon of the rendered fat from the Dutch oven and reduce the heat to medium. Add the onions, carrots, and 4 of the garlic cloves and cook until the vegetables are slightly softened, about 5 minutes.

As you will see, Russ plans to discard the vegetables, whereas we planned to eat them. With that in mind, I doubled the amount of carrots and cut up everything in bite-size chunks instead of slices, including the celery. Also, since I had three pieces of meat to brown, I sautéed the vegetables separately in half the olive oil. When that was done, I started preheating the oven (about half an hour later than Russ).

• Cut the celery in half. Tie both stalks together with the bay leaf and parsley stems using kitchen twine and insert the clove in a celery stalk, to make a bouquet garni. Add the bouquet garni and the reserved wine to the vegetables and simmer for 5 minutes.

As I've said, I treated the celery—cut in chunks—as another vegetable. I left out the rest of the bouquet garni: no parsley stems, no bay leaf, no clove. After all, I had lamb on my hands, not beef. Instead, I added 1 teaspoon of ground red chile powder and a pinch of crumbled rosemary. As to the parsley— if I'd had some, I would have used it, but we rarely buy it, because seventy percent of it ends up rotting in the refrigerator.

• Add the meat and vinegar and place a sheet of aluminum foil loosely over the meat. Cover the Dutch oven with a tight-fitting lid, place it in the oven, and cook until the meat is easily pierced with a sharp fork and is falling off the bone, 2 to 2 ½ hours. Every 30 minutes, turn the meat and stir the liquid and vegetables. If the level of the liquid gets too low, add water, a little at a time, to prevent the meat and vegetables from scorching.

I left the pot untouched for the first hour and then began the stir-and-turn routine. As predicted, the lamb took 2 ½ hours. (Even though I had drunk some of the wine, there was plenty of liquid right to the end.) Also as predicted, the lamb was tender enough to eat with a spoon.

• Transfer the meat to a plate and cover it with aluminum foil to keep warm. Pour the liquid and vegetables into a strainer over a bowl, pressing on the vegetables to get as much liquid as possible; discard the vegetables. Set the liquid aside until the fat floats to the top.

Discard the vegetables?! I'd almost as soon discard the meat! I did strain out the liquid, though, and I spooned off and discarded the fat.

• Wash out the Dutch oven. Skim off the fat from the settled liquid and return the meat and liquid to the Dutch oven. Keep warm over low heat.

• Melt the butter in a large skillet over medium-high heat. When the butter has foamed and subsided, add the mushrooms and the remaining 2 garlic cloves and cook, tossing, until the mushrooms are lightly browned, about 5 minutes.

I like mushrooms and had intended to add them as Russ

directs. But after I tasted the dish, I decided it had plenty enough going on already, with its intense, mouth-puckering, full-flavored reduction of wine, vinegar, and meat juices. Of course, I also had all the undiscarded vegetables to serve along with the meat. So, at this point, I beached my craft and let Russ sail on alone.

• Add the mushrooms to the pot roast and cook for 15 minutes over low heat to marry the flavors. Season to taste with salt and pepper, garnish with the chopped parsley, and serve.

We let everything rest in the refrigerator overnight and ate it the next day, serving it in large soup bowls (at the bottom of mine was a thickly buttered slice of sourdough toast).

Well, there you have it. Obviously, the dish that I prepared is, in spirit and—in large part—execution, Russ Parsons'. But he would not, I think, want to be held responsible for what ended up on our table, let alone have his book judged on the strength of it (at least if one sets aside the notion that "capacity to survive abuse" might be as good as any other way of judging a recipe). Also, Russ would probably tell me (and you) that I don't know what I missed by not trying it his way.

Who can argue with that? Not me. But then I didn't set out either to improve his recipe or to mess around with it; I just went and made it. Furthermore, if you happened to ask me whether you ought to try the recipe yourself, I'd answer quite honestly: "Yeah, you should. I did and I liked it a lot." And, most likely, I'd leave it at that. After all, you will be stepping into an entirely different cookbook.

When the Path to Serenity Wends Past the Stove

by Regina Schrambling

from the *New York Times*

Cooking for consolation was a recurrent theme in many post-9/11 food essays. Of her many fine articles in the *New York Times* this year, Regina Schrambling hit the mark most truly in this revealing look at how one cook sought comfort.

When a friend called to say she had suddenly felt compelled to bake an apple pie last Saturday, I understood why. Anyone who cooks even casually knows the feeling. Cooking is almost always a mood-altering experience, for good or for bad, and at its best it is do-it-yourself therapy: more calming than yoga, less risky than drugs.

The food is not really the thing. It's the making of it that gets you through a bad time.

On Thursday, I was motivated to make stew, and not because I had any real craving for meat. I needed to go through the slow process of rendering salt pork, sautéing onions and shallots, browning the beef and simmering it for hours with Cognac and stock and two kinds of mustard. Nothing about the recipe, one I have made every winter since learning it in cooking school 18 years ago, could be rushed, which was exactly what I wanted. Sometimes cooking is its own reward.

Experts theorize why it works, but to me it seems clear. Everything about cooking engages the senses. There's a physical aspect to it, even if you use a food processor more than a knife, and so at least a couple of endorphins have to be involved. But the psychological impact is even more obvious. When you're all finished, you have something to show for the time and effort: a loaf of bread, a batch of cookies, a pot of stew. On Thursday, those three hours of putting one step after another led to a kind of serenity, the feeling that no matter what was happening outside my kitchen, I had complete control over one dish, in one copper pot, on one burner.

But cooking also lets you cede control, if that's what you need. There's a reason they call it following a recipe. Sometimes it just feels calming to know that a cake needs exactly one teaspoon of salt and no less than half a pound of butter.

It's why I never try a new recipe when I cook to feel better, and I don't think most people do. The familiar is what soothes. If I'm having a dinner party, I search through cookbooks and clippings to find the most novel appetizer or dessert. When I need solace, I pull out an old cookbook with a recipe for the corn pancakes with smoked trout or the blueberry-peach cake I have made more times than I can remember.

One of the sharpest observations my sister Johanna has ever made is that there is a difference between cooking and fixing food. One is a fulfilling project. The other involves combining easy ingredients fast. Quesadillas are food you fix. Stew is cooking. It's instant gratification versus satisfaction that builds slowly and stays with you. And yet so much of life is just fixing food.

I know speed is of the essence in the cooking my consort and I do most days. We buy fish and grill or broil it. We steam corn or broccoli. We sometimes eat mesclun undressed right out of the bag. And we almost never bother with dessert.

When I cook for comfort, everything is different. I buy meat, like chuck or short ribs, and braise it for hours. I make garlic mashed potatoes, an elaborate gratin or potatoes Escoffier, with a whole stick of butter for two pounds of roasted Yukon Golds. And I get out the sugar and chocolate and bake.

The recipes that appeal most are the ones that layer on the richness, that prove more is better with butter. Abstemiousness is not an option when you're feeling low.

I have no desire for sweetness when I reach for the mixing bowls and measuring cups. I just get profound pleasure out of making muffins that are almost caffeine cakes, flavored with espresso and loaded with chocolate chips and walnuts. I like to see how different chocolate chip cookies can turn out from batch to batch. And I enjoy the whole idea of having to put together three components for something as simple as maple pecan bars, from the shortbread crust to laying the pecans over the gooey filling.

It's the reason I make céleri rémoulade every fall. I like being able to take the time to cut the celery root into tiny little strips and dress them with sour cream, mustard and parsley and then let the bowl sit until the flavors come together. And it's why I feel so compelled to roast red peppers this time of year and let them marinate in olive oil and garlic. The process of charring the peppers and peeling them is almost more satisfying than eating them on warm bread. At some point, I slip into a more mellow state of mind. I'm cooking, I'm making something, but it is not just food to be consumed unthinkingly.

In a city where any food imaginable is normally available at any time of day, cooking takes on more meaning. If we feel hungry, we can order in egg rolls or curry. But if we feel hollow, we can bake pumpkin bread or molasses cookies. Comfort food is what someone cooks for you. Comfort cooking is what you do for yourself.

And the reason you do it is very simple: cooking is the most sensual activity a human being can engage in, in polite company. My stew involved smell (onions softening, Cognac reducing), touch (the chopping, the stirring), sound (that sizzle of beef cubes hitting hot fat), sight (carrot orange against the gold-brown of

mustard and beef stock) and especially taste. Making it was a way
to feel alive and engaged.

Whoever said cooking should be entered into with abandon or
not at all had it wrong. Going into it when you have no hope is
sometimes just what you need to get to a better place.

Long before there were antidepressants, there was stew.

Searching for Lillian

by Jeanne McManus

from *The Washington Post*

Usually reporters have to go out to find their stories, but in this case a story fell almost literally in the lap of *Washington Post* writer Jeanne McManus. Thankfully, she knew just what to do with it.

A small rectangle of cardboard containing Ann Pillsbury's recipe for Hot Cross Buns cut from the back of a box and attached with a straight pin to a piece of unlined notebook paper. Four recipes on another sheet of paper, spaced evenly down the page, written in flawless penmanship, the recipe name set off to the left and underscored with a wavy line: Herb Mixture (English), Herb Mixture (French), Sage Sauce for Roast Pork and Curry Powder. On yet another page, the clean flat letters of a manual typewriter, ingredients perfectly aligned in two columns at the top, directions flawlessly pecked out and centered below. The recipe title, "Rice Spoon Bread," capitalized at the top left; the source of the recipe, "Duch. Windsor," top right.

More than 250 other pages—handwritten or typed sheets, magazine and newspaper clippings, file cards, patches of cardboard boxes, letters and notes—strained the spine of the 10-by-8-inch, three-ring binder that was slightly damp and splayed across a strip of grass at the curb of a quiet street in Takoma Park. A few feet away, a large black trash bag had spilled open, a few pieces of kitchen ware and dish drainer falling out, suggesting that the black binder had once been part of the bag's contents.

Susan Holliday, walking her dog on Buffalo Avenue on an uncharacteristically warm January morning, stopped to pick up the binder. Holliday, who runs her own public relations company, likes to cook simple meat and pasta dishes for her husband and two sons and keeps her recipes on 3-by-5 cards or taped into a file folder. She knew right away from the look of the binder that this was a recipe collection. And she knew that it should not meet the same end as the black trash bags lined up awaiting execution.

"An elderly widower in my neighborhood recently moved from his longtime home to a retirement community," she e-mailed me. "Among the piles of old stuff placed at his curb, I found his wife's 50-plus-year-old recipe notebook.

"The leather-bound binder is full of: typed recipes; handwritten recipes including carefully drawn diagrams, e.g., how to shape and serve chopped liver appetizers, chicken en papillote and a chestnut dessert from the Italian Embassy; . . . newspaper recipes and booklets . . . circa 1953 from places like St. Louis, Chicago and D.C.; recipes attributed to Jackie Kennedy and the Duchess of Windsor; and reminiscences of Maryland cooking from the early 1900s.

"Would you be interested in reviewing it?"

The next day the bursting black binder sat on my desk, the damp smell of age and the mustiness of a likely stay in a basement filled the room. No one who passed by or came into the office could resist, each carefully leafing through it page by page, past the recipe for Frankfurter Crown Roast on one page, French brined cherries on the next.

On the inside cover of the binder was her sticker, white with black calligraphy-style writing: "Ex Libris: Lillian N. Meyer."

Frederick Meyer, 84, is sitting in the sparkling clean and polished living room of his home in Silver Spring's Leisure World, dressed in casual pants, a freshly pressed shirt and comfortable shoes. Later that day he will go back to his home of 43 years, the one he just vacated on Buffalo Avenue in Takoma Park, to dig up a few of his favorite early-blooming crocuses and transplant them in the small patch of yard at his new place. On the phone a few days before, he couldn't recall the black binder, but as I opened it up before him some recollection stirred. Her cookbooks had once been in every corner of the house. "Every night she would get in bed and read—but read a cookbook," he recalls. "She was always trying new things. Even when she bought a box of angel food cake mix, she never followed the directions. She added rose extract and made it something special."

Married in 1946 in St. Louis, the couple came to the Washington area in 1958 and Frederick, a botanist, was hired by the U.S. National Arboretum where he eventually became supervisory botanist of the Herbarium, until he retired in 1991. They shared a love of herbs, with Frederick writing, researching and traveling for his work at the arboretum, and Lillian compiling "A Pinch of Herbs," writings that she illustrated with line drawings. They traveled together occasionally; when he went alone on business he invariably brought back regional cookbooks, especially from the South. She taught school for a few years in Montgomery County, but "frustrated that children weren't being taught phonics," according to Frederick, she stopped and pursued her recipes and her cooking. They didn't have a family and "it was too bad because Lillian was so good with children," said Frederick.

As her interest became a passion, Lillian's love of food and cooking came, in time, to take hold of her physically. She gained weight and struggled to diet; she became less active, then sedentary. At times, she needed oxygen to aid her breathing. In 1983, at the age of 66 she died of pulmonary problems, according to her husband.

Frederick stayed on in the house until early this year. He gathered up her cookbooks and donated 14 boxes of them to the National Agricultural Research Library in Beltsville, but the black binder was overlooked. For weeks, beginning in December, as he and some helpers readied the house for sale, there began to appear on the curb strip outside his home, black plastic trash bags, neat and tidy and tied at the top, until one January morning, when one spilled open.

Aioli from Gourmet magazine, Cherry Whipped Cream Valentine Dessert from the St. Louis Post-Dispatch, Fruit Pudding from her mother-in-law (who is referred to throughout as Mother Meyer). The recipes are both a time capsule of American cooking in the mid-1950s to the mid-1960s and a collection so personal that they are almost a diary of the woman who took the time to copy, type, collect and organize them. There is the occasional editorial comment ("Light and delicious!" of a consommé from Trader Vic's; "unusually tender and light as a feather," of Betty Crocker's Parker House rolls). But real disclosure is in the selection itself, in the acceptance of the status quo on the one hand (a friend's recipe for deviled eggs) and in the reach into the cultural, if not culinary, stratosphere on the other (first lady Jackie Kennedy's baked fruit dessert). Caught somewhere between the domesticity of the post-War American housewife and the ambition, opportunity and self-expression that eventually would be won by or allowed to women in the decades to follow, Lillian Meyer would clip the most common magazine articles ("Serve 'em Bologna Pancakes!") on one page and Chicken Creole obtained from Antoine's restaurant in New Orleans on the other. She both wanted to please ("Fred's Favorite" she notes on the Cream Tapioca recipe) and wanted to excel ("Chefs in Paris prepare and cook their pork chops in this manner," she writes of "Chef De Guoy's Baked Pork Chops Charcutiere").

In the years between 1952 and 1965, she tried tofu and sukiyaki, tuna noodle casserole and shrimp de Jonghe. She followed directions religiously or she took liberties. Mont Blanc aux Marrons, a recipe for a chestnut puree mold that originated at the famous Paris restaurant Maxim's, according to her notebook, had been handed down to her by her grandmother. But neither Maxim's nor her grandmother kept her from doing her thing: "Above is the original recipe," she wrote. "However, I like to take my chestnut paste, press through a ricer into my silver dessert bowl in 1 quick operation. Over this I pour a little bourbon or rum. Then I add a little of some to Cool Whip and mask the whole pile of chestnuts. Throw over crystallized violets if you can get them, or crystallized rose petals. . . . I use African violets a lot in my cookery. I know how to grow them, and since Frederick despises them as plants to grow he never touches them."

Lillian's recipes are now back with Frederick at his home in Leisure World, though I confess I hated to part with them. And I now look at my own collection of recipes with chilly regard. Lillian, like me, had no children of her own to inherit the part of her that is captured in her collection, the Meyer family cookie recipes, even the Norwegian Liver Sausage that appeared to have been passed down from her side of the family. I have recipes of my mother's, at 86 still a great cook, encoded in my brain. They're mostly unwritten, since she's known for the perfect roast chicken and the tender pork loin and a certain polite but assured way of dealing with any butcher, even the supermarket guy, that somehow always results in their surrendering the perfect steak or roast.

But as I flip through the three binders on my kitchen shelf and find the crab soup that I make every Christmas Eve, the old standby Roast Chicken With Mustard Sauce that my husband and I enjoy on many a Sunday night and the glazed ham recipe that I inflict on my colleagues every year at the holiday party, it occurs to me, a childless woman in the week before Mother's Day, that if there is a cherished recipe, held dear by a family member, now is the time to get it or to give it.

In her binder full of recipes, Lillian Meyer left a warm and loving legacy. And until one day in January, when Susan Holliday walked by, there was no one to inherit it.

Brownies: A Memoir

by Lisa Yockelson

from *Gastronomica*

Though common wisdom dictates that baking is an exact science, its recipes followed to the letter, Lisa Yockelson gives us an inside look at how a baking expert can tinker with a recipe—even a most beloved one.

Obsession, passion, devotion: I don't know which of these has inspired me more over the years to stir up an endless succession of batters in search of the lushest and moistest block of pure chocolate goodness to be had. I do know that a strong emotional attachment connects me to brownies, an attachment that must have begun at age seven, when I was first presented, almost as a rite of passage, with my grandmother's brownie recipe.

Grandma Lilly's recipe was the family brownie recipe. In its day, it eclipsed all others. The recipe was coveted, and the few individuals who had it refused to give it out. My mother would bring the brownies to a charity bake sale or the home of a family friend. When asked for the recipe, however, she would disavow any knowledge of it. As a teenager, when my mother's friends would slyly press me for the recipe, I pleaded ignorance. Once, my mother gave it to a friend but changed the amount of an ingredient, sabotaging the outcome. My mother was a sincere woman, but that recipe brought out a dash of deception. The friend baked the brownies and quickly figured out that they were not Grandma Lilly's brownies. The friendship, as I recall, ended then and there.

Long before I began to explore the intricacies of doughs and batters and to write seriously about baking, I baked my grandmother's brownies by rote, using the precise type and quantity of ingredients indicated in her recipe. I even assembled the batter in nine-inch round layer-cake pans, as she had done, quirky as it seemed. More than thirty years later, I cherish those beat-up layer-cake pans, whose patina has held up beautifully.

After my grandmother passed away, my mother and I went through some yellowed and frayed recipes that had belonged to her and found a few variations. The original brownie recipe had apparently endured being lost and rewritten from memory or just changed on a whim. The versions differed with regard to the amount of baking powder, vanilla extract, salt, and black walnuts, and whether the cake flour was to be measured in its sifted or unsifted state. A different oven temperature surfaced now and then. The amount of butter, chocolate, and sugar remained constant, however, as did the number of eggs. Vanilla sugar, on occasion, may have replaced plain sugar, as my grandmother used it in other baked goods. I remember seeing a few vanilla beans stored in a dark amber-colored jar in my grandmother's kitchen; she also kept a jar of vanilla-perfumed sugar near the tin of baking powder on a deep, revolving pantry shelf in a corner cabinet. The shelf, which swung in a semi-circle, fascinated me as a child.

I offer one version of my grandmother's brownie recipe below. The procedure is not unusual in any way. The dry ingredients are sifted together. The butter and chocolate are melted together and cooled. The eggs are well beaten with the sugar in the bowl of a free-standing electric mixer until somewhat lightened in consistency. (My grandmother used a KitchenAid, which was built into a sliding cabinet shelf, a basic by today's standards, but probably a luxury back then. Her stainless steel kitchen was a gem in its day, circa 1955.)

The chocolate is added to the eggs, as is the vanilla. The sifted dry ingredients are slowly incorporated, and then the walnuts are stirred in by hand. The batter is baked in two buttered and floured nine-inch round cake pans for twenty-five minutes at 350°F. or 375°F. I usually use 375°F. The cooled brownie rounds are cut into sections and the tops blanketed with powdered sugar. The round pans provide very few square brownies, other than those cut from the center. (Of course, the brownies may also be baked in a rectangular pan.)

And what do these brownies taste like? My grandmother's brownies have a delicate chocolate flavor, a pleasant aroma of vanilla, a somewhat open internal framework, and a vaguely cake-like texture. They are denser in the middle. There is a prominent crunch of oily nuts. The level of sugar in her recipe is right, but it leaves the brownies slightly granular. The thick mantle of powdered sugar is alluring and provides some relief from the slightly crusty exterior (I do love a brownie capped with powdered sugar; both my mother and my grandmother were lavish in its use, and so am I).

About ten years ago, however, I began to evaluate my stash of old, revered recipes in the context of my own baking, and the brownies so cherished in my childhood seemed insipid. The chocolate flavor was weak; the leavening excessive; the color not as intense as that of other chocolate bars and squares I had baked. The airiness of the texture failed to beguile me, and the flavor of the black walnuts overwhelmed the chocolate. My grandmother's brownies were, in essence, too tame.

What I wanted was a blissful brownie, one that haunted me. A brownie good enough to satisfy that 1:15 a.m. chocolate craving. A brownie so fudgy that it wouldn't leave crumbs in the bed at 1:19 a.m., when, propped up on a pillow, I nibbled it from a napkin. A brownie—and I say this, even now, with some trepidation—that surpassed my grandmother's brownie.

To reconfigure a brownie recipe seems easy—on paper. Improving my grandmother's recipe, however, demanded a massive reorganization, in theory, practice, and taste. Finally, an updated set of ingredients and techniques emerged. Not until I had assembled ingredients, stirred up a batter, baked, cooled, and bitten into the resulting brownie—not until I had repeated this process many times over a span of several years—did I recognize just what a brownie can deliver in terms of flavor and texture. Throughout this long period of trial and error, I held to the principle that a perfect brownie—damp, dark, and fudgy—was worth pursuing.

The first step was to figure out why my grandmother's brownies were disappointing. I realized that the extra leavening creates an internal crumb that is overly expansive. Beating the eggs and sugar as much as is indicated inflates the batter and dries out the brownies, producing a top that is a little too splintery for my taste. The cake flour (which has a lower protein content than all-purpose flour), along with the fluffy egg-and-sugar mixture and the generous amount of baking powder, makes the brownies entirely too tender, not sufficiently dense. The cake flour serves to further mute the chocolate. The composition is uneven; the brownies are somewhat dry around the edges. The black walnuts taste caustic to me (though I have written many recipes for brownies that contain nuts, when I bake for myself, I leave the nuts out).

The process of revision. I went through untold pounds of butter and a mountain of chocolate and cocoa. I juggled daredevil amounts of cake flour and all-purpose flour. I played around with the amount of salt. I omitted the leavening and gingerly reinstated it, making other adjustments along the way. I got rid of those pesky black walnuts; their musky fragrance simply belonged in another recipe. I experimented with all the premium European and American butters to be found at the market and wildly melted down pounds of the stuff, half a pound at a time. Superior butter, I found, does make a brownie that resonates with flavor. I paid nearly five dollars for eight and three-quarters ounces of *Celles sur Belle* butter. I melted it down, stirred up the batter, and pulled an exquisite batch of brownies from the oven. But surely my grandmother didn't use French butter in her brownies . . .

In short, to create a brownie that was moister and more flavorful than my grandmother's, I fiddled constantly and experimented audaciously. I altered ingredients and even adapted another mixing method. To produce a fudgier brownie, I first tried replacing a good part of the cake flour with all-purpose flour. I also used the melted butter and chocolate mixture while it was still slightly warm. Even so, the resulting brownies lacked that chocolate punch and creamy, dense texture.

Replacing some of the all-purpose flour with almost one-quarter cup of unsweetened cocoa and adding an ounce of bittersweet chocolate enhanced the chocolate flavor, but the texture was a little too coarse. I then added more cake flour back in, but the brownies were still too grainy. Next, I substituted superfine sugar for granulated sugar and reduced the volume of sugar slightly. The amount of leavening needed adjustment; after various trials, one-quarter teaspoon of baking powder turned out to be perfect, providing a gentle lift and a refined crumb that was neither dry nor lacy.

As for method, I immediately abandoned my electric mixer. Electricity, certainly valuable for the extended stretches of whipping or beating called for in other recipes, is unwarranted here. If I wanted a fudgy, dense brownie, increasing the volume of the eggs and sugar by electric beating was inappropriate. I hoped that a whisk and some mixing bowls would do nicely, and I was not disappointed.

The baking temperature of 375°F. was problematic. At this temperature, the surface and sides hardened and the inside baked unevenly. In subsequent batches, in order to obtain a softly set brownie with moistness throughout, I dropped the temperature by increments of 25°F. A temperature of 325°F. gave excellent results. The brownie batter lifted slightly and evenly as it baked and then settled as it cooled. What I had now was a dark, damp square of chocolate. But I had to be patient: if cut within an hour of baking, the brownies were hopelessly messy, so I had to give them a good two to three hours to calm down—a painful, but necessary, step.

Over the years, I baked several kinds of brownies, all dark and delicious. Like a mother with more than one child, I refuse to say which is the most beloved. One was so fudgy and dense that I had to pry the squares out of the baking pan with two spatulas. Another was creamy and nearly mousselike; several hours after baking, it settled into an ethereal softness. I packed one batch so full of chocolate that it tasted like candy, with a bit of chew and bulk. I embedded little bits of bittersweet chocolate in the next batter and slid a cookie crust underneath it. A subsequent pan of brownies—a delirious combination of cocoa and unsweetened and bittersweet chocolate—caused grown men and women to whimper audibly. No one even hinted that there might be too much chocolate.

My recipe for Dark, Deeply Chocolate Brownies yields brownies that are meltingly tender, packed with chocolate, dark, and dense. They are so moist that crumbs pressed back into their edges will adhere. When subjected to the late-night, devour-it-in-bed test, these brownies passed effortlessly.

Could I ever have imagined that my grandmother's brownie recipe—so beloved, so engraved in my mind, and so intrinsically a part of my culinary heritage—would lead to such intense scrutiny of the baking process? To this day, I'm not sure what propelled me to do all of this probing: the obsession I have with the baking process, the passion to reconnect with my own history, or simply my devotion to chocolate at its finest. I'm still dreaming up endless brownie variations. And one day, perhaps, I'll tell you about my brownie mousse squares topped with hand-rolled chocolate truffles, which may be the beginning of an entirely new brownie-meets-candy thrill. I wonder, too, what my grandmother would say about my Dark, Deeply Chocolate Brownies. She'd probably ask me for the recipe, then leave for the market in pursuit of some hefty chunks of French butter.

A Version of My Grandmother's Brownies

INGREDIENTS
Softened, unsalted butter and all-purpose flour for the
    baking pan
1 ½ cups sifted bleached cake flour
1 ¾ teaspoons baking powder

¼ teaspoon salt
4 large eggs
2 cups granulated sugar
½ pound (2 sticks) unsalted butter, melted and cooled
4 ounces unsweetened chocolate, melted and cooled
1 ½ teaspoons pure vanilla extract
¾ cups chopped black walnuts
Confectioner's sugar

Preheat oven to 375°F. Lightly butter the inside of a 13"
× 9" × 2" baking pan. Dust the bottom and sides of the
pan with all purpose-flour. Set aside.

Resift the flour with the baking powder and salt onto
a sheet of waxed paper. Place the eggs in the large bowl
of a free-standing electric mixer and beat on moderate
speed for 1 to 2 minutes to blend well after each addition. The mixture should be thick and light.

In another mixing bowl, blend together the melted
butter and chocolate. Add the butter–chocolate mixture
to the egg-sugar mixture and beat on low speed, mixing
well. Blend in vanilla extract. Continuing on low speed,
add the sifted mixture in two additions, beating until
the particles of flour are absorbed. Stir in walnuts. Pour
and scrape the batter into the prepared pan.

Bake for 25 minutes, or until risen and just set. The
outer edges will be somewhat firmer than the center.
Cool completely in the pan on a rack. With a small,
sharp knife, cut into twenty pieces. Remove the
brownies from the baking pan with a small offset
spatula. Shower the top with sifted confectioners' sugar.

Makes 20 brownies.

Dark, Deeply Chocolate Brownies

INGREDIENTS

Softened, unsalted butter for preparing the baking pan

1 cup plus 1 tablespoon unsifted bleached all-purpose flour

¼ cup unsifted bleached cake flour

3 tablespoons plus 1 teaspoon unsweetened alkalized cocoa

¼ teaspoon baking powder

⅛ teaspoon salt

4 ounces unsweetened chocolate, melted and cooled to tepid

1 ounce bittersweet chocolate, melted and cooled to tepid

½ pound (2 sticks) unsalted butter, melted and cooled to tepid

4 large eggs

1 ¾ cups plus 2 tablespoons superfine sugar

1 ¼ teaspoons pure vanilla extract

Confectioners' sugar

Preheat the oven to 325°F. Lightly butter the inside of a 9" × 9" × 2" baking pan.

Sift the all-purpose flour, cake flour, cocoa, baking powder, and salt onto a sheet of waxed paper. In a medium-sized bowl, whisk the eggs just to combine, about 30 seconds. Add the sugar and whisk until incorporated, about 45 seconds longer. Blend in the chocolate-butter mixture and the vanilla extract; at this point the mixture will be shiny and moderately thick. Resift the flour and cocoa mixture over the egg-sugar mixture and combine. Use a flat wooden paddle or a sturdy whisk to combine all the elements (using an electric mixer would aerate the batter and spoil its texture).

Scrape the batter into the prepared pan. Smooth the top with a rubber spatula to level the batter.

Bake for about 30–34 minutes, until softly set. The center of the brownies should be stable, not wobbly. Let the brownies stand in the pan on a cooling rack for 2 to 3 hours. (If your kitchen is very warm, refrigerate the thoroughly cooled brownies for 30 minutes to 1 hour before cutting.) Cut into 16 squares. Remove the brownies from the baking pan with a small offset spatula. Sift confectioners' sugar on top of the brownies just before serving.

Makes 16 brownies.

RECIPE NOTE

For crunch, ¾ cup chopped nuts, lightly toasted and cooled completely, can be stirred into the brownie batter after the sifted ingredients have been incorporated; macadamia, English walnuts, or pecans are all excellent. To drive up the chocolate quotient further, stir 3 ounces of chopped bittersweet chocolate or ¾ cup semisweet chocolate chips, tossed with 1 teaspoon of the sifted flour mixture, into the batter once the dry ingredients have been incorporated.

Growing Up with *Gourmet*

by Barbara Haber

from *From Hardtack to Home Fries*

Recipes mean more than a simple series of cooking instructions, as no one knows better than Barbara Haber, curator of Harvard's outstanding rare cookbook collection. In her book *From Hardtack to Home Fries*, she explores American culinary history through its cookbooks.

Cookbooks were one of my favorite forms of reading long before I had professional responsibilities for collecting them or thoughts of writing about them. I remember sitting on a Cape Cod beach years ago with M.F.K. Fisher's *The Art of Eating*, a title that drew stares from other vacationers whose notions of summer reading were more along the lines of novels by Agatha Christie, Danielle Steel, or Robert Ludlum. At the time, I felt special, in the know, a holder of secret knowledge about a vast, unappreciated literature that told me things about people and their lives and times that I could not always find in novels or histories and biographies. I had not yet realized the extent to which others found meaning and pleasure in reading and collecting cookbooks, whether or not they cooked from them.

The realization hit me later when I became a professional collector of cookbooks as Curator of Books at the Arthur and Elizabeth Schlesinger Library on the History of Women in America, where I am regularly contacted by people who want to donate cookbooks and food magazines they have been hoarding over the years. The gift most frequently offered is an accumulation of twenty or thirty years of *Gourmet* magazine. In almost all cases, the owners have long ago given up the idea of trying out all the recipes that looked appealing but find that putting the collection out with the trash is more than they can bear. The would-be donors are grievously disappointed when I tell them I cannot accept their gift, for the Library already has a complete, bound set of *Gourmet*. To solace them and let them know that they are not alone in wanting to find a suitable home for their magazines, I describe a *New Yorker* cartoon I keep on my office wall. It shows a woman dressed in mourning speaking to a lawyer who says, "That being your mother's wish, I see no reason we can't arrange interment with all her old copies of *Gourmet*."

Not all such collectors divest themselves of their food magazines and cookbooks when their supply gets out of hand. One woman I know rents commercial storage space to hold most of her 15,000 cookbooks, and another has turned her home and her books into a research library for the use of anyone in her small town and beyond. Some collectors try to limit what they buy, but even those that are interested only in French or Chinese cookbooks, for instance, or books about Mediterranean cuisine, can easily run out of room as cookbooks proliferate in their field of special interest. I know people who buy cookbooks as souvenirs of their travels and people who read cookbooks instead of traveling—lavishly illustrated books about the foods of exotic countries that satisfy their taste for adventure but do so without great risk and expense.

Cookbook collections can reveal secrets about their owners. One such donation came my way from an elderly woman who shared the family home with a brother who had just died. To her great surprise, she had found in his bedroom closet hundreds of cookbooks, not one of which had ever come down to the kitchen.

The books were a welcome gift to the library, for unlike many cookbooks we receive, the pages of these contained no butter stains or traces of cake batter. The collector, it turned out, was on a restricted diet and read the books as a substitute for eating the dishes that were off limits to a man with his particular health problems. Instead of food stains, what I found on the pages were lovingly composed wish lists he had written of forbidden foods such as chocolate and peanut butter desserts. As I read his lists, sometimes written in a wavering hand, I envisioned a scenario in which he would eat a real meal of lean fish or breast of chicken, steamed vegetables, and a dry salad, and then go up to his room to read his recipes and fantasize about steak and home fries, onion rings, and a salad with Roquefort dressing.

A similar picture came to mind when I examined the cookbook collection that had belonged to Ella Fitzgerald, the great jazz singer who died of complications of diabetes. Her books reflect a hearty appetite and reveal that she was a lover of soul food and other rich ethnic cuisines. It was clear that she had cooked from her oldest cookbooks, where many recipes had her marginal commentary or little checkmarks she used to register her approval of a dish. Recipes for pork stew, biscuits and gravy, chopped chicken liver, kreplach, and lasagne also had telltale stains to show that a real cook had been at work. But her newer books, acquired after the onset of her illness, were without blemish. Like our earlier donor, Ella Fitzgerald seemed to have read these books in order to bring back memories of bygone meals or vicariously enjoy the taste of new dishes she was not permitted to eat. Evidently, she was reading recipes the way trained musicians read music and hear melodies in their mind's ear.

Recipes are a link to the past, and many of us find special meaning in dishes that bring back memories of family and friends or of ourselves in younger days. The first cookbook I ever bought retains a strong connection to my teenage years, and though I have rarely cooked from it, it occupies a sentimental spot on my shelf.

It is the original *Gourmet* cookbook that I had given my mother for her birthday when I was an adolescent. For me, that thick brown classic with its gold lettering represented a sophisticated, elegant world of food that could easily have been available to our family if only my mother applied herself and learned to prepare the recipes. When weeks passed without the appearance of "gourmet dishes," I asked what was holding her up, and my mother defensively replied, "I don't understand this book." In a great, obnoxious show of arrogance and impatience, I shut my eyes, opened the book at random, and with arm held high overhead zoomed my index finger down on the page and read where it pointed: "Marinate the ham of a bear for five days in cooked red wine marinade . . ." Dumbstruck, I looked at my mother, and she looked me in the eye and said, "See?" in that victorious voice she used for such triumphs over her pretentious daughter. The notion of my mother cooking anything that had to be hunted down in a forest struck us both so funny that we exploded into uncontrollable laughter—that rare shared kind that goes on and on, fizzles, then starts up again when the laughers look at each other, and only stops when they are too weak to go on.

Much later, I understood the meaning of that episode and why we laughed so hard. I was at an age when I felt qualified to improve my mother, while she had every right to stand her ground and protect her received wisdom. I wanted "gourmet" meals, while she wanted to protect what she had learned from her mother, recipes for tasty meals that were served in a steady weekly rotation of roast chicken, pot roast, meat loaf, lamb chops, steak—the usual Midwestern American fare. Only much later, when I began research in food history, did I discover that the recipes I was trying to impose on my mother were intended for an Epicurean male readership more likely than my mother to confront and cook wild beasts. The earliest issues of *Gourmet* magazine, from which the recipes in my birthday present had been gleaned, were never intended for a female audience. The illustrations of boars' heads, shotguns, and fishing rods make it clear to me now that the magazine was geared for a readership of men who fancied themselves intrepid sportsmen.

The machismo of the old *Gourmet* was the first hint I had that cookbooks could have definite gender biases and reflect society's different expectations of men and women. Conventional thinking of that time had it that daily meals were understood to be the work of women and that any man who was interested in cooking had better be a well-paid executive chef. Outdoor barbecuing was the exception. Male cookbook writers could write about everyday home cooking and still retain their self-respect and sense of superiority as long as they first established their firemaking credentials and found some way to set themselves apart from women. This was especially true of cookbooks that came out between the 1930s and the 1960s and were filled with guy talk designed to coax likeminded men into the kitchen. As part of the inducement, the writers had to prove that male cooks were creative and adventurous, not held back as women were by fretting over level measurements or fussing about the nutritional content of food.

In his book *The Best Men Are Cooks* (1941), Frank Shay declares, "Women have reduced cooking to a science while men cooks are working to restore it to its former high estate as one of the fine arts." He snidely refers to the British Mrs. Beeton, the most famous woman cookbook author of her day, as "the nineteenth-century lady who put the blight on English cuisine." Shay takes a strong stand on salads, insisting that they be composed of such greens as romaine, chicory, endive, and cress, and that concoctions "made with mixtures of nuts, fresh or canned fruits, soft cheeses and leafy greens have no place in male gastronomy." Expectably, Shay shows no interest in planning family meals, baking cupcakes, or catering to the food preferences of children. He prefers the dangerous world of old-style barbecue, complete with pit men to watch over the fire. "No one ever expects the women to do the cooking at a barbecue," he insists. "That task belongs exclusively to certain fire-scorched men of experience." The clambake is another all-male cooking bastion Shay defends, dominated as it should ideally be by overlords who supervise the women as they gather driftwood and seaweed, collect rocks, and maybe even dig the trench where men will cook the clams and lobsters.

Despite the humorous bluster of his male persona, Shay's work is a collection of honest recipes suitable for any home cook. The book includes recipes for polenta and risotto, dishes now in vogue that were not found in most other American cookbooks of the 1940s. There are also fine recipes for all sorts of dessert pies, which apparently had some status with him as guy food, but not a single recipe for cakes or cookies, girly sweet stuff that requires unmanly exact measurements. Though it is mostly a put-on, Shay's masculine posturing disguises the fact that he wrote a good home cookbook, and it is a sign of his times that to do it he had to put women down.

Frederic Birmingham, author of *The Complete Cookbook for Men* (1961), is another writer who makes fun of women in order to establish his authority and his right to produce a cookbook. He sets himself apart from women in the usual way by trying to show that men are more imaginative and take more risks in the kitchen while women, obsessed as they are with following recipes precisely, are uninspired and predictable. As a long-time editor of *Esquire* magazine, Birmingham was groomed to stroke male egos, and he too latches onto outdoor cooking as an inveterately male prerogative, inventing prehistoric precedents in which cavemen clubbed animals over the head and cooked them over roaring flames while women stood safely on the side and watched. Birmingham also comes up with a method-acting school of outdoor cooking in which he puts himself in the place of a steak or double lamb chop and intuitively knows when it is time to turn over.

These amusing books are period pieces that illustrate the ludicrous posturing that men had to go through in order to be comfortable writing about food. Women, too, since the nineteenth century had to strike certain poses when writing cookbooks and domestic manuals and hide the fact that they may have been more interested in politics and social justice. Lydia Maria Child, known in her day as a prominent writer and abolitionist, published her most popular book, *The Frugal Housewife* (1829), to stay afloat while she and her husband Calvin, a man with no visible income, continued their work as reformers. Child knew about frugality firsthand and passed on economical tips on cooking and household management to her reading public, who evidently found them useful, for by 1832 the book had gone into seven editions and was published in England as *The American Frugal Housewife*.

Child sets a sober, cheese-paring tone as she recommends feeding the family with scraps and inexpensive cuts of meat that would otherwise have been directed to the garbage pail. "Calf's head should be cleansed with very great care," she explains. "It is better to leave the wind-pipe on, for if it hangs out of the pot while the head is cooking, all the froth will escape through it." The book projects an image of the author as a middle-aged housewife with a large brood of children. In fact, Child was only twenty-six when the book was published, remained childless her whole life, and lived a public life at a time when women were routinely relegated to the kitchen. For her, writing about food was a means of economic survival. Her real interests lay elsewhere.

Most other female cookbook writers of the nineteenth century accepted the common wisdom of the day that men and women occupied separate spheres, with women destined to run the home and stay out of the workplace. At the same time, promoting the party line created successful professional careers for women like Sarah Josepha Hale, editor of *Godey's Lady's Book*, a traditional nineteenth-century women's magazine, and for Marion Harland, author of the immensely popular *Common Sense in the Household* (1871), who made a fortune instructing women on the proper care of hearth and home. Less well known but among my favorite cookbooks of the period are novelized household manuals that had something of a vogue in the late nineteenth century. These are recipe collections crudely disguised as fiction, with plot lines that present early married life as an idyl of domestic bliss made possible by the young bride's good cooking and sense of economy. The books are clearly influenced by other sentimental fiction of the period that was written by and for women, and that was famously condemned by Nathaniel Hawthorne, who complained that "America is now wholly given over to a d———d mob of scribbling women."

Catherine Owen, who also wrote conventional cookbooks, wrote fictional accounts of women rising above straitened circumstances by earning money through their skills as cooks. Her books *Gentle Breadwinners* (1888), *Ten Dollars Enough* (1886), and *Molly Bishop's Family* (1888) are morality tales that advise women to be prepared for whatever life may dish out—loss of inheritance, dying husbands, economic downturns. Her main characters rescue themselves from poverty by opening boardinghouses or by selling baked goods commercially, playing out Owen's philosophy that superior domestic skills give women a fallback position in the event of financial catastrophe. Despite her didacticism, Owen's books are charming and delightful to read. But they are not nearly as much fun as *A Thousand Ways to Please a Husband* (1917), written by Louise Bennet Weaver and Helen Cowles LeCron. This novel centers on a year in the life of the impossibly happy newlyweds Bettina and Bob. Each short chapter revolves around a meal the couple share or one of the parties they frequently give, with lessons in domestic management shining through. Here they are having their first meal together as man and wife:

> "Say, isn't it great to be alive!" exclaimed Bob, as he looked across the rose-decked table at the flushed but happy Bettina. "And a beefsteak dinner, too!"
>
> "Steak is expensive, dear, and you'll not get it often, but as this is our first real dinner in our own home, I had to celebrate."

As she is fond of reminding Bob at every opportunity Bettina knows a thing or two about economizing, although this does not stop her from indulging her husband's sweet tooth. He loves her cookies and soon learns to make his own sweets, as we learn in chapters called "Bob Makes Popcorn Balls" or "Bob Makes Peanut Fudge." The two seem more like convent-school roommates than a married couple as they cook and eat together. Reading their story, I cannot help but picture Bettina and Bob on their tenth anniversary, each heavier by fifty pounds, as they struggle to sit side by side before their fireplace toasting marshmallows or waddling off together to a picnic with a hamper so heavy it takes both of them to lift it. Their real fate is unknown, however, for while the authors went on to write three more Bettina books, I was disappointed to find that they are not novels, only collections of recipes.

I am reminded of the Bettina books whenever people approach me to confess a guilty pleasure—that they read cookbooks "as though they were novels." I assure them I understand their appeal, have the habit myself, and tell them about cookbooks that are in fact novels. But there are also cookbooks that were written by novelists or have respectful prefaces by famous novelists. Far and away, the most high-minded example of the latter is the preface Joseph Conrad wrote for *A Handbook of Cookery for a Small House* (1923), his wife's cookbook.

> Of all the books produced since the remote ages by human talents and industry those only that treat of cooking are, from a moral point of view, above suspicion. The intention of every other piece of prose may be discussed and even mistrusted, but the purpose of a cookery book is one and unmistakable. Its object can conceivably be no other than to increase the happiness of mankind.

Jessie Conrad knew great writing when she saw it. When she published another cookbook thirteen years later, she reprinted her husband's words, explaining, "Although this preface was written for my first little book of cookery, I feel that the sentiments expressed in it apply equally well to this its successor."

A lighter note is sounded in Truman Capote's brief foreword to Myrna Davis's *The Potato Book* (1972), a fundraising cookbook for a Long Island school. Capote offers his tribute to the potato with a recipe he calls "my one and only most delicious ever potato lunch." His first ingredient, a chilled bottle of 80-proof vodka, assures us that this is the real Truman Capote talking. He pairs the vodka with a potato that is baked and slathered with sour cream, then topped with spoonfuls of "the freshest, the grayest, the biggest Beluga," a dish Capote insists "is the only way I can bear to eat a potato." I was happy to learn about this preference but somehow doubted that Capote would have turned up his nose at a plateful of hot, crisp French fries, even if they were bereft of caviar.

That Marjorie Kinnan Rawlings, author of *The Yearling*, wrote a cookbook would not surprise readers of *Cross Creek*, her memoir of life in a remote corner of north central Florida, for *Cross Creek* is full of passionate descriptions of food. What may be surprising, however, is that her editor, the legendary Maxwell Perkins, famous for his brilliant nurturing of Ernest Hemingway, F. Scott Fitzgerald, and Thomas Wolfe, provided that same service for Rawlings's book on Florida cuisine, *Cross Creek Cookery* (1942). In one of his letters, Perkins told her that she had "done a wonderfully fine piece of work," that the book "as a whole is delightful, and something altogether new." In another letter he said, "You have been wonderfully ingenious in blending the practical directions with the anecdotes, and in a way which sets all against the background. It is a most charming book."

So it is. Rawlings here brings together her talent as a cook, storyteller, and provider of local color, and spices her cookbook with her ready wit and readier opinions. She speaks throughout of Dora, her irreplaceable Jersey milk cow that produces cream that "rises to a depth of three-quarters of an inch on a shallow pan of milk" and is "so thick, when ladled off into a bowl or pitcher, that it is impossible to pour. It must be spooned out." But like so much of what is most desirable in life, Dora and her incomparable milk came with a price. Dora was the daughter of a mean-spirited cow, and she too had a vile disposition and never stopped glaring evilly at Rawlings, who responded in kind. Dora had a sister that Rawlings named Atrocia, who was even more sinister but who was sold off before she could cause much harm.

I found that reading this cookbook by so gifted a writer would be delight enough even if the recipes were not as tempting as they are. Rawlings describes her black bottom pie as "so delicate, so luscious, that I hope to be propped up on my dying bed and fed a generous portion. Then I think that I should refuse outright to die, for life would be too good to relinquish." Rawlings took care to include dishes that were true to the region, the so-called "cracker" food that local people loved. She gives several recipes for swamp cabbage (hearts of palm), a vegetable found at the core of immature trees and cooked to accompany campfire fish or game dinners. Armed with her .22 rifle, Rawlings blasted away at quail, dove, rabbit, and squirrel, which she clearly knew how to cook. She also knew how to prepare alligator tails and bear meat, although she never claims to have hunted the animals down. More conventional are her recipes that transformed the tropical fruits that grew so abundantly on her property into grapefruit marmalade, kumquat jelly, and mango chutney.

It came as no surprise to me that Rawlings was on the plump side, or as one of her acquaintances put it, "She looks like a woman who is a good cook and enjoys her own cooking." Dora had something to do with it. After a passage in which the writer proudly claims to reject desserts at the end of large meals, she concedes that for her, some desserts *are* meals: "I like to sit down on a summer afternoon and eat a whole quart of Dora's ice cream. I like to sit by the open hearth-fire on a winter's day, about four in the afternoon, and eat a quarter of a devil's food cake, with a pot of tea or coffee."

Lillian Hellman, the well-known playwright and memoirist,

was another writer who compiled a cookbook, the last work she was able to write. Published posthumously, *Eating Together: Recipes' Recollections* (1984) was cowritten with a close friend, Peter Feibleman, whom she first met in New Orleans when she was thirty-five and he a child. "Lillian was the only person I had met who didn't talk down to children," he later said. "She asked me how old I was and when I told her I was 'only ten,' she nodded and her face didn't change. 'I don't know what you mean by "only." Ten isn't so young,' she said and turned away."

The cookbook reveals another side of Hellman, who was famous for being outspoken, acerbic, quarrelsome, mendacious, and a troublemaker. Here we see her better qualities—her wit, strong ties to friends, love of laughter, love of food, and stubborn courage in the face of death. Feibleman reports one of their last conversations when she was legally blind, partially paralyzed, and unable to walk.

> "I'm no fun anymore," she said . . . trying to sit up in bed. After a long pause she added: "But I was fun. Wasn't I?"
>
> I was reading a book by the window and asked her to shut up till I finished the page I was on.
>
> "I'll shut up," Lillian said, "on one condition. When we talk, we talk about something important."
>
> "Such as?" I said.
>
> "Such as," Lillian said, "what are we having for dinner?"

Food, for someone with Hellman's combative disposition, proved to be an exquisite battleground, for it gave her a lot to fight about: what to cook, how to cook it, how to serve it, and with whom to share the meal. Hellman loved to cook, and she maintained an ambitious vegetable garden on Martha's Vineyard, where she also loved to go fishing in the dinghy she kept on the beach. She spent sociable summers there cooking for dinner guests at least twice a week, a custom she preserved long past the time that failing health would have stopped others.

Working on the cookbook kept her occupied the last year of her life and in constant touch with Feibleman, whom she loved but fought with as much as any other people she was close to. The book was conceived, Hellman says, "as a tribute to an old friendship." It is divided in two, "Her Way" and "His Way," with each author presenting favorite recipes accompanied by anecdotes. Her recipes relate to good times with friends—meals shared in Paris with Janet Flanner, or the veal dish she and Peter ate at a favorite Los Angeles restaurant where they swapped funny stories about Dorothy Parker shortly after the writer had died. Hellman gives us a wonderful recipe for Bolognese sauce given to her by the mother of a chauffeur that director William Wyler once hired in Rome. (Hellman is never above name dropping.) And sometimes she just squeezes in an anecdote whether or not it relates to a recipe. With the mention of Paris, for instance, she launches into a tirade against Simone Signoret, whose French production of *The Little Foxes* left Hellman in a lifelong rage.

For his part, Feibleman demonstrates that he too is a dedicated cook, offering such tips as never using water in a recipe when stock, wine, or beer are at hand, or using prosciutto bones instead of salt for soups, stews, casseroles, and even some vegetable dishes. His recipes relate to New Orleans and to Spain, but most of all they relate to Hellman, for whom this book was a way of feeling alive. He describes one of the last times he saw her, just after their cookbook had been turned in to the publisher. Met at the door by a nurse, he was told that Hellman was getting weaker, that her memory was fading, and that she was dying. Moving on into her bedroom, Feibleman asked, "How are you?"

> "Not good, Peter," Lillian said.
> I asked why not.
> "This is the worst case of writer's block I ever had in my life," Lillian said. "The worst case."

How like Hellman to have perceived the end of her life as writer's block.

The intimate power of cookbooks to make connections between people came home to me most recently when a college class was sent to the Schlesinger Library to seek out and write about cookbooks that corresponded to their backgrounds. As they roamed the shelves, I heard sporadic squeals that told me that students were finding cookbooks they could relate to—Irish, Italian, African-American, Jewish cookbooks with food familiar to most students from the Boston area. I noticed, however, that one young woman seemed at a loss. Speaking with a distinct Russian accent, she explained that she was new to America and had no hope of finding a book that spoke to her. I handed her a copy I found of Anya von Bremzen's *Please to the Table: the Russian Cookbook* (1990) and moved on to help someone else. But the next thing I knew the young Russian was awash in tears because she had come across recipes from Odessa, the city she had recently left. All of her pent-up homesickness broke loose when she read these recipes from her native land.

Another student I helped that day was struggling with the assignment, because, as she described herself, she was a "plain-vanilla Midwesterner of English, German, and Scandinavian background" and was sure no cookbook could speak to that. I handed her some community cookbooks from her home state, Iowa, books typical of the kind that are compiled to raise money for churches, schools, and other organizations. To her amazement, the young woman found that one of the cookbooks was from a neighboring county and she was able to recognize the recipes and the names of the some of the contributors. She too had found her place and her people in a cookbook.

Home Cooking

A Feast Made of Friendship

by Laura Shapiro
from *House & Garden*

In this *House & Garden* essay, culinary historian Laura Shapiro *(Perfection Salad)* puts a historical spin on our collective response to last September's events. What truer way for Americans to reaffirm community than by holding a potluck supper?

A week or so after the terrible events of September 11, a friend who lives near Washington went into her kitchen and started to peel, chop, sauté, and simmer. Soon, a beef stew heady with cognac was filling the house with fragrance. A neighbor baked an intensely buttery pound cake. Another neighbor made a noodle pudding, and still another made a rich mixture of chicken and broccoli wrapped in pastry. Then all the families gathered in my friend's living room, helped themselves to some of everything, and by the end of the evening everyone felt distinctly better. "It was a comfort food potluck," she told me later. "It really worked."

Potlucks do work; that's why we still turn to them when we're hungry for more than good food—when we need a feast made of friendship. The table laden with everybody's best home cooking is an American icon by now, one that goes back as far as the first Thanksgiving. While it's doubtful the Pilgrims and Indians used the word "potluck" for their communal spread of venison, duck, corn bread, and wild plums, the settlers certainly knew the term, for "pot luck" began showing up in print in England by the late sixteenth century. Back then, however, it simply meant food that was already on the stove, hence available for unexpected guests. We still use it that way, but Americans have added another meaning, inspired by the hardscrabble, homemade nature of entertaining in the New World. Potluck dinners—known on the frontier as church suppers, community dinners, or covered-dish suppers— were among the mainstays of early American social life. By the 1880s, the concept had reached New York, where a crowd of writers, socialites, and bon vivants calling themselves the Pot Luck Club held an annual dinner featuring dishes prepared by the members. According to *The New York Times,* club members used to file into the dining room in costume and march around the tables singing "See the Conquering Cookists Come" before they sat down and fell to.

But it's the potlucks of the mid-twentieth century that give the term its modern resonance. If we can believe the accounts by various well-stuffed guests, those potlucks had food that was delicious and abundant beyond imagining. Church suppers in Alabama, delineated in a report from the Alabama Writers' Project in 1941, featured fried chicken and chicken pie, baked or barbecued ham, pickles and relishes, white potatoes and sweets, breads and biscuits, preserves and jellies, cakes, pies, and custards.

Novelist and food writer Edward Harris Heth, describing church suppers in his Wisconsin hometown in 1956, rhapsodized over the ham loaves, the potato pudding, the macaroni with its "crisp, bacon-studded crust," and a local specialty known as "Mrs. Emlyn's chop suey": "It is really a baked spaghetti with chopped meat. It is redolent of celery, onions, and the goodness of ground round steak—not hamburger, small Mrs. Emlyn will tell you with a warrior's thrust forward of her chin."

And Dale Brown, in the 1968 *American Cooking* volume in the Time-Life *Foods of the World* series, included a potluck made by his family in rural New York state. "I was lucky enough to get a large slice of my great-aunt Ella's currant pie," he recalled, "filled with the tiny garnet-colored berries from her garden and so much sugar—to cut back the tartness—that sparkling crystals clung to the inside of the top crust."

Yet it's undeniable that the best cook in most families is nostalgia itself. Nobody really knows whether that fried chicken of yesteryear was as tender as memory insists, that jelly as crystalline, those biscuits truly feather light. And what about the dishes that memory simply refuses to acknowledge? Even while Great-aunt Ella was rolling out her pastry, it's more than likely that some other cook in the family was studying *Potluck Party Recipes,* a 1960 cookbook by Thora Hegstad Campbell. "Casseroles are the mainstay of the potluck," instructed Campbell, as a bell tolled mournfully for baked ham and chicken pie. True to her culinary moment, she suggested making Barbecued Corned Beef Bake, which called for canned corned beef and ketchup, layered with macaroni and peas. It probably did show up at Brown's family reunion; he just averted his eyes.

Today, when home cooking is a category that embraces everything from spaghetti doused with bottled pasta sauce to Linzer tortes baked from scratch, potluck dinners can be a merciless reflection of our culinary mores. For a food lover, there are few sights as depressing as a potluck table on which someone has deposited a store-bought pie or a take-out pizza. Please, if you can't cook, bring wine or some exotic water. And if you do cook, why not skip the lasagna and let someone else make the cole slaw? You can bring classics of another sort: a platter of short ribs, or a tureen of borscht, or a batch of Parker House rolls. Pear cobbler, spiced with star anise, will hold its own next to any chocolate cake. Our winter potluck may lack some of the favorites of the genre, but it's traditional in the best sense—a buffet of timeless dishes guaranteed to warm the spirits of all who flock to the table.

BRAISED SHORT RIBS

Serves 8

6 lbs. beef short ribs, cut into 4-inch pieces
Sea salt
Freshly ground pepper
3 Tbsp. olive oil
1 onion, peeled and finely diced
2 carrots, peeled and grated
2 large tomatoes, roughly chopped (approx. 2 cups)
4 garlic cloves, peeled and sliced
2 Tbsp. fresh thyme leaves
2 cups chicken stock
1 oz. dried porcini mushrooms, soaked in 2 cups warm
    water for ½ hour and strained through cheesecloth
    to remove grit
2 fresh bay laurel leaves
2 bottles Guinness stout
1 Tbsp. chopped flat leaf parsley

Trim excess fat from short ribs, season generously with salt and pepper, and tie each piece. Refrigerate overnight or 4 to 6 hours.

Preheat oven to 400 degrees.

Place ribs in a large roasting pan, bone side down, and roast uncovered for 20 minutes or until lightly browned. Remove and place into an 8-quart enameled pot.

In a skillet, add olive oil and sauté onion until translucent, approximately 5 minutes. Add carrots, tomatoes, garlic, and thyme, and saute for several minutes.

Add 1 cup chicken stock to deglaze the pan. Add mushrooms and laurel leaves. Remove from heat. Add vegetables, then spread evenly over ribs. Add remaining chicken stock and stout.

Cover and bake for 20 minutes. Reduce heat to 350 degrees, and continue baking for 1 ½ hours.

To test doneness: the meat should just be falling off the bones.

Remove strings, and place ribs bone side down on a serving dish; cover and keep warm.

To remove excess fat from the sauce, place in refrigerator for several hours, then skim congealed fat off the top. In a pan, bring sauce to a boil. To serve, arrange the short ribs on a serving platter, pour the braising juices over the ribs, and sprinkle with parsley. Accompany with puréed potato and celery root gratin.

PURÉED POTATO AND CELERY ROOT GRATIN

Serves 6 to 8

1 ½ lbs. celery root, peeled and cut into 8 pieces
2 lbs. Yukon Gold potatoes, peeled and quartered
½ lemon, cut in quarters
1 bay leaf
2 garlic cloves
1 onion, quartered
1 celery stalk, cut in half
1 tsp. salt
½ cup heavy cream
¼ cup milk
2 Tbsp. unsalted butter
1 tsp. sea salt, or more to taste
Freshly ground pepper
1 cup finely grated Gruyère cheese
1 Tbsp. unsalted butter to grease the dish
2 Tbsp. cold unsalted butter, cut into ¼-inch cubes

In a large stockpot, add celery root, potatoes, lemon, bay leaf, garlic, onion, celery, and salt. Cover with cold water and bring to a boil. Cook until potatoes and celery root are tender, approximately 35 to 45 minutes. Drain and set potatoes and celery root aside; discard all else. When cool enough to handle, put the potatoes and celery root through a food mill into a large bowl.

Preheat oven to 350 degrees.

In a saucepan, heat heavy cream, milk, and butter. Stir into potato and celery root purée. Add salt, pepper, and Gruyère cheese.

Butter a 12-inch oval or gratin dish and add potatoes. Top with cubes of butter. Cover with foil and bake for 20 minutes. Serve immediately with short ribs.

PARKER HOUSE ROLLS

Makes 24

1 cup milk
5 Tbsp. unsalted butter
1 tsp. salt
1 package active dry yeast (2 ¼ tsp.)
3 Tbsp. warm water (115 degrees)
3 Tbsp. sugar
1 large egg
3 ½ cups all-purpose flour
3 Tbsp. unsalted butter (approx.), melted, for brushing
    the rolls

In a small saucepan, combine the milk, butter, and salt over a medium-high heat until butter is melted. Remove from the heat.

In a large mixing bowl, combine yeast, warm water, and sugar, and stir until dissolved. Let sit for 10 minutes.

With a wooden spoon, gently stir milk into the yeast. Stir in the egg. Gradually add flour until the dough is moist but not sticky. Transfer the dough to a floured work surface and knead by hand for 10 minutes or until the dough is smooth and elastic.

Transfer dough into an oiled bowl, and turn once to completely coat with the oil. Cover and place dough in warm spot until doubled in volume, approximately 1 ½ hours.

Shape dough into a rectangle. Cut it into 4 long strips, then cut each strip into 6 pieces. Roll each piece into a ball, and place on a greased baking sheet, leaving 1 inch between the balls. Cover with oiled plastic wrap and let rest in a warm place for 30 minutes.

Grease two baking sheets.

On a lightly floured work surface, gently pat each ball into an oval. Using the handle of a wooden spoon, roll from the center toward each end of the oval, creating a valley in the center. Do not roll over the edges; they should remain thicker than the center.

Brush tops with melted butter, and fold the ovals in half so the two ends meet. Pinch the edges together and press down lightly on each roll. Place rolls on a greased baking sheet, 2 inches apart. Cover with oiled plastic wrap and place in a warm spot until doubled in volume, about 1 hour.

Preheat the oven to 400 degrees. When rolls have doubled in volume, brush tops with melted butter and bake for about 15 minutes or until golden brown. Serve warm.

The rolls may be baked a few hours ahead and reheated in a 350-degree oven.

Trading Places

by Eliot Kaplan

from *Bon Appetit*

A cross between potluck and book club, the neighborhood dining society is a fascinating phenomenon—and Hearst magazine executive Eliot Kaplan (formerly editor-in-chief of *Philadelphia* and *GQ*) went public in *Bon Appetit* with one of its dirty little secrets.

W hen Mike stepped to the front and announced a little too cheerfully how he had pureed the chilies, I thought the jig was up. It's not that Mike is an incapable fellow. He is successful in every one of his adult roles: economic forecaster, husband, father, friend. As are all the other guys in the four couples we've been sharing dinners with over the past several years.

It's just that, well, we didn't feel like cooking that weekend, or being on our best behavior. But being guys, we wanted to show off and impress our wives. As easily as possible, of course.

Now, years later, a touch of guilt lingers and dread weighs heavy as this magazine arrives in mailboxes and we're about to be revealed.

But let me step back a minute.

My neighborhood is a most unusual one, in that it actually is a neighborhood. I live on a small dead-end street of two dozen houses in a Philadelphia suburb. And people hang out together a lot. I'm not a hanger-outer. This is allowed, but definitely discouraged. Ours is a street of regularly scheduled events. My house is assigned the annual Fourth of July parade and cookout, while other homes handle the Easter egg hunt, the Christmas caroling, Oktoberfest, the Super Bowl.

Then somebody got the idea of starting a dining club. Now five couples get together for dinner every few months, with recipes solely from recent issues of this very magazine. The food, of course, is a big part of the evening, though the conversation always turns up something interesting, too. Sometimes when the wine is flowing freely, the talk can take surprising turns. Such as, Which one of the group would you be married to if not your spouse? Or: Power, Fame, Love, Money—which is your driving force?

We commiserate about job crises, take pride in the talents and idiosyncrasies of our respective children, support one another through our parents' terminal illnesses.

And after some 20 dinners, we can't complain about the quality of the meals or the relative ease of preparation. Virtually every dish has been at least a polite success.

And that's just it. When it was decided that the next party would be an all-boys' meal, we knew we could have managed. It had a barbecue theme, and what guy can't throw steaks on the grill, albeit steaks requiring a "rub"? Brian, owing to his British boarding school background, loves serving, even going so far as to auction himself off as a formal butler for charity events. Tracy is a scientist, so he should know about mixing ingredients. And George, the HR consultant, is such an expert amateur baker that he volunteers his services for friends' wedding cakes.

Mike cooks about the way a former frat boy from Pittsburgh who lugs around Rolling Rock beer might be expected to cook, and as for me, well, once my wife tired of the recipes from my mother's Campbell's soup cookbook, she seized the culinary duties in our household.

It didn't take long to convince everyone. The thought of pulling a fast one on our beloveds was too good to pass up. Only George was a reluctant convert, owing to his rock-solid Canadian nature, the implied insult to his cooking skills, or perhaps—let's admit it— terror of his wife.

A friend in the food department of a local college set us up with Francis McFadden, a student and professional chef who could use the couple hundred bucks he would pocket.

The menu was to be a mix of dishes that could believably be made by us, along with a few surprises that would draw the requisite oohs and aahs. The appetizer was wild mushroom enchiladas with *ancho* chili cream sauce, followed by a salad of arugula with prosciutto and mango. The main course would be manly rib-eye steaks with a Mediterranean rub, served with a side of grilled new potatoes with Parmesan and herbs. Dessert (attention, George!): cherry upside-down cake.

Irony Chef McFadden did not disappoint. He drove in to Philadelphia's famed Reading Terminal Market to pick the choicest ingredients from local merchants: perfectly marbled beef, prosciutto Carmela Soprano would kill for, fresh crimson cherries.

In his small apartment, McFadden rubbed the steaks with an herb blend. Like a professional food stylist, he sizzled perfect grill marks onto the potatoes with a tiny iron, then mixed the salad dressing, made two cherry cakes, and finished up the enchiladas. Then, after sizing up the aptitude of his accomplices, he covered each dish with aluminum foil and penciled on detailed heating time and temperature instructions.

We told the wives we needed to be left alone all Saturday afternoon and sent them off out of sight. After picking up the stuff from McFadden's apartment, we reconvened at Tracy's house, the scene for that night's dinner. A nice Cabernet was opened, Springsteen was cranked up on the CD, and for the pièce de résistance, Tracy started sautéing onions. "Makes the house smell like cooking," he explained.

So for two hours, we sat around prepping, if not any real food, at least each other (Remember, Mike, *puree* means to strain thoroughly), and waited to see if we could pull it off.

At seven o'clock our wives arrived, with some trepidation, some apprehension, even a little sympathy for the onerous chore they had left us with. Mike, per custom, stepped to the head of the table to explain his course, the enchiladas. The first moment of truth: Surely Mike was going to choke. There were words like *portobello* and *shiitake* involved here, *cilantro, feta, anchos.* There was draining and whisking and that damn pureeing. But Mike didn't miss a beat. Makes me think a career in the CIA could be in the offing (that's Central Intelligence Agency, not The Culinary Institute of America).

Things continued to proceed smoothly. We were cruising. Brian was oozing his best British charm as we delicately rolled slices of prosciutto for the salad. He reminded us to serve ladies first and from the left.

By now the third bottle of Cabernet had been opened, and a funny look was coming into our wives' eyes: surprise, respect, even awe. It's not a look guys get too often in their second decade of marriage.

The steaks came off the grill. I stood and declared my rub, casually mentioning its paprika, coriander, cayenne pepper, ginger and—as nonchalantly as one who has practiced 37 times can—cumin, pronounced with affect, *CUE-min.*

"George's" cherry upside-down cake was perfect, and it turned out that it actually was George's. The bum had gone and made the dessert himself, so that if we were busted, he could at least say he had done *his* job.

When the wives came back into the kitchen expecting to see a tornado, they found the place immaculate. (Naturally. The large pans and containers had long since been emptied and returned to McFadden.) We simply said that we learned from them about cleaning up as you go.

And the kitchen wasn't the only thing glowing. The radiance beaming from our wives meant that not only would our cooking skills never be mocked again, but that there might be sex tonight.

These days when we talk about our kitchen caper, we mistily recall "the night the men cooked" and look over at one another fondly. Mike lives in perpetual fear that he will be called upon to make those mushroom enchiladas again, and I keep McFadden's number close by.

The amazing thing is that despite our glee, our respect for our wives and our big mouths, our secret has never been revealed.

Until now.

Cooking Like a 3-Star Chef in Your Own Home (Almost)

by Mark Bittman

from the *New York Times*

In his persona as The Minimalist—witness his cookbooks *The Minimalist Cooks, The Minimalist Dinner, Cooks At Home*—Mark Bittman deconstructs the mysteries of cuisine for ordinary home cooks. Here The Minimalist observes a top-flight restaurant kitchen, with some surprising discoveries.

I t looks pretty straightforward, and for Harold Moore, the 29-year-old chef at Montrachet in TriBeCa, it is. Take a dry-aged sirloin and sauté it. Serve the meat on a bed of shallots in a red wine reduction sauce, with sautéed chanterelle mushrooms, a few haricots verts and some carrots.

Finally, sprinkle some tiny flowers on top of the meat, accompany it with a round of potato gratin and send the resulting plate out to the customer (or, for that matter, a photographer). There it is: honest, relatively simple restaurant cooking. A perfect French dish. The sort it would be lovely to make at home.

But without a lot of help, you can't. It is, in fact, virtually impossible for any home cook to cook like a chef. In order to make his dry-aged sirloin with potato gratin, Mr. Moore employed nine people over two days. For the final preparation, he used 10 pans and a stove area about the size of an average Manhattan kitchen.

Not even a chef can cook like a chef outside his restaurant, no matter how accomplished a slicer and dicer or how visionary an artist. "I just smoke up the house, and it annoys my wife," Mr. Moore said. Still, with some planning and a few simple techniques borrowed from the professionals, the home cook can approach the grace of Mr. Moore's $28 creation, without smoking up the house. It won't be *exactly* the same, but it will be close.

The great advantage that chefs have is a labor force. There were, for example, the two men who arrived at Montrachet in the morning to peel the Yukon Gold potatoes used in the gratin and to slice them to Mr. Moore's specifications. They left the results soaking in cream in the restaurant's walk-in cooler for another prep cook, who assembled the gratin, cooked it in a convection oven, covered it with parchment paper and returned it to the walk-in to cool. Then there was the butcher who accepted delivery of the sirloin ($120 a side, aged three months) and who cut it into steaks for the evening service, trimming fat and sinew. There was the unpaid chef's apprentice who cleaned the mushrooms, and a line cook, Bryan Stewart, who turned and glazed the carrots and trimmed and blanched the haricots verts and who, at the end, sprinkled the flowering micro beet sprouts over the meat.

There was another line cook, Pedro Espinal, who sautéed the steak and warmed the shallot sauce. There was Kevin Lasko, who cut the potatoes out of the gratin pan with an aluminum die, and gave the round to Mr. Espinal, who warmed it in the oven and browned it in the salamander, a kind of superbroiler used in professional kitchens that sits above his stove.

And throughout the process there was Mr. Moore, who poked and prodded and nudged and tasted and, eventually, smiled. "This is my job," he said, by way of slightly amazed self-explanation. "This is what I do."

And you, cooking at home? Before you finish peeling an onion, a chef is sautéeing it. While you are mincing an herb to get the teaspoon needed in a recipe, a chef is grabbing a pinch out of a little tray.

When, before tackling a new recipe, you wonder whether you should make a batch of stock, which itself might require a trip to the market, in order to reduce it so you can produce a few table-spoons of demi-glace, the chef is spooning that thick, delicious, sauce-enhancing substance out of his seemingly endless supply, produced earlier by a prep cook who arrived at 7 a.m.

A well-stocked restaurant has common herbs like parsley, dill, thyme and basil on hand every day of the year; it may also stock chervil, shiso, marjoram, lovage, baby arugula, basil sprouts or, as at Montrachet, micro beet sprouts. Veal chops are ordered cut to specifications; beef cuts are consistent and dry-aged; fresh pasta might be made on premises or delivered. And so on. Will your local fish supplier or supermarket have halibut tomorrow? The chef has someone call Maine to make sure it is delivered first thing in the morning.

And though it does not matter as much as people believe, restaurant equipment is often on a different level from what is available to all but the wealthiest home cooks. There are indoor grills and woodburning ovens; efficient salamanders (so named for the mythical reptile who lived at the fiery center of the earth) that, unlike most broilers, actually brown food; convection ovens to speed the roasting process; Fryolators that make frying, a tremen-dous challenge to home cooks, ridiculously simple; dishwashers, both human and mechanical, that take care of pots and pans almost as quickly as they are soiled; and exhaust vents that can handle real smoke.

At Montrachet, for example, Mr. Moore needs to keep the door to his kitchen open at all times. If he does not, the suction created by the exhaust hood above his stoves will pull the door open by itself, creating a breeze that blows decorative elements like flowers off his plates.

Finally, there is a fact that few people talk about but everyone knows: most chefs do not cook with your health in mind. They might fuss about organic vegetables or their steaming technique or their vegan soup, but when it will benefit a dish they load in the fat. While you might think twice about finishing a reduction sauce for four with a tablespoon of butter, the chef will finish a sauce for one with two tablespoons. Your two tablespoons of olive oil used for sautéeing four portions could easily become half a cup for sautéeing one at the chef's stove.

Mr. Moore uses butter with calculated glee, which is to say with no calculation at all. "I don't even think about the amount of oil I use," Mr. Moore said, pointing to some glazed baby carrots in Mr. Stewart's sauté pan. "For me, it's a tool, not an ingredient."

Having said all that, though, experienced home cooks know that you can produce great food that approaches the four-star restaurant level in the home kitchen. It just means you must have reasonable expectations while exercising good judgment and mastering a few special techniques.

For "judgment," I might say "restraint." Home cooks get themselves in trouble when they become overly ambitious (there is a tradition of this in the United States: it's called Thanksgiving). Without help, and I don't just mean someone to wash the dishes, it is a challenge to prepare a meal that includes more than two complicated dishes. Indeed, on anything except a special occasion, when you might set aside four hours or more to be in the kitchen, it is nearly impossible.

Great as Mr. Moore's potato gratin is, you'd need the bulk of the day just to soak the slices in cream. But the alternatives are myriad, and some, still worthy of a great restaurant, are quick enough for weeknight meals. For example, parboil those same potatoes—a step you can do in advance—crisp them in a pan, and you've saved hours. Then substitute dried porcini mushrooms for Mr. Moore's chanterelles, replace the carrots with easy-to-prepare broccoli and eliminate the time-slaughtering shallot sauce, and a meal similar to Mr. Moore's can be executed in less than two hours.

None of this means that side dishes and desserts should be store-bought; it means, for example, that you might abandon the idea of Montrachet's crisp-topped crème brûlée for dessert, as I've done here, in favor of vanilla pots de crème, a stellar dessert that predates the crème brûlée and is far simpler to make (there's no messing with propane torches to brown the top, for instance). It also means that not every dish must be served piping hot (an obsession more noticeable in the United States than elsewhere); as chefs like Mr. Moore know well, many are equally good warm or at room temperature. Steaks, in fact, can improve in the time spent resting, as the juices recede from the surface of the meat.

As for the equipment deficiencies of the home kitchen, these are largely imagined and not unlike car envy; you may want a Mercedes, but your Taurus gets you to work just fine. Similarly, you don't need a Viking stove to be a good cook, and all but the most inadequate equipment can be worked around (I have done most of my cooking on electric stoves since 1994, and have come to like them). The key lesson to remember here is not that you need a stove that produces ultra-high heat but that you should use the high heat that your stove produces.

I have talked to scores of chefs over the years about this issue, and most agree that the most beneficial adjustment home cooks could make would be to preheat skillets before beginning to cook in them. Even if you have a propane stove, if you rest an empty skillet above a medium flame for a couple of minutes before adding oil, butter or the steak you're preparing, you will begin to sauté and pan-grill like a champ.

High oven heat is almost as important, as is using the oven more frequently, even in preparing dishes that are not roasted. An oven set at 450 or 500 degrees can help you get food off the stovetop while you continue to brown it.

This has a couple of advantages. First, it can compensate for the lack of an exhaust fan, which means you can brown fish or meat in the house without setting off the smoke detector. It also means you can gain room on top of the stove. And finally, if you equip your oven with a pizza stone or ceramic cooking tiles, you can produce the kind of strong, even bottom heat that chefs gain by putting their skillets directly on the floor of their ovens.

Of the remaining issues, some are insurmountable; you will never have a bevy of workers and unlimited access to prime ingredients.

You can, of course, produce large quantities of stock and freeze some, mince enough parsley in a food processor to last a few days (and preclude the need to track down fresh, flowering micro beet sprouts with which to garnish the steak) and so on, but this does not guarantee that you will have what you need when you need it. And you can treat yourself to some chanterelles or a dry-aged steak when you see them at the market or order them from afar. That's easy enough, as long as you have the money.

But in many ways, the easiest way to make your food taste chef-created is to bring butter back into your life: steam some broccoli and top it with lemon, then steam some more and top it with lemon and beurre noisette, and see which one reminds you of your favorite restaurant.

Stirring Up Memories

by Greg Atkinson

from *The Seattle Times: Pacific Northwest* magazine

In the hands of the immensely gifted Greg Atkinson—top chef at Seattle's acclaimed Canlis restaurant and a regular writer for the *Seattle Times'* Sunday magazine— even a simple recipe piece becomes a revelation.

Choose a day when you can feel a noticeable chill in the air. It's best if the sun is shining and the leaves are turning red, or golden, or even brown. Find yourself a green kabocha squash by 11 o'clock in the morning so you can have pumpkin risotto ready in time for lunch. Kabocha is Japanese for pumpkin. Maybe you have never noticed it before, but chances are there's one at your local grocery store. It might be underneath the produce stand in a basket on the floor. It might be at the farmer's market, or in your neighbor's backyard. Somewhere one is waiting for you.

If you already have another kind of winter squash or pumpkin, take a good, long look at it. Maybe it can pretend to be kabocha long enough for you to make risotto. Buttercup squash and so-called "Sweet Mama" squash are almost identical to kabocha; they will do. Hard, dense-fleshed sugar pumpkins, red kuri squash and gold nugget squash will work, too. A butternut squash is OK, if it isn't too intent on being a butternut. But watery, stringy or thin-skinned squashes are out.

Once you have the squash, think about how it felt to stay home from school on a fall day, when the house was quiet and the light was pouring in and you had all your thoughts to yourself. Think about your grandmother. If you can't remember her, think about mine. She wore dresses even on weekdays. She had pointy glasses and preferred sensible shoes that wouldn't hurt her bunions. She laughed a lot, but she usually tried to hide it, acting straight so we would take her seriously. She cooked things up in her kitchen that she liked to eat, and if you had sense enough to know what was good, you would like them, too.

While you're reminiscing, put the pumpkin on a solid wood cutting board set atop a sturdy counter; approach with your biggest knife and most serious look. These squash have a skin as hard as life itself, and you have to cut right through it. Cut about halfway in, and if you're feeling strong and the squash seems compliant, push and push some more to cut it in half. If you're feeling weak or timid, and the knife is wedged deep in the squash like the sword in the stone, pick them up together and whack them down hard to break the squash in half; you'll feel stronger then.

Once you've cut the pumpkin in half, the rest is easy. Lay the cut side down so the thing is stable, then cut the half pumpkin in half again to make two quarters. Don't worry about the other half pumpkin for now; you won't need it. Use a soup spoon to carve out the seedy middle, then, using your knife again, cut the skin off the pumpkin and cut the peeled and seeded flesh into 1-inch cubes, or shapes as close to cubes as you can get. You should have a generous two cups of diced pumpkin.

Measure yourself a cup of rice. For now, forget what Marcella Hazan and Lynne Rossetto Kasper have said. They don't know who you are or where you live, and you don't need Arborio or carnaroli rice. Use ordinary short-grain rice from Japan. You can use the kind from Louisiana or California if you want, but I like the plain white, unwashed pearly-shaped grains from Asia. And I like to imagine I'm high above the earth looking down at the Pacific Ocean: I'm on one side, raising my cup of rice in a kind of salute and Asia's on the other side, where the sun is barely rising. Far off behind me is Italy, where the sun has already set.

Now light two burners and put a small saucepan on the back one and a nice, heavy-bottomed 3-quart stew pot on the front one. I have an enameled iron pot with sloped sides that works nicely. Put a can of chicken broth and half a can of water in the back pot; don't put anything in the front one yet. Instead, chop half a big onion while the pan gets hot. Now put a tablespoon of oil in the front pan and a tablespoon of butter. The butter will sizzle and melt in the oil. Sauté the onion until it is soft. Peel a few cloves of garlic and slice them paper thin; add them to the onion.

Add the cubed pumpkin, and stir for a minute or two to warm it up. Add the rice and stir for another couple of minutes until the rice is translucent. Think about translucent. Think about light passing part way through and not coming out the other side. Where did it go?

Stir in a half-cup of white wine. If there is no wine, stir in a half-cup of apple juice. No one will know. When the wine has hissed and boiled and evaporated, stir in half a cup of the hot broth from the back burner. And keep stirring until the rice is crying out for more liquid, until the pan begins to sizzle every time you stir and the risotto sounds like it's trying to fry again. Lower the heat a little, add another half cup of broth, and think about the salad you will serve with the risotto. Whether it's lettuce or spinach, dress it simply with nothing but three tablespoons of olive oil and one tablespoon of balsamic vinegar, salt and pepper. You can think about my grandmother's great-grandfather if you like. Desiderio Chini came over from Bologna, Italy, in 1809. Think of how he must have missed his home, the food there, the balsamic vinegar that his mother kept in a barrel in the rafters of the house. Think of how he missed the Parmigiano-Reggiano that was rubbed in his time with crushed grape seeds and ashes so the 40-pound wheels stood in black stacks in the open markets.

Sneak a short break from the constant stirring to grate some

Reggiano and think of how my old Italian ancestor must have missed the patter of his own language in his mother's kitchen. He married a 25-year-old woman named Margarita Bauve from New Orleans in 1813 and lived with her until he died in 1830. She was 42 then, and would live to be 75.

After 10 or 15 minutes, the pumpkin cubes will soften and their corners will disappear. The rice will swell and the broth will grow creamy and smooth. Keep adding broth as the rice demands it.

An African-American girl lived in the Chini household. According to family lore, she came with my thrice-great-grandmother from Louisiana and stayed in the house next door with the older children who slept there when the family outgrew the tiny house where they began. The kitchen was in a third structure, behind the two houses. The whole complex is still standing on a quiet street in Pensacola, Fla.

When the last of the broth is almost absorbed, stir in a handful of grated Reggiano, and demand that everyone who is eating with you come at once. There is a moment when risotto is at its peak, and it must not be allowed to pass. If the cheese makes the grains look flat, stir in another tablespoon of butter to make them shine, and ask someone else to toss the salad. The light will sparkle off the surface of the risotto as you spoon it into shallow bowls.

Serves 4

1 tablespoon olive oil
1 tablespoon butter
1 cup diced onion
3 or 4 cloves garlic, peeled and thinly sliced
2 cups diced kabocha, or other dense, sweet pumpkin
1 cup short-grain rice
½ cup white wine
3 cups light chicken broth, boiling hot
½ cup grated Parmigiano-Reggiano cheese
1 tablespoon butter, optional

1. In a heavy saucepan over medium-high heat, warm the olive oil and butter. Sauté the onion briefly and add the garlic. Stir in the diced pumpkin and cook until the pumpkin is hot and just beginning to brown. Stir in the rice and cook 1 minute, or until the rice is translucent.

2. Stir in the wine. When it has boiled off, add ½ cup of the chicken broth. Stir until the broth is absorbed, then add another ½ cup broth. Continue stirring and slowly adding broth for 20 minutes, or until the rice and the pumpkin are tender.

3. When the last of the broth has been added, stir in the cheese and, if desired, the extra tablespoon of butter. Serve the risotto hot, followed by a green salad.

Red Wine and Old Roosters

by Jeffrey Steingarten

from *Vogue*

> In his monthly *Vogue* food columns, Jeffrey Steingarten exhibits an irrepressible curiosity about food with a hearty appetite to match. He's like a culinary detective, doggedly pursuing the ultimate expression of a particular ingredient or recipe.

How could I have been such a blockhead, I asked myself, rhetorically. It had been right in front of me all these years, or right inside of me, to be more precise.

You know how sometimes you bite into a forkful of breakfast, lunch, or dinner—or even sometimes just a snack—and suddenly an eternal truth or universal law reveals itself to you? That's just how it happened this time. There I was, in Oxford, England, in a restaurant called Le Petit Blanc, eating a plate of coq au vin. This is, of course, one of the most famous of all traditional French country dishes—at its most essential, pieces of chicken stewed in red wine. I had eaten coq au vin maybe 200 times before. It was the first complicated dish I had ever cooked, taking many times longer to get on the table than a hamburger and requiring the purchase of unusual ingredients—a slab of unsliced bacon, dozens of tiny white onions, several bottles of red wine. I had borne the expense and effort in hopes of impressing a pretty blonde female classmate in graduate school. As I remember, it didn't work quite well enough.

Where did I go wrong? While the sauce—really concentrated cooking broth—was lovely, dark, and deep, the chicken itself came out tough, dry, and stringy. Maybe that was the problem. Or was it those slippery little white onions that worm their way into nearly every coq au vin? They are the size of marbles, take forever to peel, and are nearly impossible to bring to the lips, because when you try to spear them with your fork, they fly off your plate and onto your pretty, blonde, female classmate's fluffy white angora sweater. Perhaps it was the excess of bouncy, nearly tasteless, cultivated white mushrooms known as champignons de Paris, or just champignons, that litter most latter-day coq au vins?

The Oxford version might just have done the trick. There the chicken was juicy and meaty and full of flavor, and I finished every morsel. For the first time I understood why people have been eating coq au vin for hundreds or thousands of years. (The French believe that Julius Caesar was served coq au vin in the Auvergne in south-central France during his campaign to subdue Gaul around 54 B.C., and became a total fan.) How was the Oxford coq au vin different from mine?

And then it came to me. Coq au vin means "rooster with wine." They must have used an old rooster, a bird possessing a rich and profound flavor and flesh that stands up to endless stewing. A writer on the history of French food who happened to be at the table confirmed my hunch: Yes, of course, authentic coq au vin *must* be made with a rooster. Coq means "rooster." How could it be otherwise? When my convive had finished patronizing me, he peered into my plate and examined the scattered molecules remaining there, but he could establish nothing. I asked the waiter to ask the chef, but the chef had left for the evening.

Stewing an old rooster in wine makes perfect sense. When making chicken soup, whether my grandmother's incomparable recipe or the Chinese broth they call "superior stock," we buy a mature stewing hen weighing between six and eight pounds, whose flesh is full of savor but far too tough to roast or fry or broil. Mature hens and roosters lose their chief function when their reproductive powers fade. Something must be done with all that flavorful flesh. And the alcohol in wine is a famous tenderizer. Somehow, even then, I knew that when I returned home, my chief mission would be to bring true coq au vin to America, where nearly everybody has eaten something called coq au vin, but where nobody, I felt sure, had ever eaten an old rooster cooked in wine.

All I needed were a recipe and a rooster.

But first I had to check one fundamental fact. I telephoned my indefatigable friend Mira, who is seeking a Ph.D. in classics at Princeton. Was Julius Caesar really fond of coq au vin? Mira turned to Caesar's Commentarii de Bello Gallico (you know, the famous one that starts, "Gallia est omnis divisa in partes tres"), which I read as a boy in Latin class and which Caesar had written as a kind of campaign biography to gain popularity among stay-at-homes both in Rome and in high schools in the suburbs of New York City. There is not one bite of coq au vin in Commentarii de Bello Gallico. Caesar mentions chicken only once, and that's later, when he gets to Britain, where the people refuse to eat fowl but enjoy cockfights. As for French wine, Caesar tells us that the Gauls had a great weakness for it (though their neighbors in Brittany and Germany banned the beverage in the belief that "it makes men weak and womanish") but does not mention tasting it himself. Where do the French get these ideas?

The restaurant in Oxford had promised to fax me their recipe. Nothing arrived. If there is a cookbook written in English that tells you what to do with old roosters, I do not own it. A few of my French-language books do tell you; what shocks me is that the others use young, female birds and still call it coq au vin. When you make a chicken stew with a young (even female) bird, you can skip the marination, or use white wine, leave out the bacon, forget about the bouillon, and cook everything in just over an hour. This can be a tasty dish. But how anybody who speaks French can continue to describe it as "coq" escapes me. The level of my disillusionment with France and its people continued to mount until I could bear it no longer.

I hopped on a plane and awoke in Paris. My first stop was dinner with Mary and Philip Hyman, an American food-historian couple who have lived in Paris for 30 years and recently began work on *The Oxford Companion to French Food*, an incredibly prestigious assignment. They brought me a chapter from a book entitled *Droit [Law] et Gastronomie* (1999), by one Jean-Paul Branlard, who grapples with the legal identity and denomination of coq au vin. As you might imagine, considerable litigation has been brought on the subject. The two main issues are whether the word "coq" can include a poule, poulet, coquelet, or chapon, and whether dealcoholized wine counts as "vin." Beginning with a government decree of 17 March 1967 and continuing through a decision in Bourges in 1982, culinary justice remained unblemished: the word coq was officially limited to "a male domestic fowl of the genus Gallus, having attained its sexual maturity." But then, in 1986, the Court of Appeals in Rennes scandalously admitted both poule and poulet, claiming to prefer a definition based on actual practice over one grounded in what the judges called semantics. A few years later, the government opened the floodgates, decreeing that it is not fraudulent "to offer under the title coq au vin, elaborated dishes made from any of the fowls of the genus Gallus: poule, poulet, chapon, coquelet, or coq." [all legal translations by the author].

Some writers believe that the similarity between the words Gallus and Gallia, the Latin word for "Gaul," explains why the "coq" became the symbol of France. You can be sure that this symbolic "coq" still includes only the proud and swaggering rooster, not the effeminate poulet or castrated chapon. Why have an academy to protect the French language and then carry on like this, I asked the Hymans. They shrugged and handed me their own formula for coq au vin, using an eight-pound rooster. The Hymans can usually dig up a 300-year-old recipe for nearly anything, but the oldest they've found for coq au vin comes from 1912. They explain that before this century, cookbooks were about fine food, not country dishes. But how do they know that coq au vin was not actually invented in 1912?

And what about those ubiquitous, cultivated white mushrooms? Surely country cooking like this would call for a wild and rustic fungus, if indeed the dish is centuries old. Yes, but the Hymans tell me that the French were growing white mushrooms in large volumes by the late seventeenth century! Paris was the center of production (which explains why they are still called champignons de Paris) until just over 100 years ago, when it migrated to caverns in the Loire Valley.

My second stop was Le Coq St-Honoré, one of the two or three superpremium butchers in Paris specializing in pedigreed chickens, turkeys, and geese, most of them raised in open pasture and fed according to written guarantees. (The shop supplies, among other places, the Plaza Athénée, Taillevent, L'Espadon, the Crillon, Gérard Besson, Le Pré Catelan, and Pierre Gagnaire.) My friend Frédérick Grasser-Hermé met me at the shop, which she had already telephoned to order two substantial roosters. Our plan was to watch and interrogate the butcher, then rendezvous at Frédérick's house two days later to cook the coq au vin for eight other friends who were planning to assemble for her birthday. (Frédérick is consulting chef in charge of the menu at the hot year-old Paris restaurant Korova; her latest book is *Mon chien fait recettes* [Editions Noesis].)

The shop was spotless, all white tiles and refrigerated cases, and flooded with daylight. Our butcher was a cheerful woman named Marie-Louise Desrimais, and she brought out two twelve-pound specimens, both around two years old. Anything smaller, she said, would not be right for a true coq au vin. Our roosters had grown up on a farm in Sarthe, near Le Mans, an area as prized for fine fowl as is Bresse. Marie-Louise removed the two crests and four kidneys—prized morsels to which such extreme food lovers as Catherine de' Medici have become addicted—and discarded the heads. The long necks were chopped and saved for our bouillon, but their skin and the birds' feet were removed and discarded, not what you would do with young, tender chickens but apparently advisable in the case of old roosters. Marie-Louise then disjointed the birds, cut each meaty section crosswise into several pieces, and chopped up the carcass and wings into small chunks. We asked Marie-Louise about her own recipe for coq au vin. "Normale," she replied, and we knew just what she had in mind.

In the end, as often happens, Frédérick did most of the cooking for her birthday over the course of the next three days. Traditional, full-bore coq au vins start with a marinade made up of vegetables, herbs, and a powerful red wine. The meaty pieces of rooster—the legs and breasts resemble those of a small turkey—are steeped in the marinade for a day or more. Meanwhile, a broth is prepared from the wings, neck, carcass, and backbone, all chopped up. Some bacon—fresh or salted or smoked—is melted and the meaty pieces of rooster are browned in the fat, then covered with wine and broth, and stewed very slowly until the rooster is wonderfully tender. This can take six hours. And then those little onions are boiled or browned or both, and added, along with white mushrooms and the crisp pieces of browned bacon. At the end, the cooking liquid, now deeply aromatic with browned vegetables and rooster flesh, is concentrated into the most savory sauce you can imagine, and poured back over the pieces of rooster, bacon, mushrooms, and onions.

Frédérick's was certainly a full-bore coq au vin. But 24 pounds of rooster for ten eaters? She explained that as her recipe has evolved over the years, she has become increasingly unhappy with the breasts of the rooster, which no matter what she tries come out inedibly tough and dry. Now she uses only the dark meat, the legs and thighs. To make up for the blandness of white Paris mushrooms, she adds dried wild mushrooms to the sauce, early on in the cooking.

If I felt any reluctance to disembark at JFK, it was only because the task of finding the necessary ingredients in New York City was bound to be grueling. I needed a rooster, and I needed a big one, and not just one but many, if a delicious recipe was to divulge itself. I tried my typically patient, expert, and reliable sources for animal flesh, Lou at Balducci's and Stanley at Lobel's; both took longer than usual to conclude that a rooster was an impossibility.

My assistant Gail and I angrily telephoned the USDA to find out where all the roosters had gone. Thomas Kruchten gave us the full story. Last year, 8.4 billion chickens were slaughtered in the United States (yes, a huge number but, after all, only 31 chickens a person). Most chickens, male and female, were killed and eaten young, seven weeks old on average, and sold without reference to gender. Only 165 million of them, about 2 percent, were allowed to grow to sexual maturity. The vast majority are hens, assigned to laying eggs, some of which produce chicks. Only 5 percent of the mature chickens appear to be roosters—eight million a year, one-tenth of 1 percent of all chickens. What becomes of the other male chickens? I grew anxious and queasy at the thought that a billion of them are killed as chicks. A billion a year.

Gail despaired of ever finding enough roosters for our important work among this one-tenth of 1 percent. Me, I saw that we were practically home free. There were eight million mature roosters in America, and we needed to find only a fraction of these. I called Victoria Granof, the food stylist, who suggested that I start with an establishment on Linden Street in Brooklyn called the Knickerbocker Live Poultry Market. As so often happens, whenever you open a new door in this city, an entire world is waiting for you on the other side.

Michael Lane, 44, a graduate of N.Y.U. film school, bought Knickerbocker with his father thirteen years ago, carrying on a family trade that his great-great-grandparents had brought from

Russia more than a century before. On a good day, Michael has a thousand live fowl on hand, in cages. Roosters are child's play for him—he sells between 40 and 50 a week—but never for coq au vin. Most of his rooster customers are from India (or of Indian descent from places like Guyana), who make a special rooster curry, or are Hispanics, who prepare a rooster soup. For years the city government had limited the number of live-poultry markets to 30. With so many immigrants coming here from places where one simply does not buy dead chickens, the city lifted the numerical limit while stiffening the hygiene requirements. Sounds Solomonic to me. Now we have 76 live-poultry markets here. The USDA hates it.

Soon Knickerbocker and I had established a steady traffic in big old roosters from Brooklyn to my house, near Union Square in Manhattan. Each rooster cost $10 and arrived as I had requested it—properly dismembered with only the head, feet, and internal organs missing. Many experiments lay ahead.

First we tried Frédérick's recipe, but using both dark and light meat. She was right. The breasts were stringy and dense and dry, even when cooked ten hours. We moved on to the Hymans' method, though with dark meat only and with smoked bacon, which lent depth and complexity to the sauce, but maybe too much smoke. Then we ordered several large stewing hens on the theory that they would be more available to my readers and might yield equivalent results. The theory was wrong.

Next we tried a combination—dark meat, more wine, smoked bacon (but blanched to soften the smokiness), Frédérick's dried mushrooms—plus we browned the bony rooster pieces and vegetables to flavor the bouillon more richly. This was the best version so far.

Coq au vin is served on the same plate as a fitting starch that sops up the incredible sauce—steamed potatoes, noodles, spaetzle, or rice. Having enjoyed many meals of coq au vin over the past month or two, I would recommend nearly any form of boiled or steamed potatoes. Noodles don't absorb.

It is universally agreed that black pepper boiled in a soup or stock or stew for longer than ten minutes turns bitter and loses its aromatic and pungent properties. Yet few people correct and enhance the old recipes by leaving out pepper until the end. I rigorously held back most of it, grinding it in a pepper mill over the sauce a few minutes before serving; fresh black pepper transforms the sauce in delightful and unexpected ways, which turns both perfumed and piquant.

There followed several days of mission creep. Two goals were added. As the recipe had become just a tiny bit arduous, I rearranged it so that most of the work can be finished the day before dinner. Besides, like most stews, coq au vin seems better the next day. The second goal was more serious. The longer we cooked the rooster, the more the meat fell off the bones, leaving a pot of savory and lip-smacking rooster wreckage.

To tenderize the rooster in advance and thus shorten the stewing time, we increased the period of marination in red wine from one day to one week, and even longer. Results? Ambiguous. Our next solution was to cook the rooster pieces all in one layer and to hold down the stewing activity to a bare simmer—too gentle to agitate the meat. Our coq au vins improved.

The French, especially in restaurant cooking, use a low temperature method called *sous vide*, in which the food, cooked or uncooked, is sealed without air, and then very gently heated in a water bath. At an incredibly low 144 degrees F. and lots of time, even the toughest protein is said to emerge smooth and tender. I've had enough experience trying to maintain these stylish French slow-cooking temperatures to know how tedious and uncomfortable it is to stand at the stove for hours at a time, staring at a thermometer. But what about a Crock-Pot? I had never used a Crock-Pot, and I have always made fun of Crock-Pots and of people who use them. I threw away every Crock-Pot cookbook that came my way.

We telephoned several manufacturers, discovered that they all claim minimum temperatures no lower than 190 degrees F. Although not as mild as 144 degrees F., this *is* nonetheless below the bubbling point, will not jostle the pieces of rooster, and may also result in a slightly smoother, creamier protein, as when you poach a chicken instead of boiling it. We bought the largest Crock-Pot we could find, a six-quart Rival. Interrupting an ongoing coq au vin experiment at the post-marination stage, we poured everything into our new Rival, and tried to choose among the three temperature settings, "serve," "low," and "high."

Rival's flimsy user manual warned "DO NOT cook on SERVE setting." So I flipped the dial to "serve," waited two hours, got out my digital thermometer, took the temperature of my coq au vin twice, and learned that the Rival's absolutely minimum temperature is an admirable 180 degrees F. Eleven hours passed, most of it spent watching the immobile Crock-Pot plus additional time for reducing and defatting the sauce, and we were eating one of the two best coq au vins we had produced, deeply flavored and tender. I'll never again make fun of Crock-Pots. I apologize.

In France, coq au vin is traditionally thickened with rooster blood or, when that is unavailable, pig's blood—widely available there and sometimes found in New York City's Chinatown. These days, softened butter mixed with flour—called beurre manié—is usually substituted for blood. One day, when I cut myself while chopping an onion for the marinade, I briefly considered adding human blood. You need barely more than a quarter-cup. But that was after a long day's cooking had diminished my powers of reasoning. I had forgotten to ask Knickerbocker about rooster blood and when I finally thought of it, they said sure we have rooster blood. The Chinese often require a little container of blood with their ducks. Sadly, it was too late to embark upon a new series of experiments.

Several days ago, when our experimental work reached a feverish peak of activity, we received a fax asking for donations of food, raw or cooked, for the rescue workers and volunteers at the

World Trade Center. The nearest collection point was two blocks away at a restaurant named The Tonic, and just before dinnertime we walked over with eighteen servings of extremely good coq au vin made from four old Brooklyn roosters and five bottles of Australian Shiraz, plus a plastic tub of extra sauce. It was rumored that the chefs at the restaurant Balthazar get a police escort whenever they deliver their food to the volunteer center at Chelsea Piers, but we didn't mind. For we had succeeded in capturing the true and ancient coq au vin. How it compares to the Oxford rooster is lost in the fogs of memory. Ours emerges intact but tender, and its sauce is deep and layered and makes your mouth water just thinking about it.

When Pepe Comes Home for Christmas

by Carolynn Carreño

from *Saveur*

Operating in that curious intersection between travel piece and food writing, *Saveur* contributor Carolynn Carreño takes us on food vacations. Witnessing a Mexican family's reunion feast, she skillfully evokes setting, characters, and what's cooking.

Doña Josefina Figueras Viuda de Carreño (my stepgrandmother) steps into the living room in a pink flowered apron, dirty from the day's work. "Siempre en la cocina," she says, smiling a tired, contented smile—always in the kitchen. It is 10 p.m. on the night before Nochebuena (Christmas Eve) in Mexico City, and Josefina has come out of her kitchen, where she's been since seven this morning, because her four grown children have called for her to watch the TV update on "el Popo", Popocatépetl, the volcano 45 miles southeast of here that has been threatening to erupt. The news today is that, because of increased volcanic activity, the airport in Mexico City may close. This is of particular concern in this family tonight because *mañana Pepe viene*—tomorrow Pepe comes.

Pepe is Josefina's first child and the only one of her five whom she does not see every day of the world. (Three—along with two grandchildren—live with her in this tight but comfortable three-bedroom house, and the fourth visits every night for *cena,* the late-evening snack. Her sixth child, Rubén, lived with her as well but recently died.) Pepe lives in Washington, D.C., where, for the past 11 years, he has reported on American politics for the Mexican newspaper *El Universal.* He visits his family (my distant family) twice, maybe three times, a year. I've been here a week, on my first long visit, and the words *cuando Pepe venga* (when Pepe comes) have been repeated like a mantra ever since I arrived.

Cuando Pepe venga, his sisters tell me, we'll have a fancy lunch downtown at Casa Bell. Cuando Pepe venga, we'll go to the Ballet Folklórico, at the Palacio de Bellas Artes, where Sylvia, the oldest sister, is general manager. Cuando Pepe venga, their mother will plug in the espresso maker that Pepe gave her a few years back because the only thing she makes that he dislikes is her percolated, decaffeinated coffee, which he calls *té de café* (tea of coffee). And cuando Pepe venga, Josefina will prepare all the family favorites: shrimp soup; roasted poblano chiles stuffed with cheese and baked in rice; and, of course, Christmas standards like fresh ham with red chile marinade and roast turkey stuffed with the spiced ground pork mixture called picadillo.

Even in a country where good home cooking is commonplace, Pepe has told me, Josefina's food is exceptional. He talks of little else when he talks about going home. When he invites me to come, too, he entices me by describing the succulence of one of her specialties, tinga—shredded pork with chiles. "My mother makes the best tinga," he says, closing his eyes. "Mmmm. There's nothing like it."

Mexico City rests in a dry lake bed on the top of a plateau, at 7,350 feet above sea level. Its notorious air pollution makes breathing difficult, even painful, and turns this vast cityscape into nothing but shades of gray. There are gray parks and squares, regal gray architecture, and gray stone churches on every block. "Mexico City is an ugly city with a lot of beautiful places," Pepe once told me. In fact, the city is not ugly; it just looks ugly most of the time. It isn't until we are blessed with a clear day that I realize how different the buildings look against a bright blue sky, and how the Christmas lights, strung across streets downtown, sparkle—even from a distance.

In preparation for Pepe's arrival, Josefina, three of her four daughters, and I walk, on this crisp December day, to the *tianguis,* or outdoor market, in their neighborhood of Iztaccíhuatl. At the market Josefina is instantly transformed from a hesitant septuagenarian who takes her daughters' arms when she crosses the street into a strong, quick shopper who knows exactly where to find the best ingredients for the Nochebuena feast.

We reluctantly pass a vat filled with elote (corn)—sold slathered with mayonnaise and sprinkled with chile powder and soft, tangy queso fresco (fresh cheese)—in order to keep up with Josefina. She strides past numerous produce stands piled with romeritos, stringy green vegetables that taste like spinach, before finding a satisfactory vendor. The bagfuls she buys will go into an elaborate dish that also contains potatoes, nopales (cactus paddles), mole sauce, and fried shrimp cakes. Romeritos is a centerpiece of Christmas tables throughout the city, but it is not the first thing the members of this family will reach for. The first dish they will want and the one they will ask for seconds of is the bacalao a la vizcaína, salt cod cooked with onions and tomatoes and mixed with almonds, pickled chiles, and green olives—lots of them, because everyone in the house has a habit of picking them out before the dish makes it to the table.

Josefina crosses the central aisle, where the tails of piñatas—green and red and silver and gold—hang low, to visit the cheese man, wearing a red (yes, red) Yankees cap. He smiles and dips deep-fried tortillas into vats of crema, the sweet, buttery Mexican cream, sprinkles them with queso fresco, and hands one to each of us. While we snack, he takes care of Doña Josefina, who rattles off an order starting with many cups of crema and adding nearly every one of the cheeses he offers, including a few plastic-wrapped slices of queso americano.

We follow Josefina past a man in a black cowboy hat and elegant silver-rimmed glasses who has his boots up on a table, hiding behind a stack of chicharrones (fried pig skins) as he reads an adult comic book. She stops at a stand to buy mole pastes, arranged in little mountains of brownish red, caramel, and green. These pulverized mixtures of many ingredients—among them nuts, herbs, spices, chiles, chocolate, tortillas, and white bread—are diluted with stock, creating rich sauces. Because good-quality pastes are easily found in markets, and because, with up to 25 ingredients, they are very labor intensive, even women like Josefina—for whom "from scratch" is a way of life—choose to start with a paste and doctor it to make it their own.

On our way out, we sit down for quesadillas of mushrooms, cheeses, and tinga, made by a stout woman, her hair pulled back into a low bun. But Josefina is still shopping. A shy girl approaches us with nopales, which are reputed to have many health benefits, among them the lowering of cholesterol. Josefina gets several bags of the cactus, not only for the romeritos but also because Pepe, having acquired the dietary consciousness of an American, will certainly request a few simple nopales salads.

For the next two days, Josefina's *ayudantes* (helpers)—who include her posse of daughters and Mama, the widow of her late husband's son by his first wife (who, thanks to Josefina's generous definition of family, is an integral member of the group)—will run to the market after Josefina finds she needs more milk or a can of chiles or whatever. They will wash and peel and shell and boil. They will cut onions into a perfect quarter-inch dice, the way Josefina taught them. They will take down large pots from high shelves; they will lift heavy roasts from the oven. They will do what they are asked with tremendous love and respect and a good deal of competence. But none of them has what Pepe calls *el toque,* the touch.

On the day before Nochebuena, Marta begins the cooking by toasting dried shrimp for the romeritos, the most time-consuming dish. Josefina drains the salt cod, which has been soaking in water all night long, and then, with her small, sure hands, long nails painted pink, begins removing tiny bones. Claudia, the youngest daughter, pulls up her sleeves and takes over so that Josefina can make the marinade for the ham. Pulling out a drawer filled with bags of dried chiles, she finds one of ancho and dumps the contents into a hot skillet to toast; and a fragrant, smoky smell wafts through the small kitchen, filled with her own busy elves.

The next morning, Josefina is, as usual, the first one up. Claudia, then Sylvia, then all the others come down, one at a time, to find her in the kitchen, where she is just finishing the picadillo—a mixture of ground pork, nuts, candied citron, and spices—that she will use to stuff the turkey. Josefina gladly stops what she is doing to give the benediction to each of her grown children as they leave to do last-minute gift shopping. They stand before her, eyes closed, hands at their sides, as they must have done ever since they were small.

Josefina and Marta put the turkey into the oven, then the ham, smeared with chile marinade. Midday, the phone rings: it's Pepe, calling to say that the airport is open and his flight will be on time.

Toward evening, the daughters trickle in, laden with bags, and the whole family goes upstairs to get ready. Lilia is drying her hair and Claudia is sitting on the bed with a compact mirror, applying heavy coats of mascara and makeup, when the bell rings. The little grandsons squeal and race to open the door. Pepe's sisters, every one of them in high heels and dresses, run downstairs after the boys and then stop, standing back from the door as if they'd encountered a magnetic field. Pepe, dressed like an American businessman, with a pocket-square and cuff links, a Cohiba cigar firmly gripped in his manicured fingers, walks through the doorway as though he had walked through it yesterday evening and every evening before that. He peels his nephews off and greets each of his sisters with a kiss as he passes through them, as if parting the seas, on the way to his mother, who waits patiently by the kitchen.

He hugs her big, and she looks at him as if to inspect and admire this grown man of hers. Within minutes she's poured him a shot glass of tequila. Then it's time for her to walk the two blocks to evening mass, flanked by Rosalba and Sylvia, who, like the rest of the family, are not particularly devout but respect their mother's piety.

It is near midnight when they return. Pepe sits with his cigar, playing all kinds of poking and tickling games with his nephews while the women go into motion to get the food onto the table. At last they gather around, Pepe standing next to his mother, his arm around her shoulders, his face a near-replica of hers. She gazes happily up at her firstborn, then out at the feast and family that lie before them. Pepe reaches into the bacalao, sneaking an olive and then smiles back at his mother like a little boy who knows he couldn't possibly get into trouble tonight. It's Christmas.

Bacalao a la Vizcaína
(Salt Cod Vizcaya Style)

Serves 6–8

Salt cod appears on Christmas Eve tables throughout Mexico. In the nation's capital, the most popular preparation is this version of a classic salt cod dish from the Spanish province of Vizcaya. The Mexican interpretation adds almonds and olives and omits the Spanish original's cured ham, dried sweet red peppers, and dried red chiles.

2 lbs. salt cod, cut into large pieces
½ cup olive oil

4 medium tomatoes, cored and minced
1 medium white onion, peeled and finely chopped
3 whole cloves
¼ tsp, whole black peppercorns
¼ tsp. dried marjoram leaves
¼ tsp. dried thyme leaves
½ cup blanched almonds
1 cup large pitted green Spanish or Italian olives
3 tbsp. small pickled green chiles plus 3 tbsp. of the pickling juice

1. Soak cod in a large bowl of cold water for 6–8 hours, changing water several times. Drain. Cover cod with cold water again, then break apart into flakes while picking through cod to remove any skin and bones. Drain again.

2. Put cod into a medium pot, cover with cold water, and boil over high heat until tender, about 5 minutes. Drain and set aside.

3. Heat oil in a large skillet over medium heat. Add tomatoes and onions and cook, stirring often, for 10 minutes. Add cod, increase heat to medium-high, and cook, breaking fish up further with a wooden spoon, until mixture begins to fry, 7–10 minutes. Add cloves, peppercorns, marjoram, and thyme and cook for 5 minutes. Add almonds and olives and cook until heated through, 1–2 minutes. Remove skillet from heat and stir in chiles and pickling juice. Set aside to cool to room temperature before serving.

Runaway Brunch

by Jonathan Hayes
from *Food & Wine*

> Food writing is just one of magazine writer
> Jonathan Hayes's areas of expertise—but
> as this first-person account suggests,
> being connected to the food world doesn't
> necessarily mean being able to show off
> successfully in the kitchen.

In retrospect it may have been a mistake to invite the A-list
chefs. What can I say? It seemed a good idea at the time.

I'd decided to have a young couple I didn't know very well over
for brunch. It was an affair that snowballed; at first I invited some
mutual friends to put the couple at ease, and then people I kind of
owed a meal, and finally, pretty much anyone who I thought might
be available on short notice, until I had an archetypal Downtown
New York City guest list, including an outsider artist, a wedding
cake designer, a dominatrix and three prominent chefs. During the
several years I'd been writing about food, these chefs had not only
fed me and taught me but had also become my friends. It was my
turn to be the guy in the kitchen, and I was determined to deliver
the goods.

I needed a menu that was both sophisticated and manageable.
(Unfortunately, as it turned out, it was not manageable by *me*.) I'd
been on a baking kick and had had enough success with my breads

to become rather impressed with myself. Given my skill set, the menu was obvious: tartines, the French take on sandwiches! It'd be a snap: I'd bake my loaves the morning of the brunch, put out the fillings while the lovely aroma of fresh bread wafted through the air and then stroll into my living room to accept the accolades from my guests.

I have some excuses for what happened next. First of all, pretty much everyone I invited cruelly and unexpectedly showed up. Also, my fiancée, Cricket, and I had been at a wedding the night before, and, even though we'd ducked out early, leaving bride and groom held aloft in their chairs, I'd felt completely burned-out by the time I got home. I was too weary to make the ice creams, too exhausted to do anything other than set up one of the bread doughs for its second rise.

And then the clocks went forward for daylight saving time and I overslept, and that was where my real troubles began. Guests started to pour in just after the first loaves had gone into the oven. (It seems that while everyone has e-mail, few people check it during the weekend, when hosts are sending out CRISIS! BRUNCH LATER! alerts.) The tea-cured salmon and the ginger butter had made it to the table, but the person bringing the bagels was missing in action. The wild Manhattan yeasts that I'd cultivated for my *levain* were as energetic as a narcoleptics' convention. And still the guests kept on arriving.

The Champagne was lukewarm in the fridge, and all I had to offer was orange juice and vodka. (It rapidly became clear that orange juice and vodka are nothing to sniff at.) The guests soon became energized and sociable, like college kids on spring break waiting for the MTV remote setup to go live.

The honey-walnut bread came out of the oven and was absolutely perfect. But it needed to sit for 20 minutes. The person bringing the bagels arrived, and she had tomato juice! The bagels went out; the tomato juice was spiked with lemon juice and Tabasco, and rushed out for vodkination. A rousing success! No one even noticed that the Champagne hadn't been served yet; indeed, the mixing rhythm had become so automatic that, once the Champagne was finally chilled, it was promptly adulterated with orange juice.

The Stilton (crumbled by Cricket) and the beautifully ripened Bosc pears (bought five days previously for this very purpose and diced by a chef press-ganged into my galley kitchen for that very purpose) were put out, finally joined by the walnut bread.

The crowd, garrulous and cheery, was confused by the tartine concept. It became apparent that they were in no condition to operate my new toaster oven. Even the Lapsang souchong–cured salmon (stylishly minimal in presentation) proved puzzling to them. Luckily, one of the chefs took the lead and plunged in, slicing off thin sheets of salty, smoky fish.

The salt only seemed to increase my guests' thirst. With the salvos of popping Champagne corks, cries of "Ice! More ice!" and the smoke from my now burning sourdough bread, the kitchen was like a hospital tent at the Battle of Borodino, an impression deepened by the spray from a jug of V8 juice dropped on my kitchen floor.

One of my guests, a chef and personal hero, had arrived with a popular television expert on cooking, decorating and entertaining. As she peered into the living room, I could see her blanch; to be fair, I had not seen the living room since I'd retrieved the walnut-bread dough from its artisanal rising place on my artisanal windowsill, and for all I knew, the guests had all stripped down to loincloths, oiled up and joined in group Turkish wrestling. The television personality politely complimented my salmon. The chef complimented my *oeufs brouillés* and then asked helpfully, "Are you stressing? Because if I were you, I'd be stressing right now."

After that it was pretty much all a blur. My Robiola cheese–and–white truffle oil tartines had to compete with a copy of *Bizarre,* a British magazine lavishly illustrated with photo spreads of fetish fashion and eyeball surgery. The issue, which celebrated the recent nuptials of two of the guests, was being enthusiastically passed around. My *oeufs brouillés,* which I'd planned to serve with a spicy chorizo the color—and, for all I know, flavor—of toxic waste, were scarfed down gratifyingly quickly (although the burn of the chorizo proved such that only the guest named Lamarr could eat it).

In the kitchen, my ice cream maker obstinately refused to freeze the *ras-al-hanout* ice cream intended to go with my Winter Fruits Poached in a Vanilla–Star Anise Syrup. In the living room, the brunch table, once so festive, was barricaded by a wall of empty bottles— clear vodka bottles, thick dark Champagne bottles, tapering Riesling bottles, a few insouciantly inverted into the ice bucket. Some of the guests had started the retreat home, half-dragging, half-carrying each other down the hall and out into the street, each staggering reveler another entry on the ledger of my shame, kept assiduously by my doorman.

As the ice cream finally began to thicken, I gave up on kitchen duty. I'd baked shortbread a couple of days previously and had intended to serve it with caramel sauce, bitter chocolate and the expensive French sea salt called fleur de sel; it was apparent that this was not going to happen. The blood orange and ginger sorbet syrup I'd infused so carefully never reached the ice cream machine. I thought it had met its fate with some vodka in a highball glass, but it later showed up hidden behind the bagel bag.

Before mingling, I changed out of my chef's jacket. The jacket, a birthday gift from Cricket, is a source of considerable anguish to me. It makes her happy when I put it on, but I can't bring myself to wear it in public, as it has my name embroidered, Emeril-style, on the breast pocket. Being caught wearing it by these *real* chefs felt a bit like being surprised by one's mother while experimenting with drag in the guest bedroom.

I left the kitchen just in time to kiss the *Bizarre* couple goodbye and to give the cake designer a taste of my ice cream (at that point the consistency of hand lotion). And then it was just me, Cricket and the original couple whom I'd invited and hadn't known very well.

In the living room, the brunch table resembled a diorama of the burning of Atlanta. Little plumes of smoke rose from a smoldering end of bread abandoned in the toaster oven. There were gory spatters of salsa across the table and puddles of maroon wine staining the carpet, and a cluster of breadsticks lay where they'd fallen.

But I was finished in the kitchen. I was exhausted. I was sticky, my fingers crusted with bread dough, my left arm slightly glued to my side by *ras-al-hanout* ice cream. Cricket and I and the two diehard guests were convivially tipsy. No one cared that the ice cream hadn't fully set, or that I was serving the shortbread—intended to be an austere but sensually complex meditation on butter, chocolate, sugar and salt—with the stewed dried pears, blueberries and cranberries.

So we sat, and we ate, and we talked about politics, sex, religion, music. And about Eastern Europe, where the couple was planning to travel during the next few months. I had read an article in *Bizarre* about organ thieves in Mongolia and Georgia, and I hope my guests will be all right; I really liked them. I'm already planning their welcome home brunch.

Smoky Tea–Cured Salmon with Ginger Butter

12 servings

This recipe was included in the curriculum of the Institute of Culinary Education in Manhattan, where I learned to make it from fish expert Shirley King. It's delicious and easy. Buy the tea in bulk at a Chinese market if you can; it's sure to be considerably less expensive than at a tea shop.

1 cup Lapsang souchong tea leaves (2 ounces)
½ cup sugar
Kosher salt
Two 1-pound tail pieces of salmon fillet, with skin

1 stick (4 ounces) unsalted butter, at room temperature
3 tablespoons minced peeled fresh ginger
1 tablespoon minced chives
1 loaf cocktail pumpernickel bread

1. Line a large glass baking dish with a double layer of plastic wrap, leaving 4 inches overhang all around. In a small bowl, toss the tea with the sugar and ½ cup of kosher salt. Spread half of the curing mixture in the prepared dish. Spread the remaining mixture over the fish and cover tightly with the overhanging plastic wrap. Set a plate on the salmon and top with a heavy can. Refrigerate for 2 days.

2. In a medium bowl, blend the butter with the ginger and chives and season with salt. Spread a thin layer of the ginger butter on each slice of bread, then cut the slices on the diagonal.

3. Rinse the salmon, removing as much of the curing mixture as possible; pat dry. Using a thin, sharp knife, cut the salmon crosswise into very thin slices. Place a small slice of salmon on each bread and serve.

MAKE AHEAD The rinsed and dried tea-cured salmon can be wrapped in plastic and refrigerated for 1 week.

The Gastronauts

by Daniel Zwerdling
from *Gourmet*

Poised at the cusp of science writing and food writing, Zwerdling—a senior correspondent for National Public Radio—intently cracks the code that links science lab and kitchen.

For a group intent on nothing less than changing the course of culinary history, the foodophiles gathered in the ancient Sicilian mountain town of Erice are a rather odd crowd. Here's a *Michelin* one-star chef from Britain who makes ice cream out of foie gras and kickboxes to keep in shape for the kitchen. Over there is a physicist from the University of Bristol who has a penchant for shirts emblazoned with pictures of penguins. A 300-pound restaurateur from Philadelphia stands nearby, his arms a mass of tattoos. At the moment, they and a throng of assorted chemists, food industry scientists, and cookbook writers are huddled together beneath the weathered brick arches of a 15th-century monastery, where they are taking turns prodding soggy slices of eggplant in a frying pan.

They all have the same questions: If you salt and drain eggplant before you fry it, will that prevent it from soaking up oil, as cookbooks sometimes suggest? And will that make the eggplant less bitter, which many cookbooks suggest? The participants agree there's another question that's almost more important, at least in the spirit of this unusual conference: What are the scientific reasons why?

Welcome to the fifth International Workshop on Molecular Gastronomy, dedicated to the proposition that if you teach chefs more about the science of protein strings and hydrogen bonding, they'll be able to take their art to higher levels.

"Most chefs have no scientific background . . . none," says Jean Matricon. His rebellious white hair, bushy beard, and red suspenders make him look like a cross between a nuclear scientist and an Amish farmer; in fact, he's a noted French physicist who has spent decades trying to develop dramatic new ways of conducting electricity at super-low temperatures. At the moment, though, he's more enthralled with these slabs of eggplant. "Even the great chefs learned to cook by being told what to do, by following tradition, and by trial and error, but they don't understand *why* things happen," Matricon says. "They're too proud to ask."

One of the impromptu lab assistants, British food writer, broadcaster, and novelist Leslie Forbes, has just finished measuring the olive oil left in the pans after frying. She summarizes the laboratory method: Sliced eggplants half an inch thick. Salted them and drained one hour. Squeezed off beads of liquid. Fried slices in 20 milliliters of olive oil.

The results are striking: The salted slices have absorbed only a fraction of a teaspoon of oil. They taste fresh and light yet almost meaty, with a touch of spring to them and the faintest crackling of a crust. But the unsalted slices are greasy and limp. They've soaked up almost all the olive oil.

"This is pretty much what I expected," says a man who looks as if he might teach Shakespeare in college—and the throng looks to tweedy, bearded Harold McGee for an explanation. Just about everyone at this conference will tell you that McGee profoundly affected their culinary lives back in 1984, when he published his landmark *On Food and Cooking: The Science and Lore of the Kitchen*. McGee unearthed extensive laboratory evidence, which was essentially hidden away in academic and food industry journals, and used it to demolish some of the cherished myths of the kitchen. He's probably most famous for shattering the axiom that searing meat "seals in the juices."

At the moment, McGee is deconstructing the eggplant—which makes me nervous, since I got a C in chemistry. McGee, though, has a way of turning science into plain English. "Eggplants tend to soak up oil basically because they're constructed like sponges," he says. "Their cells contain water, but there are lots of big air pockets between the cells." And those air pockets are all-important: When you cook the eggplant, the heat squeezes the air out of those pockets, so they become like millions of empty containers—and the oil oozes into them.

When you salt eggplants before you cook them, McGee says, the salt draws water out of the cells, so the cells collapse (it has to do with positive and negative ions, but that's getting too scientific). In turn, the air pockets between the cells collapse—so there are no more empty containers to soak up the oil.

Now you know the answer: Salt works wonders on eggplant. So does any method that punctures the cells and those air pockets—in fact, McGee says he cooks eggplant slices for a few minutes in a microwave before he fries them, and it accomplishes the same thing.

And forget the canard about drawing out the bitterness. If the eggplant is bitter, any water you draw out will contain some of that bitterness, but there's so much water still left inside the eggplant that you won't taste the difference. "If you start with bitter egg-plant," McGee says, "you'll end with bitter eggplant." The scientists around him nod and harrumph.

The one-star chef from Britain nudges me and raises his eyebrows toward McGee. "That man changed my life," he says. "And my cooking."

Tomorrow, everyone will regroup for the next workshop topic: Can bakers apply chaos theory—which mathematicians use to study the origins of the universe—to learn how to get better air bubbles in a baba au rhum?

First, let's take a break.

The International Workshop on Molecular Gastronomy might never have been organized if it weren't for World War II, the atomic bomb, and a frustrated magazine editor in Paris.

Back in the 1930s, a brilliant Jewish physicist named Nicholas Kurti left Europe a step ahead of the Nazis. He ended up in Los Alamos working on the U.S. government's secret project to develop the weapons that destroyed Hiroshima and Nagasaki. People who confront disaster and dying in their work often have an acute zest for living, and Kurti went on to become an irrepressible gourmet. More than that: He became passionate about the idea that scientists spend too much time investigating arcane mysteries at the fringes of the cosmos when they could be using their genius to make life more pleasurable here on earth.

Kurti demonstrated his point in a speech more than 30 years ago to some of the world's leading scientists, at the Royal Institution, in London. He hooked up scientific instruments to a mixture of whipped eggs and sugar and liqueur, and showed how the goo's internal temperature rose and fell as he baked it. "I think it is a sad reflection on our civilization," Kurti told his audience, "that while we can and do measure the temperature in the atmosphere of Venus, we do not know what goes on inside our soufflés."

As Kurti got older, it looked as if he might never realize his dream of getting scientists and cooks to collaborate. But then he met a kindred spirit, a younger man named Hervé This, who tells me his story one evening after we've left the workshop "Parameters That Control the Texture of Gels." "At the time when I met Nicholas, I was like Dr. Jekyll and Mr. Hyde," says This. "During the day, I was editing the French edition of *Scientific American,* and at night I went home to my kitchen where I have a lab, and I did scientific experiments to improve the way we cook."

As This warms to his topic, the disconnect between science and cooking, he leans across the table to make his points; he's movie-star handsome, in a boyish way, and when he revs up, his eyes go to afterburners. "It's indecent that we cook as people did in the Middle Ages," he says. "They had whisks. They had pans. They had stoves. The microwave is the only really new kitchen tool we've had in the past five hundred years. But in the science laboratory, ooh-laaa . . . we have many tools that could do wonderful things in the kitchen."

He rattles through a veritable catalog of scientific equipment, which he actually uses to churn out dinners for his family. Forget that obsolete business of straining sauces through wire mesh and clarifying consommé by adding egg whites: This uses a chemist's filter spun from glass, and he produces crystal-clear liquids almost instantly. He would never emulsify homemade mayonnaise with a whisk—or, worse, bruise the ingredients in a processor. "I put the egg yolk and oil and other ingredients in a laboratory ultrasound box," he says, "then press a button, and in two seconds—*poof!*" The high-frequency sound waves whip the ingredients like millions of miniature beaters. "My mayonnaise is perfect.

"But I was explaining to you about Nicholas," he says. When This, the young, charismatic editor, met Kurti, the old, charismatic physicist, the two men bonded. More importantly, they agreed to launch a crusade to convince chefs that science could lead them into the new millennium. The pair tracked down a group of soul mates in the U.S. and Europe, and in 1992 they all went up to the mountaintop in Erice—and the era of "molecular gastronomy" was born.

Over the next four days, the molecular gastronomists often veer toward the surreal. A British scientist named Robin Heath shows a bizarre film that looks like something out of a 1950s horror movie. His lab, which is funded by the British government and major food companies, has cajoled some poor volunteers into sitting in front of a camera that takes X-ray movies of their heads. So we sit there like voyeurs and peer into some man's skull and jawbones projected up on the screen. We stare right into his mouth as he chews various foods, moistens them with saliva, and tosses the balls of glop around with his tongue, which looks a writhing snake. Until he mercifully swallows.

"We're learning that people perceive flavors differently depending on how they chew their foods," says Eric Dransfield, who's doing similar work at the National Institute for Agricultural Research, in France. His lab, determined not to be outdone by the British, wires electrodes to its victims' faces and jaws, and measures exactly the amount of force the various muscles of the head exert when people chew. When the researchers spike a food with bold flavors—like quinine—the subjects who chew vigorously, with lots of force, rate the foods as much more bitter than do those who chew slowly and with finesse.

Group question: Does this mean that chefs will have to tailor their seasonings to diners' chewing styles?

When you get a few dozen scientists and chefs in the same room, of course, you can't always expect the conversation to go smoothly. Or civilly. The physicists tend to wander off into the stratosphere. One day, they erupt into an argument (which starts to turn bitter) about which principles of physics are at work when you beat egg whites into fluff: Are you exerting shearing forces or extensional flow? (You'll have to look it up in a textbook.)

As Harold McGee wraps up his talk on better grilling through computer monitored heat-diffusion techniques, one of the participants looks as if he can barely stay in his seat. It's Heston Blumenthal, the 35-year-old kickboxer whose restaurant on the Thames has led British critics to rave about him and led the *Automobile Association Restaurant Guide* to recently name him Chef's Chef of the Year.

"I think Harold's experiment confirms some of the principles that I've already been working on in my restaurant," Blumenthal says. And as this muscular young man with a blond buzz cut modestly lays out his philosophy—explaining the zany method he's developed to cook his signature tenderloin of lamb, describing how chemists and physicists across Europe are helping him take meat and potatoes where no meat and potatoes have gone before—the molecular gastronomists start to murmur and trade meaningful looks. "Heston's the future of our movement," one of them whispers.

After the Erice conference, I make a pilgrimage to the Thames Valley to taste the future of molecular gastronomy. Blumenthal's restaurant, The Fat Duck, is tucked away in Bray, another lovely village with ancient credentials, and occupies a 460-year-old building that used to be a pub: whitewashed walls, splashy abstract paintings, worm-eaten ceiling timbers.

When Blumenthal took over the restaurant, he says, he served classic French dishes that he learned as a teenager, when he got himself a *Larousse Gastronomique* and cooked his way through the book. Maybe he would still be cooking that way if he hadn't gone crazy one day over a pot of boiling water and green beans. When he salted the water to fix the color—as cookbooks had taught him—his haricots turned an embarrassing khaki-yellow. He experimented further, deleting the salt and then substituting bottled water for tap. Greener beans were his. But why? He rang up the nearest physicist. Who happened to be Peter Barham, the man with the penguin obsession at the Erice conference.

"I pick up the phone," says Barham, "and I hear, 'Hello, I'm a chef. Is there any good reason why I should add salt when I'm boiling vegetables? And should I use bottled water?' " Barham trekked to The Fat Duck like a doctor making a house call, and he and Blumenthal diagnosed the haricot disease: The restaurant's tap water was loaded with calcium, and the mineral was zapping the vegetable's chlorophyll. Filtering the water solved the problem.

"I'd been rubbish at science in school," Blumenthal says, but now he sensed that chemistry and physics could help him reshape the way he cooked. He started hanging out with Barham in the kitchen, playing around with wild ideas, and the physicist introduced him to a network of European scientists who are intrigued by the notion of helping a real-life chef.

Consider the matter of the mashed potatoes and the artificial nose machine.

Blumenthal had been mulling over a problem that had been floating on the fringes of his culinary consciousness. When he made a potato purée he was never satisfied. Blumenthal flavored it as most American chefs do—with basil or garlic, or infused with truffle oil—but the flavors never seemed to burst through. He tried lime-flavored mashed potatoes, but even then, after a few bites, he could hardly detect the flavoring—it was if the lime and other flavors had simply disappeared.

So Blumenthal turned to his informal science panel for advice. Which is how he found himself sitting in a Geneva laboratory one day with a strange-looking machine hooked up to his nose.

Blumenthal had contacted the Firmenich corporation, which develops and manufactures flavors and fragrances for brand-name products around the world. Firmenich scientists told Blumenthal that if he wanted to perfect his potato purée, he needed to plunge into the latest studies on the physiology of taste and smell, and that meant he would have to learn about the brain.

For instance, scientists have discovered that we taste five basic flavors in our mouths. The taste buds on our tongue and soft palate tell us if something is salty or sour, bitter or sweet—and in the past few years, many scientists in the U.S. and Europe have come to agree with their Japanese counterparts that there's a fifth, an earthy taste known as *umami*.

But travel up the nose, to the olfactory bulb in the middle of the head: That's where we perceive countless aromas in all their subtle complexity. We "taste" them mainly by smelling aromatic molecules as they waft up our nasal passages (which is why you can barely "taste" anything when you have a cold).

So picture the inside of your mouth as you're chewing mashed potatoes: If a food molecule is as small and light as a molecular feather, and it floats easily up into your head, you'll savor it in its vivid glory. But if the molecule is so big and heavy that it just plops there on your tongue and tumbles down your throat, you'll hardly detect anything at all.

Which brings us back to Blumenthal's problem. Most molecules in potatoes are big lugs, so they sink. Worse, they have a vicious tendency to grab hold of all sorts of lighter molecules and not let go—which means that Blumenthal can add all the ingredients he wants to a pile of potatoes, and the heavier starch molecules will imprison some of them in molecular jail. Fat molecules absorb some lighter molecules in a similarly thuggish way, so when you add butter to flavored potatoes, you're doing double damage.

That, said the Firmenich scientists, was just the beginning of Blumenthal's potato woes. Many chefs (and gourmands) have known intuitively for centuries that when you eat too much of the same thing, you get palate fatigue, as they call it. So chefs serve sorbets between courses in an attempt to "refresh" the palate. They serve "tasting menus" to try to keep your taste buds on their metaphorical toes. Now, Firmenich researchers have helped develop a remarkable machine that displays the onset and progression of palate fatigue visually. They call it the MS Nose. You can buy one for less than half a million dollars.

And that brings us back to Heston Blumenthal, whom we left sitting in the Firmenich laboratory, hooked up to the MS Nose. "They put a little tube up my nostril," Blumenthal remembers. "The tube was connected to a box. And then they gave me a stick of minty chewing gum, and as I chewed it, I could actually see the mint aroma molecules that were up in my nose projected on a small screen."

The MS Nose is essentially a mass spectrometer, the kind of supersophisticated device that labs use to detect toxic chemicals. As the test subject exhales, the machine analyzes and counts the molecules in his breath, and then portrays them in a series of squiggles on a computer display. "It was strange," says Blumenthal. "After chewing the gum for a few minutes, I couldn't detect the mint anymore. But the screen showed that I still had just as many mint molecules in my nose as I did when I could sense them."

Then the researchers gave Blumenthal a new taste, a sip of sugar water. "It was perfectly amazing," he says. "I got this rush of mint flavor again—even though on the screen the number of mint molecules in my nose hadn't changed." Scientists think that the brain gets bored after it has sampled the same old flavor, and that it turns off the flavor receptors. Jolt the brain with a new sensation, and it switches the sensory circuits back on.

When Blumenthal left the Firmenich lab, he knew that he needed to ignite his customers' circuitry with unexpected flavors and textures, like fireworks that explode into new patterns just when you think they're spent. He decided to start by studding his potato purée with unexpected chunks of lime jelly.

New Problem: Blumenthal quickly realized that gelatin melts at the temperature of warm mashed potatoes, so the lime was oozing into the starch and the flavor was getting diluted. He was almost back where he started.

Next: a quick call to another scientist who's plugged into the molecular gastronomy network. Did he perchance know how to maintain gels at high temperatures? No problem: The chemist sent Blumenthal a bag of agar, a Japanese gelatin made from dried seaweed that allows him to make firm gels that shrug off heat.

Today, a waiter at The Fat Duck holds out a spoon with a dollop of ivory potato purée topped with tiny green slivers like the fins on a fish. You put the spoon in your mouth. The potatoes ooze. They melt. They soothe. And suddenly, pure lime explodes in your mouth like Pop Rocks.

Blumenthal's scientific quest bursts through in almost every dish he creates. A bite of seared foie gras, like warm loam, then the startling, briny-sweet crinkle of crystallized seaweed. A forkful of creamy sweetbreads, heady with the scent of a freshly mown field—Blumenthal bakes the sweetbreads in green hay—then the musty crunch from a dusting of pollen. Your head fills with the vapors of warm roasted crab as you begin his seafood risotto, then you reel as you bite into a cold scoop of ice cream—and reel again when you realize that Blumenthal's ice cream is the pure, cold essence of crab.

Since the conference, Blumenthal and some of the other participants have been trading e-mails, trying to figure out a way to broaden the molecular gastronomy movement. Sure, it's fun to meet every few years in Sicily, but they can pack only a few dozen people into the monastery. They dream of flexing the power of the Internet to get chefs and scientists all over the world to talk to each other, to collaborate on experiments, and to come up with new culinary ideas—just as Blumenthal works with his growing network of chemists and physicists. And that's going to require many chefs to become more open-minded—not just about using more science in their cooking but also about sharing their "trade secrets" with their competition.

Here's Blumenthal and Barham's most radical secret. (To do it safely, they employ an arsenal of technical precautions. In other words, don't try this at home.) To prepare a lovely piece of meat so that every bite is a blushing, rosy rare, Blumenthal cooks it the whole time at a shockingly low temperature. According to the laws of physics, says Barham, the meat could never, ever get overcooked.

Demonstrating this, Blumenthal turns one end of his stove down low, then sets a battered aluminum pan on top—the temperature's so low that you can touch it without wincing. He drizzles in a bit of oil, and then he props a few lamb tenderloins, with the bone and fat still cradling them, at weird angles all around the pan so only a small amount of meat touches the metal. Then, for the next hour and a half Blumenthal lets the tenderloins just sit there . . . and sit there . . . except every couple of minutes, he gives the hunks a quarter turn. The oil in the pan never spits or shimmers. You never see any juices oozing from the lamb or hear it dance and sizzle. After that hour and a half, the outer surface of the lamb looks so red and moist that it seems almost raw. But when Blumenthal's probe tells him the entire chunk is an even 135 degrees, the lamb is ready to serve.

Blumenthal is about to send an order to a customer, sliced, draped with reduced lamb roasting juices along with a crispy, caramelized lamb *onglet* (diaphragm). Before the plate is ready, though, he hands me a slice and I dangle it in my mouth. Revelation: This is what lamb should be. Ridiculously juicy. Exquisitely tender. Not a hint of tension or distress. And every bite is perfect.

FIFTEEN SECONDS OF FLAME—A STEAK'S OWN STORY
Every cook knows that when you cook a good steak, you have to make painful compromises. You learn to blast it at high temperatures because you need more than 300 degrees Fahrenheit to produce a crust with those rich, caramelized flavors that form like magic from the meat's natural sugars and amino acids. (Scientists call this process the Maillard reaction, named for the French physician who almost a century ago was the first to investigate similar reactions between proteins and sugars in the human body.) But you don't want the steak's interior to go much above 135 degrees, because that's the temperature at which it stays juicy and rare. Above that, the strands of proteins in the muscle fibers contract so much that they start to squeeze out their juices—and beef has tons of juices before you cook it; it's more than 60 percent water. Renowned food science author Harold McGee shocked the cooking world in 1984 when he used these principles to demonstrate that searing meat at high heat does precisely the opposite of "sealing in" those juices—it starts to dry them out.

So what usually happens when you throw your steak on the fire? You end up with a great Maillard crust, a juicy rare or rosy center—and then there's a dry, chewy "gray zone" in between.

McGee had a hunch that computers could figure out a satisfactory solution. He knew that Silicon Valley scientists had used mathematical simulation software to help them study how electrons move through silicon chips, so he figured they could modify the software to study how heat moves through meat. They could. McGee ran hundreds of simulations, in effect asking the computer: What's the best way to get the heat to diffuse through the meat so it cooks as fast and evenly as possible?

The computer told them that chefs are cooking their steaks, well, wrong. McGee aims a laser pointer at his computer's simulation of beef, up there on the screen: The computer shows a simulation of the inside of the cooking steaks as sedimentary layers of purple and green and yellow, each color representing a different amount of accumulated heat. And they show that when you throw a steak on the fire and just let it sit there, sizzling away, and then you flip the meat only once before you serve it, you're messing with the heat diffusion. There's such a huge difference between the temperatures on the side that's facing the fire and the side that's turned away that the heat inside your steak fluxes all over the place. (This applies only to beef.)

"But," McGee says, "the computer model shows that if you keep flipping the meat as you cook it, the heat diffuses through the meat much more evenly, so it cooks much more evenly. Our study suggests that the optimum flipping time is every fifteen seconds."

Every 15 seconds? Can McGee be serious? "Maybe that's a little extreme; it might be inconvenient,"

McGee says, laughing. "The computer model shows that flipping the meat every thirty seconds will work almost as well." And it's nice to know that another recent study, at Lawrence Livermore National Laboratory, shows that frequent flipping makes steaks more healthful, too: It reduces the amount of carcinogenic compounds that can be generated when you cook over high heat by as much as 75 percent.

Which means that short order cooks have been doing things right all along.

A Bahamian Village Welcome

by Lucretia Bingham

from *Saveur*

A frequent *Saveur* contributor, Bingham has a travel writer's knack for evoking the scene where memorable food is served. Her personal connection to this special nook of the Bahamas gave her an insider track on a very special feast.

At the sound of a timid knock, my brother opened the door. Outside, a few village children shrank back from the circle of light thrown by our kerosene lamp. Two brown-paper packages lay at our feet, radiating the most delicious aromas. One held a hot loaf of home-baked bread, split and lavishly buttered beneath its thick, nutty crust; the other package revealed a crisp stack of fried fish.

The year was 1953, and we had arrived the previous night in the remote fishing village of Cherokee Sound, in the Abacos, the northernmost island group of the Bahamas. My mother and her new husband were eschewing American suburbia for a life of self-sufficiency. He was a carpenter by trade; Mother longed to keep chickens and grow her own vegetables; together, they figured, they could build or plant whatever the family needed. Mother had promised my brother and me that we would have a wonderfully romantic time in Cherokee Sound, which was 25 miles from the nearest settlement, reachable only by boat, and home to just 312 hardy souls. For months before leaving, our bedtime stories had been *Robinson Crusoe* and *Treasure Island*—exciting books, yes, but hardly comforting. So I was not so sure about the safety of this place, especially when, moments after we had been sculled ashore, the villagers recoiled from us as if we were fearsome circus animals. But that offer of food on our doorstep finally began to make us feel welcome, and that feeling only deepened in the years to come.

Last fall, long after we had left the village, I went back to Cherokee for Cherokee Homecoming, a local festival that attracts hundreds of former villagers and benefits town projects; that year, the cause was the restoration of the town's 150-year-old limestone schoolhouse. I'd been back to Cherokee many times since my childhood, so I knew that the village, despite the recent construction of a paved road leading there from Marsh Harbour, the largest city in the Abacos, would be as pristine as ever—a place of sky and water and beaches. I knew, too, that the food would still be simple and tasty, and I was looking forward to falling into the rhythm of days still dominated by the harvesting, catching, and preparing of good things to eat.

Corella Sands, who had been one of those children outside the lamplight that first night in Cherokee and who had become a life-long friend, greeted me at the airport in Marsh Harbour, still pretty with her sweet smile, snub nose, and halo of curly hair. We drove the bumpy road to Cherokee through thick pine forests and mangrove swamps and parked outside the village, which is sur-rounded on three sides by shining expanses of water. Across the harbor, huge ocean swells smashed into lace on the reef.

Cherokee is laid out like a honeycomb, with concrete lanes threading between cottages trimmed in gumdrop colors: tangerine, peppermint pink, bright blue-green. Corella and I dragged my suitcase to the clapboard cottage in which I had lived as a child and was now renting for a few nights. Children whizzed past us on their bikes, "goin' round Cherokee", they said, to give out chicken, packaged by the festival committee, to every woman who was cooking souse, a spicy Bahamian stew, for the festival the following day.

We went over to Corella's house so I could say hello to her husband, Stewart, a craggy, tall man from another village who, years before, had come "courtin' " for Corella by boat when he heard through the island grapevine that there was a pretty girl down Cherokee way. When our conversation turned to food, Stewart shared a memory of how his mother baked bread in a six-foot-tall conical oven built of limestone, the kind that used to be in every backyard in Cherokee.

"When the coals were just right, I would lay banana leaves on them. She would lay in the bread, then I'd close the door and mud up around the cracks. To keep the 'eat in?" His voice rose at the end, not because he was asking a question but because that was the island way of asking whether I understood.

The accent in Cherokee Sound is unlike any other in the Caribbean, but I've heard a similar lilt and dropping of *h*s in a town a hundred miles north of London. In fact, most of the villagers have English roots; they are descendants of white Tory loyalists who left the United States in 1785, after the American Revolution. They came to the island thinking they would build grand plantations. Instead, the poor soil and isolation forced them to eke out an existence contingent on what they could catch and on the vagaries of wind and sea.

When I was a child, a man named Lebree would hunt wild boar in the pine forests, running them down, knifing and gutting them, then carrying them into town on his back, covering his homespun shirt with blood. Other men fished the Great Bahama Bank in handbuilt wooden smacks. We children dove down 40 feet for conchs and looked for the waving antennae of lobsters. We'd haul shoulderloads of watermelons and sugarcane in from the fields, milk the goats, and hunt for eggs under fussy laying hens. Clifton Sawyer, a hunchback with the strength of Samson in his hands and arms, taught me how to catch bait among the mangroves, then cast hand lines to snare the mutton snapper that cruised along the blue-green tidal channels.

Supplies came once a week by mail boat (less often if the weather was rough) to Mr. Arnold's tiny general store, which I loved. There were huge barrels of peppermint candy, rice, and black-eyed peas. There were salty wedges of strong-tasting, almost cheesy butter and wheels of golden cheddar, both of which came from New Zealand. There was macaroni, too, used for a favorite village dish: baked macaroni and cheese, crusty on top and sometimes fiery from tiny local red chiles known as finger peppers.

Lacking a wealth of choices when it came to ingredients, Cherokee's cooks developed a certain creativity. Fish, for instance, could be fried or boiled, or baked with thyme, stewed with tomatoes, turned into souse, or cooked with sour orange or lime juice. Rituals grew up around the few foods. Thursday was bread-baking day. Friday was chicken souse. Saturday was stewed fish with limes. If no fish had been caught, then just dumplings, potatoes, and sweet potatoes would go into the stewpot.

I slept 12 hours straight on my first night back in Cherokee, only half aware, at dawn, of roosters crowing, the chopping of a machete, and, far off, the roar of breakers. Then the sounds of women calling slid through the calm air like the silvery dash of needlefish across the flats. I was already up when Corella hailed me from my front fence, midway through her daily perambulation around the village. "Mabel be cookin' pigeons. I smelled her gravy when I opened me door this morning," she said. A few hours later, my 20-year-old daughter, Becca, arrived from California, and more people came by to say hello, including some young men who were looking to court. Becca sighed. "Maybe I'll just marry a Cherokee boy and spend all day diving off the reefs. I could do worse, you know." "I know," I said.

Toward late afternoon, people ambled toward the old school

house and the clearing next to it. Greetings rang out, and several former villagers stopped in front of me, waiting for me to see past the wrinkles and recognize, with a jolt, their freckled childhood faces. Long tables were already laden with pot after pot of chicken souse and big square pans of macaroni and cheese. One woman stood over a cauldron, frying conch fritters that were eaten as fast as she cooked them. Conch salad, a refreshing, cevichelike mixture, disappeared before I could get any.

A few men got up to make speeches, to which only half the crowd listened, and two boys kicked a ball around. A group of small children stood and sang about Cherokee food. Their eyes rolled at all the strangers and away from their teacher, who was rather desperately mouthing the words at them: "When the farmer's sown his seed,/He takes his dog, chasing through the forest, hunting wild hogs./Che–ro–KEE!" Town historian Patrick Bethel reflected on how Cherokee fishermen used to "haul" blue holes with nets. I remembered seeing those holes, freshwater springs in the middle of the ocean and so deep they were black, with the fish in them as thick as stars on a moonless night. Then the festival organizers turned the microphones off, and people gathered under the trees, laughing and swapping stories.

The following morning, desperate for conch salad, Becca and I set off to find the main ingredient. We walked out across the flats as the tide was ebbing. Several conchs scooched along the bottom, and I picked one up. It sucked itself back inside its pink curled shell, clamping its foot behind it like a tiny door. I waited. It came back out, its beady stalked eyes looking up at me. But the lip of its shell was not yet curved outward, a sign that it was too young to take, so I threw it back in. We found larger conchs among patches of sea grass. As we walked back to shore with our bucket filled, tiny waves coiled in from the deep, and with an audible sigh the tide turned.

Within a couple of hours, the flats were covered with aquamarine water. Three little boys whipped the shallows with their spears, killing minnows for bait. Even they were talking food. "I want me some peas and rice!" called one. "What's the biggest mutton snapper you ever seen?" called another. "Bigger than my daddy!"

I wanted to ask Corella and her family to dinner, but I was worried that I might not be able to catch anything for us to eat. Wind was rattling the palms and driving rollers over the reef. "If the winds are plaguing," said Stewart, "the good bottom fish hunker down just like us." But then Kenneth Albury, a childhood friend, offered some snappers from his freezer; Corella gave me guavas for guava duff, a kind of steamed pudding; Geraldine Albury, another childhood friend (and Kenneth's sister-in-law), had frozen grouper. The habit of being generous with food has not changed in Cherokee. In church that weekend, the preacher quoted from the book of Luke: "If he asks for bread, will he give a stone? If he asks for an egg, will he give a scorpion? Ask and it shall be given."

So, on Sunday, we had a feast at my house for Corella and her family, some of it cooked by me, some by Corella herself, and the majority by Geraldine: fried snapper, fresh white bread, conch salad, baked grouper, peas and rice, ambrosia fruit salad, and guava duff. Like the meal, our conversation was easygoing and satisfying, and we knew we'd go fishin' another day.

On my last night in the village, four young men passed by the house and asked us to "go sharkin'" with them. By starlight, we walked onto the long dock that stretches spindly-legged into the front harbor, baited three lines, and went back to the beach, where a fire was roaring in a half barrel beneath the pines. The boys were grilling Bahamian lobster. We ate the tails with our fingers, and they were tingling with flavor, as if all the colors of the reef could be tasted in their flesh.

One of the boys and I went to check the lines. "Something took up," he said calmly and hauled in a four-foot-long thrashing machine with skin so matte that only its flashing teeth were visible. I shrieked and hopped backward. The boy chuckled, slit its throat, and cut it loose, having caught it for sport.

Geraldine and her husband came out, and we all sat at the end of the dock, sometimes talking, sometimes not. The Milky Way was a luminescent arch. Geraldine talked about how she'd lived her whole life in Cherokee. "I never did go looking for anything else," she said, sighing, but she sounded proud.

Back in 1957, after my family had lived in the village for four years, my parents' dream of self-sufficiency soured. They hadn't foreseen the costs of kerosene and chicken feed or how difficult it was to grow much of anything, and we left. But now, as an adult, I can visit whenever I want to. And I am glad I can "coom 'ome", glad that there is still hot bread, and conch, and sour oranges, and boys who go sharkin', and friends who still welcome me with food as they did so many decades ago.

Chicken Souse
(Bahamian Chicken Stew)

Serves 8

Norma Albury made this stew for Cherokee Home-
    coming. Bahamians often stir sour orange juice into
    souse to season it further after it's cooked.

4 ribs celery, trimmed and cut into ½"-thick pieces
2 large yellow onions, peeled and chopped
2 small red bell peppers, cored, seeded, and cut into 1"
    pieces
2 tbsp. allspice berries
1 tbsp. freshly ground black pepper
1 5–8-lb. stewing chicken, cut into 2" pieces, neck
    reserved
2 small hot red chiles, such as bird's-eye, stemmed and
    halved lengthwise
2 bay leaves
4 ears shucked corn, quartered

3 carrots, peeled, trimmed, and cut into ½"-thick
  rounds
2 medium waxy potatoes, peeled and cut into 1" pieces
Salt

1. Put celery, onions, bell peppers, allspice, black
pepper, and 3 cups water into a large pot and bring to
a boil over high heat. Add chicken and neck, chiles, bay
leaves, and 7 cups water and return to a boil. Reduce
heat to medium and simmer until chicken is cooked
through, about 1 hour.

2. Add corn, carrots, and potatoes to pot and simmer
until potatoes are soft, about 30 minutes more. Season
to taste with salt. Discard bay leaves and chicken neck
before serving.

The Child's Physiology of Taste

by Stephanie Hartman
from *Gastronomica*

Hartman's tongue-in-cheek parody of the precepts of famed French gastronome Brillat-Savarin smartly uses academic wit to dissect the eating habits of *brattus Americanus*, circa twenty-first century. Those of us who regularly eat with kids know how true her words can be.

I. Aphorisms of the Child

1. The introduction of a new dish does more to promote children's misery than the necessity of a bath.
2. The pleasures of the table are better enjoyed under the table, with only a comic book for company.
3. We can learn to feed ourselves, but if we never learn we shall always be fed.
4. He who eats a vegetable without first striking an advantageous deal with the parent is a fool.
5. Animals feed themselves; men eat; but only children can spatter food on the walls.
6. Tell me what you eat, and I shall tell you whether you are a weirdo.
7. If eating from the dog dish is fit for man's best friend, it is fit for man's progeny.

8. A meal not served on one's favorite plate is like a birthday cake without frosting.

II. Definition of Taste

By taste we mean that faculty by which food is rejected as unfit for consumption. Numerous variables, however, including color, texture, and unfamiliarity, may prevent the food from getting even so far as the lips. In occasional circumstances, taste can also be the sense that brings one into contact with substances that provide nourishment and entertainment.

Interestingly, a food may be tasted without being consumed, much as wine tasters avoid inebriation. One may instead, after masticating the substance into either a chunky mass or a smooth paste, retain it in one's mouth until afforded the opportunity to project it outward, such as when the parents' attentions are elsewhere.

III. The Aesthetics of Presentation

1. It must be well understood that foods must never intermingle or otherwise come into contact with other foods on the plate. Such contact results in cross-contamination severely detrimental to the enjoyment of any of the foods.
2. A piece of food is always inferior to the whole. It is not gluttony to demand the entire bagel, apple, sticky bun, or cookie a foot in diameter; generally one wishes to take only one bite and throw the rest on the sidewalk.
3. Small foods are desirable when they are miniature, and therefore cute, versions of other foods; consider tiny cupcakes or cocktail wieners. (A broken-off piece of bagel is not cute. The difference here should be clear.) Small, discrete foods, such as Goldfish, Teddi-Grahams, and the like, are also acceptable. Individual packages, bowls, or Tupperware containers will prevent unfortunate mixing.
4. Sprinkles, chocolate syrup, whipped cream, and the like are to be considered an essential component of the dish they adorn.

Ideally these should be applied until the shape and color of the underlying food are thoroughly obscured.

5. It is advisable to exercise caution with representational foods, like ants-on-a-log or Mickey Mouse–shaped pancakes. These can be desirable, reinforcing as they do the sense of food as entertainment. But consider the case of broccoli set on end to resemble tiny trees; such a presentation may be no more than a stealthy way to introduce healthy foods into a meal, thus violating the integrity of the diet.

IV. THE METHODS OF CONSUMPTION

1. Enjoyment of many foods is heightened if they are first remade according to the eater's vision, in a triumph of culture over nature. Thus peas may be arranged into long lines much as a gardener's labor orders a patch of wilderness into a personal Eden. Formless mashed potatoes and gravy can become a mountain crossed with rivulets, or a Power Ranger, much as Michelangelo's David materialized from a block of marble. An irregular ice cream cone can be licked smooth and pointy; the supple plasticity of American cheese can be folded and broken into innumerable triangles. Once these and other creations bear the civilizing stamp of the maker, they can be demolished with the greatest satisfaction.

2. Reorganization and relocation of the food may be required. It is pleasing to arrange M&Ms by color, and to remove all McDonald's fries from their paper sleeve before any are eaten— particularly when traveling by automobile. Reorganization can also be an end in itself. For example, Cheerios may be placed at one-foot intervals over the entire surface of a rug. Experimenting with more random arrangements is also to be encouraged.

3. Food does not need to be eaten if the television program is particularly absorbing; it may instead be pushed around on the plate, reduced to smaller pieces, or transferred to other locations, as above. As long as the plate assumes a different aspect

than when it was presented, a meal can be said to have taken place.

4. It is kind to allow the parents to offer vegetables in order to assuage their consciences, but it is not necessary to go so far as to eat them.

5. Any food particularly beloved by one's parents as children, and thus invested with nostalgia, should be scorned and either left untouched or brutally chopped up.

6. The dog is always hungry and needs just a little extra something, which the adults are too hard-hearted to provide.

V. Different Ways of Preparing a Proper Sandwich

There is essentially only one way to prepare a sandwich. The bread must be white, and the crusts removed with care, or the sandwich will be less flavorsome. The result can be cut into squares or triangles, but if the adult fails to perform this act according to the preferences of the child, the whole process must begin anew. Fillings may include cheese (orange, pre-sliced, and yielding in texture), bologna (pink, pre-sliced, and yielding in texture), or peanut butter and jelly. The last, however, is fraught with dangers: one must consider the relative merits of creamy and crunchy, the proportions of ingredients, their relationship to the margins of the bread, and the variety of preserves.

It has been suggested that foreign substances, such as lettuce, tomatoes, or other vegetables, or pickles, mustard, or other condiments, may be introduced into sandwiches. These have been proven unsatisfactory.

A night's rest under a couch will often improve a sandwich's flavor by allowing it to season properly.

Here the child lets her pen drop, and goes to harangue her mother for a hot dog.

Someone's in the Kitchen

From Grits to Gaul

by James Villas
from *Between Bites*

> Holding forth for decades in *Town & Country* and *Esquire*, as well as in books like *from My Mother's Southern Kitchen*, James Villas has been a major force in the American culinary world. His new book-length memoir recounts his career with a characteristic blend of joie de vivre and curmudgeonly charm.

O n a rainy, chilly October morning, Jimmy and another Fulbright helped me load a gigantic steamer trunk, suitcase, and portable Royal typewriter (all my worldly goods for a whole year) into the VW in preparation for the 350-mile drive down to Grenoble. Leaving Paris and my friends was traumatic enough, but lighting out on my own into *la France profonde* with little idea of what awaited me was nothing less than frightening. Before I left the U.S., my worldly father, who had already exposed me somewhat to fine dining in New York, Chicago, San Francisco, and even London, said he'd read in *Holiday* magazine about a good restaurant he thought was called La Côte d'Or in Saulieu, a small town almost equidistant between Paris and Grenoble and on my direct route. Maybe, he suggested, I could stop there for lunch.

Not, mind you, that I'd ever heard of or cared about Michelin except as a company that produced good tires and road maps, meaning that I certainly had no copy of the legendary red restaurant guide that would have verified the name and location of the restaurant (and that would one day become my bible in France). Nor, as I made my way guardedly down Route Nationale 6 in the pouring rain with visions of the Alps and French classrooms and lofty scholarly endeavors running through my brain, was I in the least bit aware that at Sens and Auxerre and Avallon and elsewhere in this part of Burgundy existed some of the finest food and wines in the entire country. My most immediate and anxious concerns were getting to Grenoble, finding a place to live, getting officially enrolled at the Faculté des Lettres at the university, and meeting the distinguished professor Léon Cellier.

SAULIEU the sign read through the flapping windshield wipers. It occurred to me that I was peckish, so slowing down, I looked from side to side through the fogged windows, hoping to catch sight of the restaurant Daddy had mentioned. I saw nothing in the village that looked like a restaurant, but across the busy highway from a gas station I did notice the name Hôtel de la Côte d'Or in gold letters framed in a blue band on a nondescript, yellowish, two-story building. Not really caring where I ate, and thinking that in this hotel I could probably get a good omelette with *pommes frites* or a *croque-monsieur* like those I'd had in Paris, I slammed on the brakes and turned into the small parking lot. I did find it strange that next to me was a majestic silver Bentley, but after throwing on a corduroy sports jacket over my crewneck sweater, I made sure the doors to the car were securely locked and raced through the drenching downpour for the hotel entrance carrying only my new and very French satchel containing my important papers and documents.

The lobby couldn't have been less ostentatious or more welcoming: a plain tile floor, wood-paneled walls covered with what looked like lots of family pictures and menus and certificates, simple chairs, a tiny bar, and a desk behind which was a rack of mailboxes and room keys tended by a middle-aged, slim, neatly dressed lady.

After we'd exchanged the appropriate *bonjours,* I huffed, *"Quel temps!"* casually whisking the sleeves of my wet jacket with my hands.

"Oui, c'est affreux," she agreed, rolling her gutteral "r" and pronouncing the difficult "eu" in ways I could only envy.

"I was hoping to have a little lunch," I informed in my most careful French. "Maybe an omelette or sandwich."

Madame appeared somewhat taken back. "Does Monsieur have a reservation?"

Now it was I who was a bit surprised as I uttered, "No."

"I'm sorry, Monsieur," she continued politely, "but we serve no sandwiches in the restaurant." She hesitated a moment, glancing again at me suspiciously before looking down at a thick notebook. "But due to the weather, we have had quite a few cancellations today, so if Monsieur would care to be seated in our dining room and see the menu . . ."

"Ça va," I confirmed offhandedly, now aware of the intoxicating aromas of food wafting in the air and even more hungry.

Coming from behind the desk, she then ushered me into the restful, almost homey, half-empty restaurant and seated me at a small table next to a window outside of which I could hear cars and trucks speeding by on their way to Paris or Lyon. Across the room was a large display table with baskets of fresh fruit, an assortment of cheeses with a little tag stuck in each, and a huge, rosy ham positioned on a silver stand. The impeccable white tablecloth was heavy starched linen, the small vase of flowers unassuming, the silver brightly polished, and the glassware thin and elegant; and just before a plainly dressed, dark-haired lady arrived to ask if I'd like an apéritif and hand me a menu, it suddenly dawned on me that every man in the place except me was wearing a necktie.

This slight shock was nothing compared with the jolt in the pit of my growling stomach when I started to study the menu and saw the strange dishes and hefty prices. *Timbale de Morilles Chatelaine, Quenelles de Brochet Mousseline, Gratin de Queues d'Ecrevisses, La*

Potée Morvanaise—I'd just as soon have been trying to decipher Sanskrit. In Paris, I'd had complete meals in bistros for no more than seven new francs; here that was the price of a single appetizer. Remembering that my solvency was all of ninety-three dollars a month, my first urge was to escape with some outlandish excuse to Madame and continue driving till I found a humble café. Then I recognized *Le Coq au Vin à l'Ancienne* priced at eight francs, and detected a half-bottle of some Beaujolais for two francs, and was delirious over the fragrances emanating from the next table, and—damnit, I was starving to death.

I tore off a piece of bread from a rugged loaf nestled in cloth in a wire basket and spread butter on one end. The bread was tangy and chewy, the butter sweet, with a slight hazelnut flavor like none I'd ever tasted, not even in Paris. I was beginning to relax.

Pad in hand, the lady returned to the table while I was sipping Pernod and eating bread and listened as I indicated that I'd have just the *coq au vin.*

"Et pour commencer, Monsieur?" she inquired, a sudden expression of extreme disappointment or pity on her smooth face when I shook my head. She then smiled, placed a carbon copy of the order on the table, and left.

In a few minutes, a tuxedoed waiter brought the bottle of wine, uncorked it, and very ceremoniously poured a little into the wide-lipped glass for me to taste. It was fine, I nodded with confidence, feeling rather proud of myself and actually quite taken with the wine's fresh and intensely fruity flavor. My eyes followed another waiter carrying a large silver tray to a table of four smartly dressed diners across the room, and as I watched him and a helper begin to carve and serve what looked like two chickens or ducks, I couldn't help but also catch sight of a short, stout, mustached man in a white chef's uniform peeking through what must have been the kitchen door. At first I assumed he was observing all the action with the fowl, but soon it became perfectly clear that the object of his attention was . . . me.

"The chef would like for you to taste his *terrine de gibier*," whispered the waiter, placing a small, meaty rectangle in front of me and a china pot of mustard and ceramic jug of what looked like miniature pickles on the table. Baffled by both the gesture and the word *gibier* (and innocently wondering if I'd be charged for the starter), I nonetheless thanked him and cut into the pâté. Slightly gamy, coarsely textured, and so subtly seasoned that no particular agent could be identified, it was remarkable, and when I added a touch of hot mustard and bit into one of the salty pickles and took a sip of the wine, the sensation was startling.

After a great flurry of scraping bread crumbs off the tablecloth, changing the silver, and replacing my napkin, the waiter then rolled over a handsome wooden cart on top of which rested a large, shiny copper pot, two covered copper containers, and a plate of what appeared to be heart-shaped pieces of bread. By now I should have suspected that I was in no ordinary hotel dining room. I didn't, nor was I fully prepared when the waiter formally announced *"Le Coq au Vin à l'Ancienne pour Monsieur"* as if I'd ordered foie gras studded with diamonds, served a first portion topped with the beautiful fried croutons rubbed with garlic, and spooned a few buttered green peas and parsleyed boiled potatoes from the other containers into separate china bowls. The stew, which also contained tiny onions and mushrooms, was almost black, and although I'd had *coq au vin* before in the States, even at the famous Pavillon in New York, and indeed in simple Paris bistros, I knew the second I took my first bite of this robustly rich, smooth, incredibly sapid chicken that I'd really never eaten *coq au vin*. What I was also certain of was that while I ate, the same pudgy man in the white uniform would crack open the kitchen door and glance in my direction.

For maybe forty-five minutes, I slowly relished my meal, at once aware that this had to be what genuine French cuisine was all about and, as the alcohol asserted its authority, slightly depressed that I had no one with whom to share this special moment. In years to come, life would be such that I'd learn to appreciate dining alone and actually prefer solitude to inordinate conviviality, but when you're in the flush of youth, and accustomed to family security and the fellowship of friends, and blindly in love, nothing can be so dispiriting—especially far away in a foreign land—as finding yourself truly enjoying something like a great meal with nobody else to partake in the experience.

Just when I had begun feeling a little sorry for myself and wondering whether I could afford at least a cup of wonderful filtered coffee, the waiter appeared again, this time with a glistening apricot tart and bowl of *crème fraîche*. "*Avec les compliments du chef,*" he pronounced proudly before asking if I wouldn't also like a cup of coffee. I was dumbfounded. Who was this chef sending out food I hadn't ordered, and why? Had I perhaps been mistaken for another customer? Cutting into the luscious tart, the second question was answered when I suddenly realized that, except for an extremely well-tailored man with a striking woman who looked remarkably like Princess Grace, I was the only person left in the restaurant and that it was almost three o'clock.

After the coffee had been delivered, I'd no sooner tapped a cigarette from my pack of Winstons than a waiter materialized from nowhere with a heavy gold lighter at the ready. Across the room, the handsome couple finally got up to leave, only to be met at the entrance by both the mysterious chef from the kitchen and the kind lady who'd seated me. There was momentary chitchat, a cordial bowing and shaking of hands, and the customers left. Knowing that I too had to get back on the road, I was about to signal for the check when I noticed the plump chef heading toward my table.

"Did Monsieur enjoy his lunch?" he asked pointedly in rapid but articulate French. His voice was soft but authoritative, his small mustache perfectly trimmed, his fingers short and stubby, and there were heavy bags under the most melancholy brown eyes I'd ever seen. He appeared to be at least in his early sixties.

I assured him it was one of the best meals I'd ever had, then inquired timorously if he'd been the one who sent out the appetizer and dessert.

"And what did you think of Dumaine's terrine?" he diverted my question, a smile on his comfortable, lined face.

"What kind of terrine?" I almost stammered, figuring he was either using another term for *gibier* or referring to some abstruse moniker like those I'd seen attached to so many French dishes on menus.

"*La terrine Dumaine,*" he repeated proudly, his expression lighting up even more. "*My* terrine. My *terrine de gibier.*"

I finally understood and said it was extraordinary, like nothing I'd ever tasted—though I couldn't begin to identify the seasonings.

"Ah, that's the most important aspect," he continued, withdrawing a rumpled pack of Gauloises from a pant pocket and lighting one with a match. "Are you English?"

"American."

"*Ah, américain.* Well, *jeune homme,* for an American, you have curiosity—I can tell. And you speak French well. This must be your first time here."

"Actually, it's my first trip to France," I clarified, wondering whether I should ask him to sit down. "I'm a student—a Fulbright scholar—and I'm going to study at the University of Grenoble."

He didn't seem at all impressed. "Ah, my wife and Madame Bonino were right. A student, though my headwaitress had the impression you were English or German or Scandinavian. We get lots of Americans here, lots—especially in summer. I like the Americans. Without the Americans during the war, we wouldn't be here talking now, and I don't forget that. I remember. And the Americans love good cuisine. They're not critical enough, in my opinion, and most believe that great cuisine must be complicated and rich, but yes, the Americans generally appreciate good food."

After that rapid and slightly intimidating lecture, I pointed to the other chair and asked if he'd like to sit down. He ignored the question, as if he hadn't heard it or didn't understand my French, simply tapping an ash into the crystal ashtray.

"Would Monsieur like a cognac?" he offered.

I shook my head with the legitimate excuse that it might make me sleepy and I had a long drive ahead of me.

"And the *coq au vin*. Did Monsieur enjoy the *coq au vin*?"

I'd learned the delightful French gesture of kissing the tips of my fingers. "Monsieur Dumaine, that has to be one of the most delicious, most memorable dishes I've ever eaten," I exclaimed truthfully. "But one question: Why is the stew so dark?"

"Blood," he almost boomed. "Chicken blood—plus pureed livers. It's the only way."

I wasn't about to let him detect my squeamish astonishment.

"*Ah, le coq au vin*," he then almost sang. "There's still nothing like a real *coq au vin* when it's made correctly with a fat rooster that's cooked slowly for a long time." He seemed to be almost in a trance, his sad eyes again sparkling. "*Ecoutez,* I've been preparing *coq au vin* for over forty years, and I think I'm only now finally getting it right."

The man was intriguing me—his forthrightness, and honesty, and . . . passion for food. But skeptic that I already was, I wondered even more why he was being so attentive to a total stranger.

"The flavor of that chicken!" I continued with equal enthusiasm. "How can any chicken have that much flavor? I live in the South in America, and we make wonderful fried chicken, but never, Monsieur, have I tasted chicken with this amount of flavor."

Still standing and smoking, he raised a hand in the air and shrugged the way only the French do. "But Monsieur, that was a mature *poularde de Bresse,* the finest chicken in all the world. You've never before eaten *poularde de Bresse*?"

Of course, I'd not only never eaten a Bresse chicken, I'd never heard of it and had no idea even what or where Bresse was.

Opening his eyes wide, he appeared actually shocked. "*Ah, jeune homme,* you'll pass by the Bresse region on your way to Grenoble, and I can tell you . . . *écoutez* . . . there'd be no Burgundian cuisine without our great *poulardes aux pattes bleues.*"

Pattes bleues? The expression threw me.

"*Pattes . . . vous savez, les pieds,*" he clarified knowingly. "*Elles ont des pieds bleus.*"

Blue-footed chickens. I thought I'd heard everything, but blue-footed chickens?

He seemed surprised that I was surprised, but this only inspired him to begin a short discourse on how these unique blue-footed chickens are bred, their special diet of corn and dairy products, how their breasts are larger than those of ordinary chickens, and why they must be killed at exactly the right age. At one point during his fervid declamation, I once again signaled for him to take a seat, but again he refused, just as he rejected my offer of a Winston with another wave of the hand and the curt comment, "No taste." Across the peaceful room so devoid of artifice, a waiter stood in almost military silence, and I also observed that, from time to time, the dark-haired lady whom I took to be Madame Bonino would appear at the entrance as if she needed to speak with him. He took no notice of either.

He lit up another Gauloise, then hesitated again as if puzzled by something. "You mentioned *le poulet frit* in America. What is fried chicken? I've never heard of chicken being fried. It sounds horrible. You must mean sautéed chicken."

I assured him that I did indeed mean fried chicken, battered and fried in oil like *pommes frites,* and that it was one of the great specialties of the South—especially when my mother first soaked it in . . . I didn't know the word for buttermilk so began scrambling words.

"*Ah, babeurre,*" he finally determined with more interest. "But your chickens. I understand that American chickens are all commercial, and killed too young, and have no flavor, so . . ." He frowned as if truly disgusted, ". . . how could any chicken dish be good without good chicken to start with?"

Although I remembered as a child in North Carolina eating

chickens that were farm-raised and how much better they tasted than those bought in supermarkets, I had to admit it was a subject to which I'd never given much thought. To Monsieur Dumaine, such irreverence was nothing less than a cardinal sin.

"*Ecoutez*," he almost bolted, "nothing matters more in cooking than the quality of ingredients. Without superlative ingredients, even the most brilliant chef can produce only second-rate cuisine. My sole comes all the way from Boulogne. I use only butter from the salt marshes of Normandy. And just right here in my own region, we have Charolais beef around Mâcon, and fat pigs from over in the Morvan, and, of course, the Bresse chickens used to make dishes like your *coq au vin*. Ah, *non, Monsieur*, there's no great cuisine without great ingredients, and I use only the best—no matter the cost." His puzzled expression returned. "Buttermilk fried chicken, you say?"

That he was proffering this astonishing culinary edification to a young intruder who had only scant knowledge of what he was talking about impressed but also daunted me, such that I felt compelled—especially since he insisted on remaining standing—to suggest that I was taking up too much of his precious time and really should be leaving. Nonsense, he said, basically. He could tell that I was interested in food, and he loved nothing more than discussing *la grande cuisine* with someone eager to learn more about it, and he felt he had . . . a mission, a duty . . .

All at once he reached up, opened one of the frosted windows, and shut it again. "The rain is worse than ever, and you should not be driving," he declared as if addressing a son or telling one of his kitchen helpers not to cut a piece of meat in so-and-so manner. "Why don't you stay in the hotel tonight? Our rooms are not expensive, and we've had so many cancellations. Ah, then you could have a nap, and Dumaine would prepare for you maybe a simple *omelette aux fines herbes* this evening since you've had a large lunch, and . . . you're interested in *les poulardes de Bresse*, are you not?"

I uttered a nervous "*Oui, Monsieur*," my brain reeling.

"*Eh bien*," he continued, "I'm due to see my chicken woman

early tomorrow morning—I haven't been too happy recently with the size of her chickens—so after a nice breakfast of fresh brioches and apricot preserves, you'll follow me in your car down to the farm and I'll show you our special chickens—the finest in the world. It's on your way to Grenoble, not far off the main highway."

Now my head was really spinning. I knew I had exactly four days to find an apartment in Grenoble and get settled before class registration. I knew there would be other Fulbrights to meet, and that in three days there was a scheduled conference with our local adviser, and that Professor Cellier was expecting me. Exactly what would a night in this hotel cost me? Was breakfast included in the price? And could I really afford another meal in the restaurant? On the other hand, I reasoned, I'd have to pay for a hotel in Grenoble plus dinner, and it was stupid trying to drive at least another 150 miles in the pouring rain, and . . . when would I get another chance to see those blue-footed chickens?

Southerner that I was, I'd already led something of an impatient, rebellious life, so it didn't take too much further self-debate before I found myself being led by Madame Dumaine up the narrow stairs of the hotel to a room that was plain but neat. I did indeed take a good nap before soaking in a hot tub and returning to the dining room at precisely eight o'clock ("The only thing my husband demands and expects is punctuality," Madame had warned) for a soft, golden, creamy omelette. And what I remember most was hearing the faint clanging of pans in the kitchen after I returned to the room and leaning out the window far enough to watch a busy pastry chef go about making bread and croissants and brioches for the next day. At least for the time being, my apprehension over what lay ahead for me abated, and the loneliness of being away from those I missed was relieved by the consoling reality of a few kind people who seemed to care about me, amazing food and comfortable lodging in a quaint country inn, and the ubiquitous sounds of a language that I loved and was now being forced to speak at every encounter.

The Grand Dame of Southern Cooking

by Rand Richards Cooper
from *Bon Appetit*

> Novelists often turn into delightful food writers when, like Cooper (*The Last to Go, Big As Life*), they bring storytelling sensibilities to bear on the subject. Esteemed cook and cookbook author Edna Lewis has been long overdue for a appreciative portrait like this one.

In the mid-1980s, fresh from college, I lived briefly in Manhattan in a Hell's Kitchen apartment. I spent my mornings trying to write fiction; afternoons I'd go out walking. Often my walk took me past a southern restaurant down the block. Approaching the open kitchen door, I'd slow down, swimming through the glorious aroma of fried green peppers and onions and celery, honey and ham and God knew what else. On that bleak street, my poor-man's feast had a magical, comforting effect. Though I'm from New England, the smell of southern cooking somehow made me feel at home.

It's amazing to think I owed that feeling to one pioneering woman: No one has done more to take down-home cooking beyond the Grits Belt than the indomitable Edna Lewis—the granddaughter of slaves, a chef and cookbook author, who is the unofficial ambassador of southern cuisine. Her groundbreaking career was capped in 1999 with her designation as Grande Dame by Les Dames d'Escoffier, an organization of women culinary professionals from around the world.

Edna Lewis's life is a great American story. Born in 1916 in Freetown, Virginia, a tiny farm community founded by her grandfather, she went to New York and became a chef at a time when women chefs, let alone black women chefs, were few and far between. Her landmark 1976 book, *The Taste of Country Cooking*, was one of the first cookbooks by an African-American woman to reach a wide audience, and is credited with helping spark a national interest in genuine southern, country-style cooking and its roots.

"Edna Lewis is an icon," says Barbara Haber, a food historian and curator of books at Harvard's esteemed Schlesinger Library. "She commands enormous respect and affection."

As a food writer Lewis is warmly personal. She offers helpful kitchen shortcuts—tips and tricks as well as techniques—like how to boil corn in its husk, and how to add a bit of country ham to perk up greens. We feel we're getting the friendly benefit of years of trial and error; we hear the echo of mistakes made. If you're making coconut layer cake, she advises, buy two coconuts, in case one is bad. To judge when the cake is done, try listening to it: The liquids in the cake make bubbling noises that grow faint when it's ready; if it's too noisy, put the cake back in the oven. This is the very essence of comfort food—cooking with all of the quirks left in.

Lewis organized *The Taste of Country Cooking* with menus set to the routines of rural life: "A Spring Breakfast When the Shad Were Running," "Making Ice Cream on a Summer Afternoon," "Morning After-Hog-Butchering Breakfast." These slices of seasonal life evoke a world of persimmon beer and country-fried apples, watermelon-rind pickles and smothered rabbit and Saturday-night yeast bread. The rhythm of farm work and holiday feast follows the back-and-forth between people and nature, revealing a regional cuisine's original connection to the soil. Lewis's advocacy of natural foods reflects not the zeal of a convert but the living memory of being a farm girl in Freetown, where the woods and orchard and garden were her supermarket, and a box behind the kitchen stove served as a makeshift nursery for hatchling chicks.

In the book, Lewis chronicles bygone rural folkways and food-ways, such as the practice of planting root vegetables in the dark of the night. She also paints forgotten figures of rural life, like the itinerant hog killer, a traveling butcher who appeared each year at the first cold spell. It is all precisely detailed, yet heightened by mystery, seen through the thrilled eyes of a child—a blending of procedure and rapture that make the book an American original.

It was at the urging of Judith Jones, her editor at Knopf, that Lewis wove her recipes around childhood stories, giving the book its glow of luminous recollection. She wrote of the bliss of a spring morning, red sun rising behind thick fog, "the velvety green path of moss leading endlessly through the woods," and of rushing out after a summer storm to look for turtles washed up from rain-swollen streams—turtles that might end up in that day's pot of soup.

Further on, Edna's father plows the field, and she follows along, walking barefoot in the new furrow, "carefully putting one foot down before the other and pressing it into the warm, plowed earth." Her father sings; the plow turns up roots of a sassafras bush that will become tomorrow's tea; her brother and sister return the call of a nesting bird, "Bobwhite, bobwhite, are your peaches ripe?"

It's all incredibly lovely, and indeed, *The Taste of Country Cooking* is one of those food books you fall in love with. "You talk about it," says Haber, "the way you talk about a work of fiction." This dream of a rural childhood paradise was written by an urban exile—a woman in late middle age (Lewis turned 60 as the book came out), guided by the "memory of good flavor" back to "a time and a place that is so very dear to my heart."

Lewis retired as a chef in 1992—her last position was at Brooklyn's venerable Gage & Tollner—and now lives in Atlanta, where she's co-authoring a new cookbook with Scott Peacock, of the Watershed restaurant. She and Peacock share an apartment, and their affectionate collaboration has won them renown as the Odd Couple of southern cooking.

"Scott is my buddy," says Lewis. "And he's a great cook. Tuesday night is fried-chicken night at his restaurant. People go wild for it."

On the phone Lewis has a girlish laugh and rambles warmly about her early years in New York City—taking a job at the *Daily Worker* and joining political demonstrations ("I was a radical," she chuckles), going to a party where her friend Ken Scott, the designer, had decorated his apartment walls with cookies. "Life is great," she says, "when you're young and free and can do anything."

These days, at a young 85, Lewis is still spry and active, attending the occasional culinary event and helping Peacock with her biography. "I'm in awe of Ms. Lewis," says Peacock. "There's simply no one else like her."

People who know Lewis can't say enough about the life she has led, or about the woman herself. "Edna is both a grand lady and an unpretentious person," says John Egerton, author of several books on southern cooking. "Every place she's gone, she has touched and inspired people." For decades, aspiring young chefs have profited from her guidance, Egerton notes. "Edna has always been free with her skills and techniques. She doesn't create masterpieces to be observed only from a distance. She invites you in."

Perhaps that helps explain what makes southern cooking so magical, even to non-southerners. Comfort food isn't just taste, after all, but a whole set of relations. The relentless specialization of modern life has taken its toll on home culinary life, eroding skills and weakening the chain of cooks passing along family lore in the form of favorite recipes. Not only our kitchens, but our lives, our very selves, are decreasingly well-equipped for home cooking.

And thus—the deep, near-mythic resonance of Lewis's life and vision, with its ecstatic unity of food, farm and family. Her personal memory cues our collective one, inviting us back to a place we're only half-aware we left behind.

A Week in the Gramercy Tavern Kitchen

by Steven A. Shaw
from fat-guy.com

If the term "gourmand" hadn't existed, it would have had to be invented for Shaw, a lawyer-turned-foodist who presides over his own lively, opinionated website devoted to high-end restaurants.

PART I: FIRST NIGHT

"You call that a brunoise?"

Matt Seeber, Gramercy Tavern's sous-chef, has had the misfortune of being placed in charge of me for the next week. With a flick of the wrist, my personal drill sergeant casts my last half-hour's work in the garbage. "If the chef saw your sorry excuse for a brunoise, he'd send you packing." He unholsters a 10" chef's knife. "Good thing celery is cheap," he growls. "I'll show you again." In a blur of activity, Matt hones his knife on a steel, splits a celery stalk down the middle, lays the halves on the cutting board, trims them into rectangles and, moving his knife in smooth horizontal strokes, shaves each rectangle into ⅟₁₆" slivers. He then dices each sliver into identical ⅟₁₆" cubes. It takes him five minutes to parse one celery stalk—about 4,096 cubes, by my computation. This is the dreaded brunoise (pronounced "broon-WAH!" in kitchen-French), which will be the bane of my existence in the days to come. "Got it? Okay, I need about a quart. Then you can do the carrots."

Three hours later, I move on to peeling several hundred boiled fingerling potatoes with a paring knife. The potatoes are still hot, and they scald my fingers as I try to hold them—but just try peeling them cold. Then I prepare the bayaldi, a huge baking sheet of razor-thin, alternating one-inch circles of zucchini, yellow squash, eggplant and tomato laid over caramelized onions. My feet are getting sore from standing on the hard, slippery, tile floor (even though I wore what I thought were my most comfortable shoes), my back is aching from bending over the counter and it's only my first day. Now it's time to make dinner.

At 5:30 p.m., as Gramercy Tavern's first customers are seated, Tom Colicchio, Executive Chef, takes his post on "the pass," a worktable at the front of the kitchen where every dish passes before his eyes and receives its final garnish before being dispatched to the dining room. One of the floor managers sticks her head into the kitchen. "Nineteen menus," she says, indicating how many customers are seated and studying their options. In the dining room, the section captains are answering questions, taking orders and passing the handwritten order slips off to their waiters, who enter them into a computer.

As the table receives the evening's amuse bouche, the little printer on the pass comes to life and spits out the first order of the evening. Chef Tom snatches the ticket and calls out the appetizers for table 235: "Ordering one partridge, one tartare, two green salad, one urchin." The kitchen springs to life. Jonathan, the steely-eyed line cook in charge of partridge, foie gras and a few other meat dishes, begins the partridge salad appetizer—two boneless cylinders of partridge breast, wrapped in cabbage and served with a consommé. At the same time, Juliet, at the shellfish station, starts to heat the sea urchin fondue and mashed potato mixture, while Hector, at the garde manger ("gahrd mahn-ZHAY," where cold food is prepared) station, unrefrigerates a portion of tuna tartare with cucumber vinaigrette (leaving it in its steel mold) and prepares to toss two green salads.

When the hot dishes are almost finished, the chef calls "finish tartare, salads," at which point Hector unmolds the tuna and plates the salads. Chef Tom garnishes the partridge with coarse salt and fresh marjoram and sprinkles the urchin (served in its shell) with chopped chives. With a final command of "pick up!" three runners grab the orders (quickly glancing at a copy of the order ticket to see which guest gets which dish, and in what sequence—the ticket even indicates, by a "W," which guests are female) and deliver them to the dining room. With a red pencil, Chef Tom notes the time the appetizers went out. The meat entrees are already cooking, while the fish will get started in a couple of minutes.

The first order of partridge gets sent back. "What's the matter with it?" Chef Tom asks the captain. "She says it's not what she expected," he replies (this is, incidentally, the first night of the Autumn menu, and almost every dish is new). Now, everybody in the kitchen has tasted this partridge dish and the consensus of these professional cooks (and me) is that it's great. Chef Tom sighs. "It's going to be a long night." The partridge order is replaced with a salad of cured hamachi.

Meanwhile, other orders are pouring in. Within an hour, Juliet is "in the weeds" (swamped) because 23 customers have spontaneously and simultaneously ordered lobster in the past few minutes—and the red meat station is inundated with orders for "beef, MR," and "lamb, MR." Chef Tom relinquishes the pass to Matt and ambles over to assist Juliet (this kind of thing, which happens every day, doesn't constitute a crisis in Tom's world). He looks at the 23 spice-rubbed lobsters waiting to be sautéed. "We need more skillets."

"What do you mean they're not ready?" Matt says to a waiter, as he stares down at two plates of monkfish ("monk" in kitchen-speak) destined for table 245. "She's got one bite left of her app. and they're just staring at each other, all starry-eyed," reports the waiter. Matt puts the two plates aside and turns to me. "Looks like we're having monk for dinner." He surveys the accumulated order tickets and sees that table 220 has two monkfish orders in the works. "Eric, how long on those other two monk?" "About five." "Okay, fire two more—four all day. Make those first two real nice for the starry-eyed lovers." 245 gets 220's monk and 220, which was ahead of schedule anyway, suffers only about a one-minute delay.

By 11:30 p.m., when things finally quiet down, the kitchen has served three or more courses each to over 240 guests. But even as the exhausted line cooks clean their stations and Matt wraps the little printer in cellophane (to keep it dry), there is still plenty to be done over at the pastry station. Christina and Connie—two of the assistant pastry chefs—will be baking apple tarts and lemon soufflés to order for at least another hour, and they'll be cleaning their station until 1:30 a.m. Claudia Fleming, the head pastry chef, will be in at about 5:00 a.m. to start the next day's desserts.

For a midnight snack, I have a big plate of leftover mashed potatoes (perhaps the most rewarding part of working in a restaurant kitchen is the virtually unlimited opportunity for snacking—this is basically my idea of heaven), plus a glass of Bruno Paillard Champagne and two Advil.

PART II: SHOPPING AND COOKING

A Trip to the Greenmarket with Senor Modesto

Modesto is Gramercy Tavern's produce buyer. I don't know if that's his first or last name—everybody just calls him Modesto. A visit to the Union Square Greenmarket with Modesto is like a trip to Disneyland with Mickey Mouse as your tour guide. Modesto is King of the Greenmarket. After four hours of sleep, I meet Modesto at the restaurant's loading dock at 7:00 a.m. Today, I'm trying a different footwear strategy: Timberland light hiking boots and

Thor-Lo socks. We grab two hand-trucks and walk the three-and-a-half blocks to the Greenmarket—just long enough for me to realize that my boots are going to be a complete failure.

Modesto is a big guy, but he moves like a water bug. I scramble to keep up as we approach the first stalls. Modesto sees a pile of leeks and he's off like a shot. He picks up a bunch, sniffs them, squeezes them and holds them three inches from his eyes. "Nice," he rules. "How many you got?" he asks the woman behind the table. "About 50 pounds, Modesto." (Everybody knows Modesto by name.) "Okay," says Modesto, turning away (apparently, this indicates that he wants to buy them all). "How about some yellow tomatoes?" the woman calls out, but Modesto is already two stalls down, tasting radish sprouts. I've lost all track of time, and it's not until I see Modesto talking to two farmers dressed as cows that I realize it's Halloween. One of the cows conspiratorially hands Modesto a small envelope of tomato seeds. "I send these seeds back to my family in my country," confesses Modesto. "I hope they grow there." But every time I try to ask Modesto where his country is (Mexico or somewhere in Central America, I assume), he's gone.

At the Paffenroth Gardens stand, where Modesto makes his largest purchase of the day (about 300 pounds of assorted herbs and vegetables), Alex Paffenroth has hot, home-made tamales waiting for me and Modesto in the back of his truck. "Just one each?" Modesto accuses the burly, silver-bearded Paffenroth. "Yeah, just one—you're getting too fat and," gesturing towards me, "the gringo don't look like he's starving either. Now get on out of here so we can pack up your stuff." Modesto and Paffenroth exchange hugs and bone-jarring pats on the back, and we're off.

In season, Gramercy Tavern gets most of its produce at the Union Square Greenmarket (during the winter months, of course, the restaurant works with commercial produce distributors). This reliance on the fortunes of small farms can lead to some interesting situations in the kitchen of the "What am I supposed to do with all this salsify?" variety, but Tom Colicchio is a fanatic when it comes to fresh, seasonal produce. In keeping with this spirit of unpredictability, all the while, Modesto is making his purchases without any sort of shopping list. He doesn't even have a pencil. So I ask, "Modesto, how the heck do you know what to buy?" He holds up four fingers and explains, "Four years! Four years I do this! I know what to buy."

At the end of our tour, we circle around to pick up Modesto's orders, all of which he charges on Gramercy Tavern's accounts. Nearly every farmer has an apple, a muffin or some other treat waiting for Modesto—all of which he and I consume with great relish. It takes two men six trips each to get the produce back to the restaurant.

Modesto deftly maneuvers his cart around every crack in the sidewalk, while I keep getting stuck. As I collapse in a chair back at the restaurant, Modesto taunts, "This is nothing! In summer, I do this all day."

A Week on My Feet

It's Marathon Sunday, and a group of 20 Australian runners is having a dinner party in Gramercy Tavern's private dining room. I'm wearing running sneakers.

Gramercy Tavern maintains a separate area of the kitchen that services only the private dining room, which can accommodate up to 24 guests. That way, when it's time to make 24 lobsters, the rest of the kitchen doesn't grind to a halt. On this night, Matt and I are assigned to cook for the party (or, rather, Matt will cook and I'll try not to chop my fingers off). But first I have to make the brunoise.

At least half of what goes on in a restaurant kitchen is prep work, and it's dizzyingly boring. I've got the brunoise job down to about two hours now (fifteen minutes or so is the goal for a real professional cook), but there's plenty more to do. I spend almost an hour arranging tiny, overlapping, paper-thin slices of potato on gigantic cookie sheets (this is similar to the bayaldi I made the other day, so for all intents and purposes I'm a seasoned veteran).

In the end, these potato shingles get cut up into small rectangles and used as a garnish. You can barely even see it on the plate because it's partially concealed by a piece of bass. Then again, none of this vegetable work is nearly as rough as the afternoon when Matt foisted me off on one of the prep cooks in the basement and I butchered and tied two dozen whole loins of lamb, the same number of rabbits and several quail.

Gramercy Tavern is known for unpretentious American cuisine with little elaborate preparation, yet most dishes require about ten elements when plated. If you look at one of the simplest—a piece of sirloin with mashed potatoes (potato puree, actually)—it seems pretty basic. But on the plate you have a dollop of sauce (which took all day to make) hidden under the steak; a ring of potato puree around that; a couple of sliced fingerling potatoes on the side; some sautéed sprouts on top of the steak; two pieces of braised leek (a real hassle—leeks are very difficult to clean); a little pile containing two pieces of salsify and one slice of black truffle; another little pile of lentils and pearl onions; and multiple fresh herbs (plus coarse salt) sprinkled on the various components of the dish (not to mention the various stocks and seasonings needed to braise the leeks, cook the lentils, etc.).

The separate private party facility has an unanticipated benefit, which is that it's a great place for a beginner like me to observe. Because the private-party cook knows in advance exactly what he will be making (private party menus are usually preset or limited to a couple of choices), he can prep and cook everything in an orderly progression from start to finish (whereas, for the line cooks responsible for the regular dining room, the orders come in seemingly at random and everything is bedlam). For a private party, you have to start the meat two courses before it's going to be served. But you must be prepared to delay things if the party is going slowly on account of people getting too festive or going outside for long cigarette breaks. And you need to be prepared to speed things up if, later on, they all of a sudden announce that they have to leave by a certain time. We had both experiences.

Twice, Matt had to "hold fire" (stop cooking) on the two whole beef tenderloins we had in the oven. Later, when the revelers revealed their secret deadline, Matt had to expropriate one of the pastry assistants to help us plate the cheese and dessert courses right away. It didn't seem to bother him. "Ha! This is nothing. The best is when six more people show up in the middle of the meal."

Downstairs, in the men's locker room, I peel off my now-dirty chef's whites (which will be laundered overnight in Long Island City and delivered to the restaurant at 6:00 a.m.). I engage a few of the cooks in a discussion of my foot problem. "Shit yeah, that's the hardest part of the job," they all seem to agree (the cooks spoke to me with some candor because Tom and Matt were the only ones who knew I was a journalist—Tom thought having a reporter around would make the cooks nervous so they were told I was the chef's friend who's a lawyer and wants to spend a few days in the kitchen). One faction supports clogs as the best choice, while another favors clunky, black, rubber-soled shoes of the cop-on-the-beat variety. Small, iconoclastic minorities speak out in favor of work-boots and running shoes. One of the female cooks adds, from the hallway, "I've had good luck with support hose."

PART III: NIGHT AND DAY

A Night at the Fulton Fish Market

Eric, Gramercy Tavern's main fish supplier, is to the Fulton Fish Market what Modesto is to the Greenmarket. Eric's company, EMS (Early Morning Seafood), supplies fish to a select group of New York's top restaurants, including Gramercy Tavern, Lespinasse and Union Pacific (try the halibut at all three restaurants and you'll see how different the same fish can taste when prepared according to three drastically different recipes).

Matt and I (along with two of the cooks) meet Eric outside the Fulton Fish Market at 2:00 a.m. We enter a bizarre nighttime world where, under blazing arc-lamps, miniature forklifts zoom around like evil bumper cars with fangs, and large men with rusty hooks slung over their shoulders smoke cigarettes and drink coffee while tossing around 150-pound crates of fish like they're bags of feathers. I'm wearing work boots.

It's the first day of diver-scallop season. Eric has just returned from Maine. He and his wife, Pat, drove up there the previous morning, spent all day on a boat with a team of divers who hand-harvested very large (eight to a pound, when shucked) scallops, and drove back all night with two big coolers of scallops in the trunk of their Volvo. At lunchtime, Gramercy Tavern will be serving New York's first diver scallops of the year.

We enter a small shed off to one side of the Market. Inside, six men in yellow slickers are butchering gray sole at an alarming rate. Three swift cuts and the fillet is off the fish. One more cut and the flesh separates from the skin. Matt and I look on in wide-eyed amazement. "Now those are some knife skills," he admits. When we next see Chef Tom and tell him that we spent the night at the Fulton Fish Market, he immediately asks, "Did you check out the guys with the knives?"

As we chase Eric around the Market, I can't help but conclude that people who purchase food for a living are faster than normal humans. Eric is frantically trying to find skate that meets his exacting standards. We visit a dozen vendors, and Eric keeps asking, "Is this the best skate you got?" Finally, one of Eric's friends says that a shipment is just coming out of JFK Airport and that the truck will arrive in 40 minutes.

We sit on a couple of crates of frozen salmon (not destined for Gramercy Tavern, which uses only fresh fish) and eat some sand-wiches (salami, cheddar cheese, olives, capers and mustard on Balt-hazar's cranberry nut bread) that Matt and I prepared earlier. Eric looks at his sandwich. "What's with the fancy-schmantzy bread?

Doesn't anybody use white bread anymore?" He takes a bite. "Hey, you know, this is pretty good."

I ask Eric what he does during the day. "Oh, Pat and I have a restaurant in Jersey." He senses my incredulity. "We don't sleep much." We finish our meal with some leftover Gramercy Tavern desserts.

At about 6:30 a.m., all the vendors in the Fulton Fish Market will pack up their trucks and depart. The sidewalk will be hosed down and almost all traces of the market will disappear. The space will be used as a parking lot for the South Street Seaport. You could walk through the market by day and, eerily, never be aware of its existence.

Work boots are a total failure. I'm sticking with a combination of running shoes and Advil.

The Chef's Night Off

It's Tom Colicchio's night off and Matt is in command, so of course all the VIPs decide to show up at once. Within moments of opening the restaurant, an order ticket shoots out of the printer with a special notation at the bottom: "4 VIPs—Chefs from Restaurant Taillevent, Paris." Thirty seconds later, "3 VIPs—Kevin Costner & Friends," followed by, "7 VIPs—Friends of Chef Tom." Matt shrugs. "Same thing happened last week—David Bouley showed up, along with a bunch of other industry people. It's a conspiracy."

For me, this is the most interesting moment of the week. As a restaurant critic, I always wonder how much a restaurant can do to improve the cuisine for a VIP table. In the case of Gramercy Tavern, at least, the answer is: Not much. VIP treatment at Gramercy Tavern basically consists of a little extra food. Perhaps the kitchen will send out half-portions of urchin between the appetizer and entree, or perhaps an extra dessert course. The actual preparation of the food, however, is unchanged. To Jonathan, on the line, it's just another order of foie gras. Or perhaps he spends an extra second selecting the specific piece of foie gras for the chefs from Taillevent. Looking at the foie gras orders coming over the pass, though, they all look the same to me. In one case, Matt walks over and prepares a dish himself, leaving Marco, another sous-chef (and now the head chef at Colicchio's other restaurant, Craft), in charge of the orders—but it seems mostly a symbolic gesture. The line cooks make these dishes all day. Matt's final product, for all his skill, can't possibly represent a substantial improvement.

Indeed, in the course of a week—during which I observe almost every order that goes through the kitchen—I never see any secret, special, VIP-only dishes or anything of that sort. The kitchen always keeps a piece of salmon on hand for one very special customer—but that's about it. Nor is every request from a VIP table granted.

A waiter reports, "245 wants four side-orders of escarole." Matt shakes his head. "What do I look like, I'm made of escarole here? Offer them spinach." He explains to me: "If I had it, I'd give it to them, but we make maybe one head of escarole for the whole dinner service." Technically, Gramercy Tavern doesn't even offer side dishes—but the kitchen tries hard to accommodate all customer requests, VIP or not. All night, shouts of "SOS" (sauce on the side), "All Meat" (no vegetables), and "Veg. Entree" (a vegetable plate) can be heard in the kitchen.

In five years at Gramercy Tavern, Matt has heard just about every special request in the book. "233, table of two, wants to do the tasting menu but wants a substitution for every course." I think Matt's head is going to explode, but he just says, "Fine. They can have whatever they want as long as they both get the same courses."

It's my last night in the kitchen. By now, my brunoise is almost good enough to satisfy Matt. "You're leaving? But we just got you trained," says one cook. "You're okay—for a lawyer," quips another. I'm just happy to be getting off my feet.

Back in the Dining Room
My wife, Ellen, and I are customers again, and my feet feel great. I'm sitting there, looking at my appetizer, wondering whether

Jonathan made it . . . and whether he knew he was making it for me . . . and whether, if he knew, he would care. Does my order ticket say "2 VIPs—Former Gramercy Tavern kitchen flunky/food critic Steven Shaw & wife, Ellen" or am I just a regular civilian again? Who's on the pass? Is it a good night in the kitchen?

Ellen asks me what I think of my appetizer.

I take a close look.

"Nice brunoise."

A Rogue Chef Tells All

by Gabrielle Hamilton
from *Food & Wine*

When the cult of celebrity chefs threatens to overwhelm the food world, the hype-free perspective of Gabrielle Hamilton (chef/owner of the Manhattan restaurant Prune) is like a breath of fresh air.

Sometimes when I look through the food magazines, watch the cooking shows and read the current crop of books about restaurants, being a chef looks so appealing that I think I'd like to be one too. But even though I've been cooking professionally for over 20 years and now have my own restaurant, Prune, in New York City's East Village—which has gotten enough good press to make my head swell—I'm starting to see that I'll never be a real chef.

If I were a real chef, I'd be at the farmers' market every morning in my crisp, white, conspicuously monogrammed jacket, handpicking organic produce so vital it practically bursts into song. Anything I couldn't find there would be delivered to my door just hours after it was picked by my own private forager—a former stockbroker who had tired of the grind and discovered the simple joys of mushroom hunting. A short time later, I'd be back in my kitchen, its walls lined with freshly polished copper pans, tossing off words like *fond* and *entremet* and *concassé* with my staff of culinary-school graduates while we washed the lettuces by hand in mineral water and dried each leaf individually with a chamois cloth.

When this was finished (a leisurely two hours before service) we would all sit down to an intimate and convivial staff meal, passing big platters of nutritious, well-prepared and delicious food that, we would all agree, one could write a book about. And even if I had flown off the handle earlier that day—thrown a fish or a pot, indulged myself in a peevish chefly tantrum—I would know I had only deepened the respect of my underlings and that all was now well.

If I were a real chef, I would have trained my staff to answer anytime a diner inquired, "Yes, madame, the chef is at the restaurant tonight. The chef is always at the restaurant." I might be cooking at a benefit in Chicago or having my photo taken dining al fresco at my country home, but my staff would never let on.

But hands down the coolest part about being a real chef, the part that really attracts me, is that I would no longer have to cook. What with the perfection of my artisanal, seasonal, locally grown and handpicked ingredients, I would merely coax, nudge or show-case. No need to weary myself with all that labor; no need ever to *tourner, sauter, flamber, dépouiller* or *remouiller.* Fish would jump out of pristine local waters, gills pulsing, and land on my wood-fired grill long before rigor mortis had time to set in. Each turnip, radish and carrot, rich soil still clinging to its roots, would speak for itself.

FROZEN LIMAS AND CANNED CHICKPEAS

No, I'm afraid I'll never be a real chef. To begin with, I am confined by nature and by geography. The growing season here on the East Coast is short and, like some of my most cherished friends, rather undependable. Spring arrives by the calendar around March 21, but outside the wind howls, cold rain falls, and there is not a green shoot in sight. I crave favas and shad roe as much as the next guy, but the beans aren't growing yet and the shad aren't running. No sooner do I put peas on the menu than their short season ends. I still have a taste for tomatoes in October, but we may have had frost by the middle of September and the market would be bereft of anything but Hubbard and turban squash.

It sounds so romantic when the real chefs talk about using only locally grown produce, but I don't know how to do that where I live. I accept the need to order ingredients from Israel and South America and Holland and New Zealand. If I relied on my forager, the ex-stockbroker, we'd be eating rutabagas eight months of the year. You love your seasons, but they really try you.

That said, the one season I can count on is winter. Like a U.S. Treasury bond, it hangs on a long time and has a low yield. Going to my greenmarket any time between late October and early June is like passing through some Soviet Gulag. Nothing is available but cabbage and potatoes and softening apples. A few die-hard farmers cheerfully sell wreaths and bathroom potpourri they have fashioned out of dead flowers and fruits; I have to avert my eyes. In winter, the only market I go to daily is my local Key Food supermarket.

Actually, I'm a fan of supermarkets. They've become so good over the years that the average home cook could re-create anything I make in my restaurant with supermarket ingredients. Hellman's mayonnaise. Goya cooked chickpeas. Bird's Eye frozen Fordhook lima beans. We use them all at Prune. Goya cooked chickpeas are constant, standardized, reliable. To pick through a bag of dried chickpeas, sort them by size, get rid of the twigs and pebbles, train my staff to cook them the same way every day (perfectly tender, correctly seasoned) and to dedicate two hours' worth of burner space in my tiny and already burdened kitchen would be a bad business decision. I will continue to let Goya make the chickpeas, just as I let Lafite make the wine; I don't feel the need to crush my own grapes.

Having smartly saved myself all that work by opening cans of chickpeas, you'd think I could give my staff a decent meal on time. At Prune, staff dinner is adequate—sometimes delicious—but invariably late and often repetitive. I never have anything appropriate to feed my heavily pierced and tattooed youngest waiter, who's currently going through her vegan phase, because I am not a particular friend of vegetarians and I have lamb scraps to use up, frankly. The other waiters—a brigade of actresses who are always watching their weight and reapplying their lip liner—just want salad anyway. You can tell them a thousand times to eat now because they will be hungry later, but they won't listen. And midway through service, I find them standing over the garbage can back in the kitchen performing gruesome and debasing acts of carnage on a chunk of steak that some patron has left on his plate.

I cannot remember the last time we all sat down to eat together, much less with forks and napkins. I eat every meal of the day with my fingers, standing up or crouching down on the rubber kitchen mats out of sight of the night's first customers. I've never seen a picture of a real chef doing that.

BAND-AIDS AND LIGHTBULBS

But I have seen chefs screaming in the kitchen, and I've even read that these fits, inordinately rageful and intent on humiliation, are all part of the great familial bond of life in a restaurant. When I hear about a chef reaming out his staff, I can only think that he could use a good day off. If his menu looks exactly like a dozen others in town—all $40 foie gras and wild baby whatever—and his tables are empty, he needs to get out and see the eager people queuing up for a Nathan's frank and let that spark his imagination. And his staff and his customers need to let him do this.

Nothing makes me feel more trapped in my own kitchen than when a customer claims to have had a disappointing meal in my absence, as if the food didn't taste as good on my day off. Is the fish going to be better if Eric Ripert poaches it himself? Poaching the fish is not my job, at least not every night. My job is to make sure that my line cooks have the tools, the training and the confidence to cook the food the way I do. My job is to accept and reject plates, keep the portions consistent, taste for salt, make salads, wipe down counters, make sure the walk-in refrigerator is clean and organized, administer Band-Aids to my dishwasher, change light-bulbs, scrape dried egg yolk off the floor and, like a good sheepdog, yap at the heels of cooks who arrive late. And to take all the credit, of course.

A well-run restaurant will be as good on Tuesday as on Friday, whether the chef is there or not. I do cook a lot of the fish here, but I am also confident that, when I am busy making a cobbler, or cutting the meat, or finishing paperwork in the office, or even out having a sliver of a personal life, the fish will be as good as if I'd poached it myself. So if I miss you tonight, I'll see you on your next visit; please try to be glad for me if I am home getting some rest. I need to read books that have nothing to do with food, to walk down a city street, to see what people are wearing, what painters are painting. I want to see the austere amber light of an October day, to chew on the August humidity and to endure the harsh January winds. I want to crave soup or watermelon, leafy greens or braised meats, depending on the weather. I don't want to learn about the change of seasons from the faxes my purveyors send me.

Mostly, though, the way I know I will never be a real chef is that I am still cooking. My ingredients may be good but they need my attention. My razor clams from Maryland, my figs from Israel, my corn on the cob from Ecuador—ordered by telephone and delivered to my door the next day by José and Manuel, who seem to have discovered the simple joys of stacking the heaviest crates on top of the softest tomatoes—are sometimes beautiful and at other times only adequate. The figs and radishes look excellent today. But some not-great artichokes will need to be braised into something that is great; the fading lettuces will need reviving, a very good vinaigrette and perhaps a piece of cheese. Today's corn is not going to speak for itself, unfortunately. It's going to need more than coaxing; it's going to need something more like translating. So tonight I will have to do something very unfashionable and un-cheflike: I will cook.

The Count of Cuisine

by Betty Fussell
from *Saveur*

Culinary historian Betty Fussell (*My Kitchen Wars*) has chronicled many waves of food fashions over the years; in this profile she deftly captures a elusive chef who resists most labels.

In a pretend-Italian hotel called Bellagio, I look across a fake lake called Como to a faux tower called Eiffel and feel lucky that the steak on my plate is real. In the virtual geography of Las Vegas, food may be the only real thing left—except for money and the giant numbers game that sucks it up. And yet there's some conjuring going on here, too: the creator of this seemingly down-to-earth American steak house, called Prime, is one of New York's finest French chefs, and his Las Vegas debut is typical of his skill as a gamester who keeps diners on their toes.

"I love blackjack; that's my game," Jean-Georges Vongerichten says, when I ask him whether he gambles when he flies to Vegas—which he does for four days every two months, to check on his tables. It's a world Vongerichten understands because it's about numbers, and he's addicted to numbers. I am not surprised when Vongerichten tells me that geomancy, divination through numbers, is an essential part of his private life. He depends on geomancer

Jerome Brasset, "the crystal-ball guy", as he calls him. "Right away I connect. I go to him for everything." His Prime menu is a study in numbers: seven types of red meat, five sauces, six flavored mustards, 11 potato sides, six salads, six desserts. (As a footnote, he also offers chicken, lobster, and dover sole.)

Other well-known chefs have installed more-predictable versions of their best known brands in Vegas: Sirio Maccioni replicated both Le Cirque and Osteria del Circo restaurants from New York, Todd English transported Olives from Boston, Wolfgang Puck brought Spago from LA. But when Vongerichten's partners, the advertising team of Bob Giraldi and Phil Suarez, asked him how he would like to fill one of the dozen restaurant spaces in the megalopolitan Bellagio, he surprised them. "Steak house," he said.

"It was brilliant," says Giraldi. "Gamblers. Guys. Broads. Hotels. Money. Steak." And in the high-adrenaline atmosphere of the casino, Vongerichten is onto a sure thing. I was told that Prime is the biggest cash cow of the restaurants in his empire and that sales swelled to $14 million in 1999. (Note: Jean-Georges and his partners refuse to release any more-recent figures on this or his other enterprises.)

Vongerichten is young, he's hip, and he likes motorcycles, Prada shoes, the Knicks, jet airplanes. He's airborne one week out of four and has plotted unique game plans for each of his restaurants, five in New York and six more around the globe. And, like others of the world's finest chefs, he is in the business of fine cuisine. While Americans in particular cling to a *nostalgie de la vie pastorale* in which the master chef lives above his studio and daily turns out masterpieces for a favored few, 40-odd years of wanderings by France's celebrity chefs—Bocuse, Vergé, Ducasse—should have exploded the myth that an haute kitchen demands the constant presence of the master. "Maintain quality" is the mantra of Vongerichten's Rat Pack, the key staff members who travel with a batterie de cuisine that includes cell phones, computers, digital cameras, and archived databases. Given the speed of technology and a global economy, regionalism and authenticity are rapidly being replaced by *la cuisine sans frontières,* whose lingua franca is English—American English—and whose pilot is arguably Vongerichten, who has changed the rules of the game in a very American way.

When I first met Jean-Georges Vongerichten, in 1986, he was the executive chef of Lafayette, the restaurant in Manhattan's Drake hotel. The menu had been conceived by Louis Outhier of L'Oasis, at that time a three-star restaurant on the Côte d'Azur, and even though Lafayette's menu was haute French—foie gras, salmon, lobster, caviar—it contained enough surprises to quicken the pulse. In every dish was discovery: the sea urchin roe was puréed and molded under a ginger vinaigrette; the sea bass was wrapped in zucchini flowers; the brie sprouted black truffles. When Vongerichten emerged from the kitchen, I was surprised not by how young he was (29, looking 20) but by how French he seemed, his accent so clipped he was hard to understand. His food was too much fun, too exuberant, to be French; he'd transmitted his passion for food onto the plate directly, or so it seemed, without pomp or circumstance.

By the time of my next visit to Lafayette, after the crash of '87 had ended Wall Street's party, Vongerichten had changed the menu entirely. Instead of the traditional three courses, he now offered four "building blocks" of equal weight and importance—Bouillons, Vinaigrettes, Huiles Parfumées, and Jus de Légumes—that could be arranged in any order. Juxtaposition was more important than sequence; instead of a narrative, he offered a painting. And the food itself had changed, too. Juices—of carrot, zucchini, fennel, and any other vegetable or fruit whose liquid could be extracted—came to the fore. But Vongerichten did not invent liquid cuisine. In France, a new generation of nouvelle chefs had progressed from *cuisine du terroir* to *cuisine de l'eau,* and Jean-Georges inhaled such ideas easily and instinctively, then exhaled them, in translation, for American palates. It's less that Vongerichten "invented" a fashionable style than that he radically restructured the nature of the meal to reveal the essence of flavors displayed in different contexts. He imparted a sense of risk and adventure and freedom to experiment with flavors and textures that broke open the mold of classical French culinary thinking and felt American to the core.

Jean-Georges Vongerichten is as hybrid as his moniker. His first name joins his mother's Jeannine to his father's Georges; his surname, too, represents a grafting—like the half-German, half-French history of his native Alsace. He looks like a Frenchman, but sculpted by a German woodcarver, with symmetrical black eyebrows, precisely carved mouth, long, indented upper lip. He was born in 1957 in the village of Illkirch-Graffenstaden, on the outskirts of Strasbourg. The river Ill, which named his village, also christened Auberge de l'Ill, the three-star restaurant where he began his apprenticeship, at 16, under the discipline of chef Paul Haeberlin.

As the second of four children and the eldest son of a coal merchant, Vongerichten was expected to take over the family business, but even as a boy he was fanatically tidy and avoided coal in favor of the kitchen. Watching his mother and grandmother prepare lunch for 40 employees each noon, Jo Jo, as the family called him, became so obsessed with food that they nicknamed him "The Palate". His other obsession was clothes. "At night he always folded his little pants, his little socks, and if the band of the socks or pants was not exactly right in the morning, he would not get dressed or go to kindergarten," his mother recounts. "He would stay in the corner and sulk." Yet Vongerichten remembers that he was a wild kid, getting into trouble, hating everything in school except the two things he was good at, numbers and geography. He believes that the strict regime of Haeberlin saved his life. "Otherwise I might have ended up a gangster or who knows what," he says.

He showed talent from the outset, Paul Haeberlin remembers, and earned his professional certificate. At 19 he went into the navy, fulfilling his mandatory military service; afterward, he headed to L'Oasis, where he met Outhier's style of improvisation. "At Outhier's there was nothing on the stove, nothing in the kitchen," he recalls. "You came in, and then you cut the fish, made your sauce from scratch, sprinkled on some herbs—it was spontaneous." He'd found his métier.

After two years Vongerichten left to continue his apprenticeship, first under Paul Bocuse in Collonges-au-Mont-d'Or and then with Eckart Witzigmann in Munich, but he was forced back to prepping and quickly grew restless with the restraints. When Outhier called him and asked whether he'd go to Bangkok to the Oriental hotel, Vongerichten replied, "I'm your guy." Romance blossomed as well as career: his girlfriend, Muriel Prévost, a hairdresser he'd met in the L'Oasis hometown of La Napoule, came to visit, and when she became pregnant, they got married and eventually had two children. (They divorced after a decade, and Muriel moved with the children to live on the Côte d'Azur.) After two years cooking in Thailand, Jean-Georges left to execute Outhier's French menu in six-month and yearlong stints at restaurants in Singapore, Hong Kong, Lisbon, Geneva, London, Boston, and, finally, New York City—where he finally encountered an energy to match his own.

When he left Lafayette to open his own place, in 1991, he surprised everyone by abandoning the four-star game for a bistro, Jo Jo, in a pocket-size town house on East 64th Street that felt like a grown-up's playhouse—with tiled floors, mirrored walls, and a menu laid out like a child's primer: Soup, Salad, Pork, Salmon, Chicken, Chocolate. Of course the Salad was composed of fresh asparagus with morels and dressed with both hollandaise and a soy vinaigrette, the Pork was in a clay pot with potatoes and riesling, and the Chocolate was his fun cake, the individual kind that leaks molten chocolate when you poke it with a fork.

Vong was Vongerichten's next venture. Designer David Rockwell fabricated a scene at 200 East 54th Street that looked like a collage of old Siam—full of glittering mosaics, gold-leaf walls, louvered shutters behind orchids and palms. Vongerichten's combinations of Eastern and Western flavors and ingredients defied geography and needed to be explained as well as tasted in order to be understood. The waiters would instruct the diners, bite by bite: Dip the lobster daikon roll into the rosemary-ginger sauce, the prawn satay into the fresh-oyster sauce, the crab spring roll into the tamarind.

Something else was interesting about Vong, too: it could be replicated. "With a computer you can have a Vong anyplace because it's a very precise cuisine, more than 150 spices," Vongerichten points out. Every recipe is carefully formulated so that the spices, the sauces, will produce exactly the same flavors in London that they do in New York. In 1995 he and his partners opened a Vong in the Berkeley hotel in London, in 1997 in the Mandarin Oriental in Hong Kong, in 1999 in downtown Chicago. The world was Vongerichten's oyster, with a full range of dipping sauces.

If Vong is a game based on multiplication, the restaurant Jean Georges (without the hyphen), which he opened in 1997 in the Trump International Hotel and Tower on New York's Columbus Circle, is a subtler and more complicated game of division. Here Vongerichten ingeniously solved the problem of how to combine 24-hour room service with a four-star restaurant. He laid out two separate spaces—restaurant Jean Georges and Nougatine café—and connected them with a theatrical show kitchen, all of it designed by Adam Tihany to make a cool understatement as geometric and urbane as a martini glass. The nitty-gritty working kitchen, which would also handle room service, went into the basement. Vongerichten's tasting menu is like an edible autobiography. Here are Outhier-inspired dishes like turbot sauced by the sweet yellowish vin de paille of Château-Chalon. Here are later innovations like orange dust for the langoustine, made by pulverizing sugared and dried orange zest. Here are Vong-ish desserts—six crèmes caramel with flavors like green tea and ginseng.

On Sunday, his day off, Vongerichten stays home in his apartment on the 11th floor of Tribeca's historic Textile Building with his fiancée, Marja, and their year-old baby, Chloë, and collapses, as he says, like "a soft vegetable". He's never cooked a meal there, he admits, and grabs breakfast at a local Starbucks. Any vacations he takes he spends exploring new flavors in new topographies: in 1998, he went with Mark Bittman, coauthor of his third cookbook, *Simple to Spectacular,* to Vietnam to research an Asian cookbook based on Vong's recipes, which he hopes will be published in the winter of 2002.

Personal earnings of $3 million for 2000 placed Vongerichten third on *Forbes* magazine's list of millionaire chefs, after Wolfgang Puck and Emeril Lagasse. Despite the boom in business, he's kept standards high, maintaining, as he puts it, his own "flavor". "What you want in a restaurant is consistency with your flavor," he says. "When you put your recipes in the hands of somebody else, you've already lost 20 percent of yourself; then if that person adds his own 20 percent, you're down 40 percent. If your key workers are trained by you and have been with you for 16 years, you close that gap."

As the chef's empire grows, the question becomes, At what point does it expand so much that the cooking no longer has his own "flavor"? Already he considers restaurant Jean Georges a one-shot—"it's too demanding." He worries that the inevitably rising costs of four-star dining may mean that no one in the future can afford to produce it. His solution has been to invest in real estate—he bought a building on Perry Street in Greenwich Village and constructed 28 apartments within it—and aims to open a hotel one day. Hotels are cheaper to run than restaurants and require less personal energy, he figures. Of course, he can put in a small restaurant, he says, perhaps one that does only vegetables. That would be a predictably unpredictable next move.

What's Eating Georges Perrier?

by Benjamin Wallace

from *Philadelphia* magazine

> Wallace's gutsy profile of one of Philadelphia's most celebrated restaurateurs sheds an unblinking light on the restaurant business—especially on how even the most celebrated temples of gastronomy must fight every day to maintain their luster.

Everybody wants to fock Georges Perrier in the ass," Georges Perrier was saying. Lunch at Brasserie Perrier was winding down, and the owner's voice filled the bar. The voice was almost cartoonish; French-accented, octave-leaping, disdainful of syntax, it swung from soft, chiding singsong to asphyxiated growl to contralto screech. "Fork Georges Perrier in the ass!" the voice barked, as if Perrier were a fairground pitchman goading patrons to step right up and try their luck.

Customers drinking coffee glanced over at the 58-year-old man who just a few years before was almost never seen out of his chef's whites. Now, sitting at a table in the second-built of his three restaurants a few weeks before September 11th, he wore the finely striped monogrammed shirt, tasseled loafers and Cartier wristwatch of the businessman he had become. Perrier was meeting with his publicist and his graphic designer, talking about having new menus printed and griping that everyone—printers, florists, *everyone*—tries to gouge him on pricing. He looked around wildly. *"Ohhhhh,"* he said. "Eeets Georges Perrier! Ah theenk I weel put mah deek in hees ass!" He scooted back in his chair, squared his hips to the table, and made a downward thrusting motion with one fist. "Ah yes," he said, "let's fock Georges Perrier in the ass!"

Perrier left the restaurant and hobbled east on Walnut Street. His usual hybrid of swagger and waddle—he isn't much taller than five feet—now featured a limp. In July, at the home of a friend of his girlfriend, he'd opened the door to what he thought was a bathroom but turned out to be the basement. He skied down a staircase, broke both his heels, and spent the next three months in a wheelchair. Three months later, it still hurt to walk.

Today, he was going to drive out to Wayne for a late lunch at Le Mas Perrier, the Provençal restaurant he'd opened a year before. After lunch, he planned to spend the rest of the afternoon getting ready for a political fund-raiser he was to host at his home that evening for gubernatorial candidate Ed Rendell. But first, he had some paperwork to do. He limped along Walnut Street toward his corporate offices, past Le Bec-Fin and the intersection with Georges Perrier Place, a kiss from his adoring adopted city on the occasion of its favorite restaurateur's 50th birthday, in 1993.

Upstairs at his office, he talked business with an administrative employee—details of upcoming banquets, catered weddings, that night's fund-raiser—then went into the small room where his desk sat. One wall boasted a framed Xerox of a *New York Times* article from 1974. Written by Craig Claiborne, then the newspaper's all-powerful food critic, the article put Le Bec-Fin on the gastronomic map. Accompanying the story was a black-and-white photograph depicting a leaner, darker-haired, 30-years-younger version of the man in whose office it hung. Now, Georges's hair was graying, showing flashes of silver and a streak of white. His midsection had sprouted a potbelly.

Elsewhere in the room, other laurels from Georges's career were on display. In the course of Le Bec's 31 years, national magazine surveys had deemed the restaurant the best in the country, and in 1976, Georges was inducted into an elite fraternity of the world's greatest French chefs. Of particular importance to Georges were the five stars Le Bec was routinely awarded by the Mobil Guide, putting it in a highly select circle.

Now it had been cast out. In January of 2000, without ceremony or explanation, Mobil removed Le Bec's fifth star. The demotion devastated Perrier just as he was embarking on the creation of Le Mas, a $3 million project. Stunned, he eventually made the wrenching decision to try to reinvigorate the kitchen of Le Bec by turning it over to a young French chef from New York, Frederic Côte. In short order, Perrier suffered other setbacks, including the breaking of his heels and the filing of two sexual harassment and sex discrimination lawsuits against him. (He has denied the charges, and the cases are pending in federal court.) But losing the star hurt the most. On a shelf beside his desk, Georges had propped the Mobil 2000 plaque awarding Le Bec its shrunken constellation, the phantom fifth star taunting him with what he had lost and what he hoped to recapture. He was considering ripping out Le Bec's longstanding Louis XVI appointments and redecorating in a more contemporary style. A portrait of Napoleon hung on the wall behind him.

Life was simpler when Perrier had only one restaurant and cooked every night. Now he is a CEO with a small empire to run, a personality customers want to see and talk to, a brand whose name opens wallets. He tries to visit each of his three restaurants every day, and he regularly hosts charity dinners at his home. Beside his desk, a folded-up padded table awaited his weekly massage. His chef's jacket hung on a wooden stand.

Georges sat, head bent over a stack of checks that needed his signature. Le Bec-Fin alone has 96 employees, to whom he pays more than $2 million annually. His total payroll encompasses 250 people—he is the patriarch of an oversized family. He doesn't talk about it publicly, but there are employees he has supported through rehab two and three times, and he has silently helped others in more generous ways. For years he paid for an employee's asthmatic son to travel each summer to the Alps to clear his lungs.

Georges began scrawling his signature on the checks. "What the fuck is that?" he said suddenly. "WENDY! What is that shit—US Bancorp! What's that?" His assistant, sitting in the next room, informed him it was one of his credit-card bills. He resumed flipping through the checks, signing his name with a ballpoint. "Fucking shit," he said. "WENDY!" She appeared in the door. "Who the fuck is Jennifer Bellezzi?" A hostess at Le Bec, Wendy informed Georges, and yes, she was owed a week's vacation; she had been working for him for more than a year.

Georges finished with the checks, then drove his dark-green Mercedes sedan home to Haverford to pick up his assistant. He is a terrible driver. He had a Rolls-Royce once, but he totaled it. He views seatbelts as an imposition. Beneath his dashboard, he'd installed a radar detector. As he headed for his house, hitting speeds of more than 80 miles per hour, his stop-and-start driving unsettled the contents of his passenger's stomach, while Georges blithely honked at other cars, screaming "Asshole!," and complained about how many bad drivers were out there.

At his home, a formally decorated ranch house with a pool, he and his assistant, Liliane Nino, a middle-aged woman who worked for Air France for many years, climbed into an SUV driven by his chauffeur and headed for lunch at Le Mas. There, he would fuss over flowers, hook his arms through those of a pair of matrons to escort them on a tour of the restaurant, sign another stack of checks, discuss the restaurant's wine-by-the-glass program with a manager, and have a light lunch of warm lentil salad and mahimahi à la Provençal.

In the wake of his forced convalescence, during which he'd crawled around his bedroom on all fours and had to be carried downstairs at Le Bec by three employees, he was reasserting himself, as he had several times before in his career. In the early '80s, feeling Le Bec drifting, he'd fired the chef and resumed oversight; just two years back, he'd purged Brasserie Perrier of several employees following a period when he felt he'd ceded too much authority to a manager. Once more, he wanted to be in full command. "Now we work again," he said as he and Liliane rolled toward Le Mas. "We are working again. I am retaking control. I'm taking charge. The old Georges Perrier burn in fire now. This—" He held up a hand to command attention. "This is the new Georges Perrier."

On a Thursday evening a few weeks later, after the first dinner service at Le Bec-Fin, Georges went downstairs to eat at his Bar Lyonnais, which occupies the floor below Le Bec. His lawyer, John Pelino, was sitting at the bar with his wife. The three talked for a while; then a manager asked Georges if he was ready for his table. "Please, please don't push people," Georges said. "Don't be pushy. You very like my mother."

"You are crabby today," Karen Pelino said. "What are you crabby for?"

"I need sex," Georges said. He looked down the bar in the direction of a middle-aged blond woman who was sitting by herself. "Did you hear what I say, Lisa?"

"I heard you," the woman said wearily, as though she'd heard it before. Georges grinned and sidled up behind her chair, draping his arms around her neck. Then he took a seat at a table where Liliane and an old friend, Joel, were already sitting. They began talking about the troubled restaurant industry.

Georges's business, already suffering from the slump in the economy, had fallen even further after September 11th. More than half his banquet bookings for the month had been canceled. He understood why—he himself had scrapped a planned September trip to France to visit his parents—but that gave him little comfort. "I wanna take a gun, I wanna shoot myself," he said, "but it's not gonna do anything. I wanna jump out the window, but it's not going to do anything." He mused aloud, as he sometimes did, about opening a neighborhood restaurant and charging $10 an entrée.

The waiter brought appetizers.

"Are they okay in the kitchen upstairs, without me, for five minutes?" Georges asked.

"Yes," the waiter said.

"They okay? Eh? They okay?"

"We're okay," the waiter said.

After Georges lost his fifth star in January 2000, TV trucks showed up at the restaurant. He had what he calls "a nervous breakdown," then suffered a deep spell of depression. Despite wielding only a minute fraction of the clout of the Michelin guides in Europe, the Mobil guide is the closest American approximation to that tyrannical system, which over the years has driven French chefs to bankruptcy and even suicide. "I was devastated, because I have it for so long, and suddenly is not coming anymore," Georges said after finishing his order of steak frites. "You say, 'What I have done wrong?'" He began to act out. One night, eating at La Parisienne on the Main Line, he pronounced the coq au vin "an insult" and spilled a glass of wine on the table, prompting the owner to accuse Georges publicly of "insecurity and jealousy" and demand an apology.

As Georges talked about the lost star, his eyes teared up. He said he had been desperate to understand how this terrible event could have befallen him, and he undertook an internal investigation. He convened a staff meeting where he asked if anything had happened in service that could have brought this about. He said he wouldn't be upset; he just wanted to know. No one said anything. He consulted a medium in Chicago, an older woman named Beth whom he has been calling for several years for help in making decisions. (For instance, she gave him the go-ahead to do the Le Mas project.) Anytime he is considering making an important hire, he gives Beth the prospect's birth date, and she consults her zodiac. When it came to the lost star, Beth told Georges that someone who worked for him was responsible.

Finally, a friend at the Mobil guide called Georges and, in a breach of Mobil protocol, explained what had happened. It turned out Georges's astrologer was right. On the night when four Mobil officials ate at Le Bec, a waiter and a busboy had argued near their table. Three times, the Mobil officials asked the employees to take their argument elsewhere, as it was disrupting their meal. Georges's source at Mobil provided him with the date of the incident, enabling him to review the checks from that night and figure out who was working. Georges deduced which check belonged to the Mobil party, and his secretary was able to figure out who the busboy had been.

In the course of denying everything, the busboy said it wasn't his fault—the waiter had provoked the argument. Georges met with the waiter, who'd worked for him for 16 years, and said he couldn't believe that a customer had had to ask him three times to stop arguing. Georges couldn't understand this, he told the waiter, and he was also upset that the waiter had lied to him by not owning up to the offense. Georges said he wouldn't fire him, but one more mistake and he'd be gone. A couple of months later, a customer called to complain about pushy service from the waiter, and Georges dismissed him.

As part of a campaign to restore Le Bec to five-star status, Georges hired a new manager, Nicolas Fanucci, who had worked for Alain Ducasse and who vigorously set about updating and refining service at Le Bec. But when Mobil announced the awards again in January 2002, Le Bec still had four stars. "So, I been punish, I guess," Georges said. "It's not so much tough because I lost the star. It's tough for my ego. This is an ego thing. Because you say you not part of the family of the 18 best restaurants in the nation. Now, I'm four-star. I'm same as the Brasserie. I'm same as Neil Stein. I'm the same as Rouge. Rouge have four star. I mean, do you think I should be the same as Rouge? Four star to Rouge and four star to Georges Perrier? You comparing cauliflower to roses. Rouge can be very good, but don't compare to Le Bec-Fin."

With Mobil set to announce the stars once again in January 2002 and a new chef running the Le Bec kitchen, Georges thought he had a better shot this year. "I hope we will have it back," he said, "because it will bring some more happiness, a little bit, from my misery that I have since this. . . . We will get the five star back. I know we will. We have work all year very very very hard to get it back. So if we don't get it back, then that proves to me we have not done good enough job."

After finishing his dinner with Liliane and Joel, Georges ran into the Pelinos again, this time outside Le Bec. It was 11 o'clock, and they were now with John Pelino's daughter Clare, Perrier's longtime publicist.

"You were cooking on the line tonight?" Clare asked.

"Yes, I was cooking on the line," Georges said. "Nobody believe I cook on the line, but I was cooking on the line."

Georges had spent the first dinner service moving restlessly around the claustrophobic Le Bec kitchen—seasoning a piece of red mullet, whisking a saffron sauce, keeping himself busy—but some things he could no longer do. Since 1995, when he reached into a Robot Coupe commercial food mixer to change a blade and cut four fingers to the bone, his right hand had given him trouble. Despite four hours of microsurgery and months of rehab, the finer knifework, like cutting the tomato diamonds that accompany his *galette de crab,* was now beyond him.

And he was lately something of a stranger in his own kitchen. In the spot on the hot line that had always belonged to Georges, Frederic Côte now stood. Georges had hired him away from Daniel Boulud, the renowned New York chef, after a three-hour phone conversation in which he'd sought Boulud's advice, and after Georges's astrologer had concurred that it would be an auspicious hire. Now, when line cooks said "Chef"—which for decades meant Georges—they were looking at his tall, dark-eyed, goateed young successor. As Côte and his crew busily plated updated versions of Le Bec classics as well as such new Côte creations as an olive soup and a potato *brûlée,* Georges had stood off to one side, sipping at a glass of Vittel water.

On the sidewalk outside Le Bec-Fin, the Pelinos begged Georges to come to their house to see the new kitchen Karen was near completing. After trying out different excuses—"I been up since 5:30." "You don't have any good wine"—Georges relented, but first told how he had come to the rescue at a charity auction at Fort Mifflin the night before. "They couldn't sell shit at that auction," Georges said, "and then they say, 'Georges Perrier, cooking demonstration for 10.' " When it didn't draw the minimum bid of $2,500, Georges upped the ante, saying he'd do it at his home, and for 20 people. That went for $4,000, and then Georges agreed to do another one for the underbidder, for $3,500, raising a total of $7,500.

"They're going to call you St. Georges," Karen Pelino said.

"Georges, that's huge," Clare Pelino said. "That's huge."

"I'm too good," Georges said.

"They should be kissing your feet," Karen Pelino said.

"Yes they should," Georges said, then thought better of it. "They should send me some customer," he said. "That's what they should do."

He got into his Mercedes—his driver had gone AWOL a few days before—and noticed a white slip of paper on the windshield. He had been ticketed on Georges Perrier Place. "That's not right," Georges said. "That's my fucking street. Fucking ticket on my street. Ridiculous I get a ticket. Piss me off." He pulled into traffic, still muttering. "I hate to get ticket. A ticket on my car. Stupid city." He spat out the window. "I'm annoyed. Annoyed. So annoyed. I don't care about the ticket; it's just the principle."

• • •

The following night, Georges didn't work in the Le Bec kitchen, on Chef's orders. It was a particularly busy Friday, the first busy night since September 11th—157 covers expected—and Côte had asked him to give the cooks some breathing room. So Georges shuttled restlessly around the restaurant, adjusting the thermostat ("Is it cold?"), giving a young line cook just back from doing a *stage* in Lyons a punch in the chest ("Do you learn something?"), answering the Le Bec phone ("I should be in reservation business") and making cameo appearances in the kitchen. ("We busy tonight. . . . Fire these fucking people! . . . I need pickup!. . . Go! Go! . . . I hope you have lot of lobster. . . . Holy cow! . . . Chef, Table 8 is a friend of mine.") Then he switched to front-man mode.

Georges's presence in the Le Bec dining room had long been a part of the restaurant's appeal; people calling to make reservations would demand to know whether he would be there. Tonight, he greeted an Eagles executive, drank champagne with a society couple who'd been coming to his restaurant for years, seasoned the sauce at tableside for a couple of regulars who'd ordered the lobster press, kneaded the shoulders of a longtime customer and offered his recommendation of the lobster and the rabbit, toweled off a vacated table, abused the service bartender ("Your bar is pretty shitty tonight"), and otherwise kept himself busy.

Around 9 p.m., his girlfriend, Andrea, arrived. Tall, dark-haired and 32 years old, she wore a long, sleeveless black astrakhan coat, an expensive-looking silk blouse, and pointy heels. She and Georges embraced and went downstairs to have a glass of wine. They decided to have dinner at the Brasserie.

Domestic happiness was one of the pleasures Georges had sacrificed in his long marriage to the restaurant. He'd been married for 11 years to an American woman—they were divorced in 1982—with whom he'd had a 28-year-old daughter, Genevieve, an actress living in Brooklyn. For many years, his relationship with his daughter was strained. Throughout her childhood, he worked from 7 a.m. to 2 a.m. and saw her only on Sundays, except for those occasions when she'd toddle around the restaurant. (Once, she fell into a pot of hot stock; she was immediately plucked out and swaddled in a tablecloth filled with ice.)

Georges felt guilty about the years when he wasn't around to raise Genevieve, and recently they had become very close, having had a candid conversation about Georges's lapses as a father. "I say, 'Za, I feel bad,' " Georges recalled. " 'I love you, I always have love you. But I know I have not been a father that you expect, and I'm very proud that you came out the way you are. You are a wonderful daughter. And you have wonderful *qualité*. And when I have not give you what I can give you, like a normal father can give you, because I wanted to succeed so much, I sacrificed everything for the restaurant, and not enough for my family.' For years, I never took a day off. I worked seven days a week. . . . But you know," Georges said now, reflecting on it, "restaurateur life is not a normal life. I don't think so, by any means, you can be a restaurateur and expecting living a normal life, 'cause it's not gonna happen if you care about what you doing." Then he seemed to have doubts again. "Everyone needs a parent when they young," he said.

Georges never remarried. Since his divorce, he'd had a string of young, pretty girlfriends. He seemed to have more in common with Andrea, a culinary-school graduate who once worked in the kitchen of the Four Seasons' Fountain restaurant and now advises wealthy people on their diets. She'd first met Georges downstairs at the Le Bec bar, and they had been dating since April.

Earlier in the evening, Georges appeared anxious, but Andrea's presence seemed to relax him. As he perused the Brasserie menu, weighing what to have for dinner, Andrea teased him about his eating. "Diet is against my religion," Georges said. They ordered Belon oysters to start, and a basket of bread was put out. Since the opening of Le Mas, Georges's restaurants have made their own bread.

"C'est bon," Georges said.

"C'est très bon," Andrea said.

As they ate, Georges never stopped monitoring the room. From time to time, he got up from his seat and went into the kitchen to yell at the hustling crew—part cheering fan ("Go! Go! Go!"), part galley master ("C'mon. C'mon. Gimme fuckin' food! Pickup!")—before returning to his seat at the bar. Once, when he noticed a family that seemed to need attention, he flagged down the maître d' and asked what was going on. Another time, he left the Brasserie for 20 minutes to go down the street to Le Bec, where a customer was celebrating his 40th birthday in the mezzanine room; there, Georges performed a trick he has done many times, including on *Late Night with David Letterman,* opening a bottle of champagne with a saber in a single stroke.

As he sat with Andrea at the Brasserie bar, she ran her fingers through his hair. He seemed momentarily content. He smoked a Davidoff cigarillo. Around 11 p.m., he rubbed his eyes and said, "I feel very tired." On the TV screen above the bar, a Flyers game had given way to a Dennis Rodman interview. "Look at thees asshole," Georges said to the bartender, who happened to be the brother of actress Kim Delaney. "Patrick, how can a woman go out with a man like this?"

Andrea kissed Georges's forehead. Then he left to look in at Le Mas before going home to sleep.

Sometimes, to get away from the ever-encroaching distractions of his own business, Georges eats down the block from Le Bec at the restaurant of Susanna Foo, who has been highly acclaimed for her singular fusion of French and Asian cuisines. Like Perrier, she has published a glossy coffeetable cookbook. Their restaurants, along with Neil Stein's Striped Bass, are the mainstays of Rittenhouse Row. Unlike Georges, though, Foo has never expanded beyond her one restaurant, and she can still be found in the kitchen every day.

Lunching there a few weeks after his dinner with Andrea, Georges was having trouble finding something on the menu that he wanted to eat. "I cannot have spring roll, it's gonna be too greasy," he said. "Maybe I can have the steamed veal dumpling. I only eat the inside. And maybe I have the Mongolian lamb. And I will told them no, no, no, no nothing on the lamb. Just the lamb."

For three months after his accident, he was unable to exercise at all. He still hadn't been able to resume playing tennis, but in the past month, he had begun working out three times a week with a personal trainer, and three days ago, he'd gone on the Atkins diet. Already he had dropped from 173 to 165, he said, and he wanted to lose at least another seven pounds. "I start feeling better," Georges said, "and I'm start to feel my energy, and I start to feel I can walk again. I feel already I look great." He sucked in his stomach and patted it. "I got a pretty good control of my body," Georges said. "I have no bad habits. Yes, I love wine. That's a habit. I love good wine." He has about 1,200 bottles in his home cellar.

The waiter arrived with appetizers and put them in the wrong places. "No, you got it wrong, sir," Georges said. "Wrong. You could not work for me. Bad."

The waiter corrected his mistake.

"I forgive you," Georges said.

The physical and existential wages of being a chef began when Georges signed on as an apprentice. Born into a bourgeois family in Lyons, the son of a jeweler father and a biologist mother, he deeply upset his parents with his decision, at age 14, to become a chef. He left home and didn't return until his apprenticeship was over, three years later. The apprenticeship was hard. Wake-up was at 5:30 in the morning, and work ended at midnight. The chefs were tough. "They kick your ass, they hit you, they bang you, they dig you," Georges said, sitting on a banquette at Susanna Foo. "It was hard, really really hard. It was bad. It was too bad. I cannot talk nicely about it, because it was not nice." His left wrist still bears the scars of an incident when, late in getting a fire going, he tried to accelerate the process by pouring oil directly onto charcoal, burning himself badly.

Georges weathered additional abuse from his fellow apprentices, who came from working-class backgrounds and resented their middle-class peer. "It was traumatic," Georges recalled. "They have tough time to accept me. And they let me know and make me cause great pain, but I'm not going to discuss here. It was very difficult, and I have to fight very hard to stay. But I prove them wrong, because when the apprenticeship came [to an end], I was the number one apprentice."

Georges then worked at two of the great mid-century restaurants in France. La Pyramide, founded by the legendary Fernand Point in Vienne, was the first restaurant in France to win three stars from Michelin, and before Georges arrived it had already graduated such giants of modern French gastronomy as Paul Bocuse, Roger Vergé and the Troisgros brothers. Georges rose to *saucier* at the restaurant, then went to work at Oustau de Baumaniere, a Michelin three-star in Provence.

Now, at Susanna Foo, he pushed his plate of lamb aside and pulled a gilt Le Bec matchbox from his pocket. The sulfur heads were pinched off, and Georges started picking at his teeth with a matchstick. Foo stopped by the table and asked about the lamb.

"Very good," Georges said, "but I, I, I'm on diet, so ... Wonderful."

"I wish I have a restaurant like this," Georges said, after Foo had walked away, "because, you know, there is five gram of meat." He pointed at the remains of his stir-fry, a hillock of purple cabbage and white disks. "It's only vegetables," he said. "I wish I have a restaurant like this."

He quizzically regarded one of the gummy disks. "What is this?" he said, poking it. "I gotta ask. Is like a starch. What is that?" He pulled at it. "What is that? Is a noodle? Eh?" He took the disk between his fingers and pulled it in opposite directions. "Very starchy. It's like ... *élastique*. I gotta ask the waiter." He flagged one down and interrogated him. "Thank you," Georges said, satisfied. "Chinese pasta."

Georges likes to stay up-to-date by reading other chefs' cookbooks. He said he admired Chicago chef Charlie Trotter's, and he had read the book by Thomas Keller, chef-owner of the French Laundry, three times. Located in the Napa Valley, the French Laundry, regarded by some critics as the best restaurant in America today, was the one restaurant Georges had never been to that he wanted to visit. "And he's a very nice man," Georges said of Keller. "I never met him, but I know some customer went there, and [he] says, 'We not have the pleasure to have Georges, but you can told him: "We want to thank him for what he has done toward the industry. Because of him, this is what we are now."'" That was nice of him. Really very nice man. I have never meet him. I love him."

Patrick Feury, Susanna Foo's chef de cuisine, came over to pay his respects to the master. "How are you," Georges said. "Nice to meet you." Feury mentioned that he'd had dinner at Le Bec a few nights earlier, and it had been wonderful. He was staring at the uneaten food on Georges's plate. "I'm sorry I didn't eat much, because I'm on diet," Georges explained. "And I can only eat meat. And I was afraid to ask to only have meat on my plate."

Georges had arrived at an age of heightened health concerns, and over the summer he'd driven to Washington, along with Jean Banchet, the 61-year-old former owner of Le Francais in Chicago, to visit their friend and fellow chef Jean-Louis Palladin, who lay dying of lung cancer in the hospital. Georges also co-hosted a fund-raiser in New York to help pay Palladin's health-care costs. "It is sad," Georges said, leaning back on the banquette. "Great chef. Great talent. You know, I think I learned that you have to enjoy the life. All the bullshit that we have every day means nothing. It means absolutely nothing. Today you are here, and tomorrow you can leave. So you gotta take the life a little bit not so seriously, much more relax."

"I'm sorry I didn't eat much," Georges said, on the street outside Susanna Foo. "But . . . they were five gram of Jamison lamb. How much they charge for that? It was prix fixe? Five gram of meat." He chuckled at the thought.

• • •

The next Tuesday morning, around 7 a.m., Georges arrived at Pennock flower wholesalers in Germantown. He was with his assistant Liliane and Jean Banchet. Before Banchet left the kitchen of Le Francais a few years ago, it had five Mobil stars. Banchet and Georges are best friends; they talk every day on the phone. Now, Banchet was staying at Georges's house for two weeks. He had short black hair and a goatee. On this morning, he was wearing a black knit sweatsuit and Nike cross-trainers, while Georges wore baggy jeans, an untucked Academy of Music T-shirt and a blue fleece jacket.

Ever since Georges had decided he could save money by doing the flowers at his restaurants himself, he'd been spending a full day each week personally buying and arranging them. But Liliane was clearly in charge of the operation. At the Pennock warehouse, she gave Jean and Georges errands, and they went off to freezer rooms to count out roses and orchids and birds-of-paradise. Nicolas Fanucci, the manager at Le Bec, showed up to help transport the flowers, and everyone scattered. Nicolas took a carful to Le Bec, Liliane drove a load to Brasserie, and Jean Banchet and Georges got into Georges's silver Pathfinder and made the delivery to Le Mas. Then they headed for Center City.

They were having fun. As they passed a road crew on a tree-lined back road, Georges eyed a worker standing idle. The worker was dark-skinned and had a wispy beard. "Are you *terroriste?*" Georges asked through the glass, cackling madly. "He look like *terroriste,*" Jean agreed, laughing. When they got into town, Georges went off to Le Bec to arrange flowers, while Banchet headed to Tower Records.

Later, Banchet arrived first for lunch at Brasserie. During his fortnight here, he would talk to Georges's chefs and managers, eat at his restaurants, spend time in his kitchens, then report to Georges. But his friendly advice extended to all areas of Georges's life, including romance. "I think he miss somebody at home," Banchet said. "He have to have somebody he love at home. This is what I think is most important." Banchet had been married to the same woman for decades; she'd run the front of the house at Le Francais. "You know," he said, "if you have nobody at home, you go home, you watch TV, you read the newspaper. This is boring, you know what I mean? Nobody to talk with." Banchet said he wanted to protect Georges. "I don't know if Andrea is the right one," Banchet said. "I don't know. I say: Find somebody simple, modest, low-key, which is not after your money. When they see all this, they see the house, they see the restaurants, I'm sure they say, 'Jeez, I don't have to work anymore.' I tell him: 'Don't look always for beautiful.' He like these young chick looks like a hooker."

When Georges arrived for lunch, he was clearly stressed. Sitting at the table with his friend Jean and his assistant Liliane, he squeezed his eyes shut, winched his head around on his neck, chain-smoked Davidoffs, and nervously worked a matchstick in his teeth. Liliane solicitously put a hand on his cheek. Georges and Liliane and Jean were speaking among themselves in French when a new waiter walked past. Georges asked who he was, and upon learning that he was working part-time at Stephen Starr's Alma de Cuba, next door, said: "Wonderful. Give him a job. Take him out of there. Take him out of there. Come here."

The waiter took a few tentative steps forward, and Georges began grilling him: Was Alma busy? During the week? It was? "Hmm," Georges said. "I'm impress. I'm very impress that so many people like starches." The Nuevo Latino cuisine of Alma de Cuba makes generous use of starchy fruits and root vegetables like yuca and taro and plantain. "I don't like starches," Georges said. "What, you gotta have everything for everybody? Only starches. How many starches." His face twisted into a sneer, and his voice turned demonic. "More starches!" he shrieked, pounding the table. "Get me more starches!"

A waiter took dessert orders.

"Starches, eh?" Georges said, having trouble letting go of the topic. Then he abruptly changed tones again. "No, no," he said, "it's a great restaurant. I like the restaurant. It's good." He chuckled darkly. Georges was upset because he had heard that Starr had described Le Bec-Fin as "stale" to a former Le Bec chef applying for a job.

"Steve Starr," Georges said, "Steve Starr." He chewed on the name as if it might be a rancid piece of meat. He was getting worked up. Suddenly he held up an index finger, and his eyes seemed to lock onto something no one else could see. "I declare war on Steve Starr!" he announced. Jean and Liliane were silent. "I don't give a shit," Georges continued. "It's true. It's a war. It's a fucking war. I declare the war! It's a war!"

He placed his declaration squarely in an honorable gastronomic tradition, invoking the feuds of his mentor, Paul Bocuse, who had once dismissed chef Alain Ducasse as a souped-up BMW beside his own well-engineered Mercedes. Of Michel Guerard, pioneer of a lighter, more diet-conscious style of French cooking dubbed *cuisine minceur,* Bocuse snipped: "I'm a chef, not a doctor."

For 30 years, Georges had waged relentless war against imperfection and inconsistency, maintaining Le Bec as the longest-running act in French-American gastronomy. Now, he was fighting to reclaim Le Bec's fifth star, and in December, Esquire would name Le Mas Perrier one of the 23 best new restaurants in the country (which wouldn't stop Georges from firing its chef shortly after the magazine hit newsstands). Georges wasn't about to raise the white flag for a local theme-restaurant impresario.

"I think it's not fair for Steve Starr to say that to one of my chef," Georges said. "I really do. Because it reflect on me." Why not call Starr and clear the air? "Listen," Georges said, minutes after declaring jihad. "You want me to start a war? I start a war if I start to say something. I will have more enemies than I have friend. You know how many enemies I have? They hates my guts. Everybody hate my guts." Georges sucked in the last of his cigarillo, pressed it out in an ashtray, and went upstairs to continue making beautiful flower arrangements.

Don't Mention It

by Calvin Trillin

from *The New Yorker*

Every restaurant reviewer someday faces the dilemma of recommending a beloved restaurant only to see public exposure spoil the joint. The delectably droll Calvin Trillin plays out this mini-drama in his portrait of a Greenwich village restaurant that's idiosyncratic to the max.

I suppose Kenny Shopsin, who runs a small restaurant a couple of blocks from where I live in Greenwich Village, could qualify as eccentric in a number of ways, but one of his views seems particularly strange to journalists who have had prolonged contact with proprietors of retail businesses in New York: he hates publicity. I've tried not to take this personally. I have been a regular customer, mainly at lunch, since 1982, when Kenny and his wife, Eve, turned a corner grocery store they had been running on the same premises into a thirty-four-seat café. Before that, I was a regular customer of the grocery store. When the transformation was made, my daughters were around junior-high-school age, and even now, grown and living out of the city, they consider Shopsin's General Store—or Ken and Eve's or Kenny's, as they usually call it—an extension of their kitchen. Normally, they take only a brief glance at the menu—a menu that must include about nine hundred items, some of them as unusual as Cotton Picker Gumbo

Melt Soup or Hanoi Hoppin John with Shrimp or Bombay Turkey Cloud Sandwich—and then order dishes that are not listed, such as "tomato soup the way Sarah likes it" or "Abigail's chow fun."

When Kenny gets a phone call from a restaurant guidebook that wants to include Shopsin's, he sometimes says that the place is no longer in operation, identifying himself as someone who just happens to be there moving out the fixtures. Some years ago, a persistent English guidebook carried a generally complimentary review of Shopsin's that started with a phrase like "Although it has no décor." Eve expressed outrage, not simply at the existence of the review but also at its content. "Do you call this 'no décor'?" she demanded of me one evening when I was there having an early supper—the only kind of supper you can have at Shopsin's, which has not strayed far from grocery-store hours. (Aside from a Sunday brunch that began as a sort of family project several months ago, the restaurant has never been open on weekends.) She waved her arm to take in the entire establishment.

I looked around. Shopsin's still looks a lot like a corner store. It has an old pressed-tin ceiling. There are shelves, left over from the grocery store, that are always piled high and not terribly neatly with ingredients and supplies. There are always newspapers and magazines around for the customer who might need reading material while eating alone. A table setup might include a constantly varying assortment of toys and puzzles—a custom that started when the Shopsins' children were young and continues for the more or less grownup customers. The counter, which no longer has stools, is taken up mainly by buckets of complimentary penny candy. One wall has, in addition to a three-dimensional advertisement for Oscar Mayer beef franks, some paintings of the place and its denizens. The portrait of Kenny shows him as a bushy-haired man with a baby face that makes him look younger than he is, which is nearly sixty, and a girth that may reflect years of tasting his more remarkable creations; he's wearing a Shopsin's

General Store T-shirt, folded over in the way the cognoscenti know how to fold it in order to form the words "Eat Me." A large sign behind the tiny kitchen that Kenny shares with his longtime assistant, José, says "All Our Cooks Wear Condoms." When I had taken in all of that, or whatever part of it was there at the time, I said, "I absolutely agree, Eve. A reviewer might comment on whether or not the décor is to his taste. Conceivably, he could prefer another type of décor. But you can't say that this place has no décor."

Normally, mentions of Shopsin's in print are complimentary, in a sort of left-handed way—as in *Time Out New York*'s most recent guide to the city's restaurants, which raved about the soups and described Kenny ("the foul-mouthed middle-aged chef and owner") as "a culinary genius, if for no other reason than he figured out how to fit all his ingredients into such a tiny restaurant." To Kenny's way of thinking, a complimentary mention is worse than a knock. It brings review-trotters—the sort of people who go to a restaurant because somebody told them to. Kenny finds that review-trotters are often "petulant and demanding." Failing to understand that they are not in a completely conventional restaurant, they may be taken aback at having the person next to them contribute a sentence or two to their conversation or at hearing Kenny make a general remark in language not customarily heard in company unless the company is in a locker room or at being faced with deciding among nine hundred items and then, if they have selected certain dishes, having to indicate the degree of spiciness on a scale of one to ten. (Before Shopsin's began restricting its serving staff to Eve, it employed a waitress who narrowed at least that choice by refusing to take an order higher than a six, on humanitarian grounds.)

Ken and Eve have found that review-trotters often don't know their own minds. If a customer at Shopsin's seems completely incapable of deciding what to order, Eve will, in the interest of saving time, reveal her own favorites, which these days happen to be three

dishes with chicken in them—Chicken Tortilla Avocado Soup,
Pecan Chicken Wild Rice Cream Enchilada, and Taco Fried
Chicken. But she doesn't do it with a song in her heart. Kenny is
less flexible. "If somebody comes in here and is flabbergasted by
the number of things on the menu and tells me, 'How can I
choose?' " he has said, "I realize that they're essentially in the
wrong restaurant."

The place can handle just so many people, and Kenny was never
interested in an expansion that would transform him into a super-
visor. "The economic rhythm of this place is that I run fifteen
meals a week," he used to say before Shopsin's offered Sunday
brunch. "If I do any five of them big, I break even; if I do ten of
them big, I'll make money. I'll make a lot of money. But if I do fifteen I have to close, because it's too much work." Kenny requires
slow periods for recouping energy and ingredients. The techniques
that enable him to offer as many dishes as he does are based on the
number of people he has to serve rather than on what they order.
That's why he won't do takeout, and that's one of the reasons parties of five are told firmly that the restaurant does not serve groups
larger than four. Pretending to be a party of three that happened
to have come in with a party of two is a very bad idea.

Not all the rules at Shopsin's are based on the number of meals
that the kitchen has to put out. For years, a rule against copying
your neighbor's order was observed fairly strictly. Customers who
had just arrived might ask someone at the next table the name of
the scrumptious-looking dish he was eating. Having learned that
it was Burmese Hummus—one of my favorites, as it happens, even
though it is not hummus and would not cause pangs of nostalgia
in the most homesick Burmese—they might order Burmese
Hummus, only to have Eve shake her head wearily. No copying.
That rule eventually got downgraded into what Ken called "a
strong tradition," and has now pretty much gone by the wayside.
"I realized that the problem was not that they were trying to imi-
tate the other person but that they weren't capable of ordering

anything themselves, and it was just unnecessary cruelty to point that out to them," Kenny told me not long ago. He said he was getting more and more people of that sort.

"Why is that?" I asked.

"The country's going that way," he said glumly.

Because Shopsin's has a number of rules and because Kenny is, by his own admission, "not a patient person," it's common to run into people who are afraid to enter the place. I've escorted a number of them to their first Shopsin's meal, in the way a long-time businessman in a Midwestern town might escort a newcomer to Kiwanis at noon on Wednesday. Since the "Seinfeld" Soup Nazi episode became part of the culture, people sometimes compare Kenny to the brilliant but rule-obsessed soup purveyor who terrified Jerry Seinfeld and his friends. Kenny would say that one difference between him and the Soup Nazi is that the Soup Nazi is shown ladling out his soup from a steam table; at Shopsin's, most soups are made from scratch when they're ordered.

Some people think of Shopsin's as forbiddingly clubby, chilly to outsiders. Actually, Shopsin's does not have a crowd, in the sense of a group of people who go in assuming they'll run into someone they know—the way the old Lion's Head, a few blocks uptown, had a crowd, built around *Village Voice* writers. At a play reading once, I was surprised to run into a Shopsin's regular I hadn't realized was an actor; all I'd known about him was that he doted on a dish called Turkey Spinach Cashew Brown Rice Burrito. Still, there are a lot of regulars, and they seem more at home than they might at a conventional restaurant. "You're really not allowed to be anonymous here," Kenny has said. "You have to be willing to be who you really are. And that scares a lot of people." One evening, when the place was nearly full, I saw a party of four come in the door; a couple of them may have been wearing neckties, which wouldn't have been a plus in a restaurant whose waitress used to wear a T-shirt that said "Die Yuppie Scum." Kenny took a quick glance from the kitchen and said, "No, we're closed." After a brief

try at appealing the decision, the party left, and the waitress pulled
the security gate partway down to discourage other latecomers.

"It's only eight o'clock," I said to Kenny.

"They were nothing but strangers," he said.

"I think those are usually called customers," I said. "They come
here, you give them food, they give you money. It's known as the
restaurant business."

Kenny shrugged. "Fuck 'em," he said.

Anytime there seemed to be a threat of my becoming entangled
in a piece of unauthorized publicity about Shopsin's, I have
resorted to rank cowardice, spooked by the fear of a lifetime banishment that might not even carry the possibility of parole. Once,
I asked Kenny if an acquaintance of mine who'd been eighty-sixed
some years before but greatly missed the place and its proprietors
could come in for lunch with me sometime. "Sure, she can come
in for lunch," Kenny said. "And I'll tell her she's a scumbag bitch."
I told him I might hold off on that lunch for a while.

In the mid-nineties, I got a phone call from a reporter named
D. T. Max, who was doing a piece for the New York *Observer* on
Shopsin's, without the cooperation of the proprietor. After
assuring him of my belief that reporters have an obligation to talk
to other reporters on the record and informing him that I had
been quoted by name insulting most of the people I've ever
worked for, I told him that in this instance I intended to be
exceedingly circumspect and to keep Kenny informed of everything I said. Max was most understanding.

When I did report back to Kenny, I was asked what information I had surrendered. "Well, the subject of Egyptian Burritos
came up," I said. Egyptian Burrito was then listed on the breakfast
menu, although I'd never eaten one. On the rare occasions that I
had been to Shopsin's for what people in some other trades might
call a breakfast meeting, I'd always allocated my calories to Shred
Potatoes, a fabulous dish that Kenny claims to have stolen from a

short-order cook in the Carolinas through intense observation that required only ten minutes.

"And?" Kenny asked.

"Well, he seemed interested in what an Egyptian Burrito was," I said.

"So what did you say?"

"I said, 'An Egyptian Burrito is a burrito, and inside is sort of what Kenny thinks Egyptians might eat.'"

Kenny considered that for a moment. "Well, that's accurate," he finally said. He sounded relieved. By chance, though, the *Observer* piece ended with an anecdote, accurately gathered from someone else, that involved me: One morning, a Sanitation Department officer had come in to ticket Kenny for some minor infraction like wrapping his garbage incorrectly or putting it in the wrong place. Kenny, who was at the stove, lost his temper and threw a handful of flour he happened to be holding at the sanitation officer, who thereupon summoned a police officer to write a citation. When I was told about the incident at lunch that day, I asked Kenny, "What was the citation for—assault with intent to bake?" A couple of months after Max's piece appeared, Kenny said he had finally concluded that I, frustrated at not having been able to work the assault-with-intent-to-bake line in anywhere, might have instigated an article in the *Observer* just to get it into print. I had a defense for that: within days of my exchange with Kenny about flour-throwing, I had, without mentioning any names, eased the anecdote into a newspaper column that was on a completely different subject.

Yes, I've managed to write about Shopsin's from time to time, always observing the prohibition against mentioning its name or location. That is one reason I've never been offended by Kenny's refusal to recognize a reporter's God-given right to turn absolutely everything into copy. In a piece about Greenwich Village a few years ago, for instance, I asked a restaurant proprietor "who tends not to be cordial to people wearing suits" what the difference was between the Village and uptown, and he said, "I don't know. I've never been uptown." Kenny has never objected to any of the mentions. He has always thought of us as being in similar fields, and, as someone who has to be prepared every day to turn out any one of nine hundred dishes a customer might ask for, he has a deep understanding of waste not, want not.

In the mid-seventies, in fact, when my daughters were little girls, I wrote an entire article for this magazine about a corner store in the West Village which was run with rare imagination and a warm feeling for community—a store with a rocking chair and bean-counting contests and free circulating paperback books. At that time, the store struck me as being about as close as Greenwich Village got to the Village conjured up by reading, say, "My Sister Eileen"—even to the point of having a proprietor, described in the piece as a young man from a prosperous background who'd always had what he called "a little trouble with authority," capable of making occasional allusions to Camus or Sartre as he sliced the roast beef. At the time, Kenny owned some dazzling old gumball machines, and I simply referred to Shopsin's by the name my girls always used—the Bubble Gum Store.

So why am I calling it Shopsin's now? Because not long ago Kenny told me that it was no longer necessary to abide by the rule against mentioning the place in print. The building that Shopsin's is in, an undistinguished five-story brick structure that consists of the restaurant and eight apartments, changed hands several months ago. Kenny, who was faced with having to renegotiate his lease, at first treated the situation philosophically. When I asked him what the new owner, Robert A. Cohen, of R. A. Cohen & Associates, was like, he shrugged and said, "He's a real-estate guy," in the tone that New Yorkers customarily use to mean that asking for further details would be naïve. Then Kenny and Cohen had a meeting at Cohen's office. ("I went uptown!" Kenny told me, as a way of emphasizing a willingness to put himself out.) According to Kenny, Cohen offered the Shopsins a one-year lease at more or less market rent. He also offered a three-year lease, contingent on one of their daughters vacating a rent-stabilized apartment she occupies in the building. A one-year lease is obviously not practical for a restaurant, and the attempt to include Kenny's daughter in the transaction did not please him. All in all, I would say that Robert A. Cohen was fortunate that the offers were made when Kenny wasn't holding a handful of flour.

Kenny decided that he would leave at the end of May rather than sign a new lease. He hopes to reopen nearby. He is aware, though, that the tone of his business has a lot to do with the physical space it has occupied for more than thirty years, including what I suppose you'd have to call the décor—the old-fashioned booths that Kenny ran across and cut down to fit his space, the music from tapes he puts together himself from songs of the twenties and thirties (supplanted, occasionally, by a modern Finnish group that concentrates on the tango). Kenny says that what really distinguishes his place from other restaurants is the level of human involvement in every detail. As he has put it, "I've been peeing on every hydrant around here for thirty years." In other words, the Shopsin's my daughters have known—Kenny's, Ken and Eve's, the Bubble Gum Store—can no longer be affected by publicity because it will no longer exist.

The God of New York real estate is an ironic god, and he works in ironic ways. What propelled Ken and Eve into the restaurant business in the first place, twenty years ago, was a bump in their rent. They figured that their choices were to start opening on weekends or transform the store into a restaurant. By that time, Kenny was doing a good business in takeout sandwiches like chicken salad and egg salad. "Zito would bring me over bread and I would just have a line out the door every lunchtime," he recalled not long ago. "Essentially, if anyone asked me what I did for a living, I said I sold mayonnaise—mayonnaise with chicken, mayonnaise with shrimp, mayonnaise with eggs, mayonnaise with potatoes. The key was that essentially you sold mayonnaise for eight dollars a pound and everything else you threw in for free." He had also been making what he calls "restaurant-style food to take out of a non-restaurant"—turkey dinner every Wednesday, for instance, and chicken pot pie. When Ken and Eve closed the store for the summer—because they had young children, Shopsin's was the rare Village business that often observed the *fermeture annuelle*—Ken, a reasonably adept handyman who had worked as a building superintendent before he went into the grocery business, turned Shopsin's General Store into a restaurant. When it opened, the menu listed a conventional number of more or less conventional dishes, although there was some hint of the future in items like Yiddishe Melt (grilled American cheese on rye over grilled Jewish salami) and Linda's Frito Pie, a Texas specialty whose recipe has to begin, "Take a bag of Fritos . . ."

Kenny had Frito Pie on the menu because one of his customers, who's from Texas, was comforted by the knowledge that less than a block from her house in Greenwich Village she could order a dish that most Texans identify with the snack bar at Friday night high-school football games. The menu grew because of what customers wanted or what Kenny was struck by in reading cookbooks or what new ingredient he happened across or what he figured out how to do as he taught himself to cook. "I don't make too many decisions," Kenny once told me. "I react." Lately, for instance, a lot of dishes have been inspired by the tchotchkes he's bought on eBay. Because of some tortilla bowls he snapped up for a bargain price, he is now offering Mexican moo shu pork, which can also be ordered with chicken or turkey and has something in common with a former dish called Thai Turkey Torpedo. Some large plastic bowls split in two by a curving divider led to what he calls Yin/Yang Soups—a couple of dozen soups and a couple of dozen kinds of rice that can be ordered in any combination, like Sweet Potato Cream Curry Soup with Piña Colada Rice or Toasted Pumpkin Seed Soup with Ricotta Pignoli Rice.

There is almost no danger of a customer's ordering Plantain Pulled Turkey Soup with Strawberry BBQ Rice only to find out that there isn't any more Plantain Pulled Turkey Soup and he might have to settle for, say, Mashed Potato Radish Soup. In the twenty years my family has been eating at Shopsin's, putting our meals on the tab we established when Ken and Eve were selling milk and paper towels and cat food, nobody at our table has ever ordered anything the restaurant was out of. When I asked Eve recently if that held true with other customers, she said that she thinks she remembers running out of chicken cutlets sometime within the past year.

"I think I have everything all the time," Kenny says. "That's part of the system." What does happen occasionally is that Kenny gets an idea for a dish and writes on the specials board—yes, there is a specials board—something like Indomalekian Sunrise Stew. (Kenny and his oldest son, Charlie, invented the country of Indo-malekia along with its culinary traditions.) A couple of weeks later, someone finally orders Indomalekian Sunrise Stew and Kenny can't remember what he had in mind when he thought it up. Fortunately, the customer doesn't know, either, so Kenny just invents it again on the spot.

As the menu at Shopsin's grew, I half expected to come in for lunch one day and find Kenny being peered at intently by a team of researchers from the institution that foodies are referring to when they mention the C.I.A.—the Culinary Institute of America—or maybe even a team from the other C.I.A. The researchers would have their work cut out for them. It's true that if you listen to Kenny talk about cooking for a while, you can see the outline of some general strategies. For instance, he freezes pre-portioned packages of some ingredients that take a long time to cook and then pops them into the microwave—"nuking 'em" for a couple of minutes—while he's doing the dish. He fiddles with his equipment, so that he's drilled out the holes on one burner of his stove and rigged up a sort of grid on another. He runs a new idea or a new ingredient through a large part of his menu. ("I love permutations.") On the other hand, Kenny has said, "There's no unifying philosophy. I do a lot of things special, and not only do I do a lot of things special but I commingle them."

To get an idea of Kenny's methods, I once asked him how he made one of Eve's favorites, Chicken Tortilla Avocado Soup, which he describes as a simple soup. "When someone orders that, I put a pan up with oil in it," he said. "Not olive oil; I use, like, a Wesson oil. And I leave it. I've drilled out the holes in the burner so . . . it's really fucking hot. . . . On the back burner, behind where that pan is, I have that grid. I just take a piece of chicken breast and throw it on. The grid is red hot, flames shooting up, and the chicken sears with black marks immediately and starts to cook. If there were grits or barley or something, I would nuke 'em. . . . At that point in the cook, that's what would happen if this were Chicken Tor-tilla Avocado with barley in it. For this dish—this is a fast dish—I shred cabbage with my knife. Green cabbage. . . . I cut off a chunk and I chop it really finely into long, thin shreds. I do the same with a piece of onion. Same with fresh cilantro. At this point, José has turned the chicken while my back is still to the pan. I throw the shit into the oil, and if you rhythm it properly, by the time you have the onions and everything cut, the oil is just below smoke. Smoke for that oil is about three-eighty-five. After three-eighty-five, you might as well throw it out. It won't fry anymore; it's dead. But I turn around just before smoke and I throw this shit in. And what happens is the cabbage hits it and almost deep-fries—it browns—and now we get a really nice cabbage, Russian-type flavor. The onions soften immediately, and I now turn back and I take one of any number of ingredients, depending on what they've ordered, and in this particular instance, for someone like you, I would add crushed-up marinated jalapeño peppers to about a five, which is about a half a tablespoon. They're in a little cup in front of me. . . . In front of me, in, like, a desk in-out basket, I have two levels of vegetables that don't need to be refrigerated and I have plastic cups full of garlic or whatever. So now the soup is cooking. So then I reach under the refrigerator. On the refrigerator floor there's another thirty or forty ingredients, and I'll take for this particular soup hominy—canned yellow hominy—and throw in a handful of that. Then I go to the steam table and take from the vegetarian black-bean soup—it has a slotted spoon in it—a half spoon of vegetarian cooked black beans. And then I switch to the right, because the spice rack is there, and I put in a little cumin. Then I take the whole thing and I pour chicken stock in it from the steam table. And at this point José has already taken the chicken off the flame. The chicken now is marked on the outside and the outside is white, but it's not cooked. It's pink in the center. He cuts it into strips, we throw it into the soup, a cover goes on the soup, it gets moved over to the left side of the stove on a lower light and in about three minutes José takes a bowl, puts some tortilla chips that I've fried the day before in the bowl with some sliced avocado and then pours the soup over it. And that's Chicken Tortilla Avocado Soup." There are about two hundred other soups.

Presumably, Kenny can arrange his ingredients around a customized stove in some other storefront. Presumably, it will be convenient to our house. The last time I discussed the move with him, he mentioned a couple of possibilities. One is convenient, but it's somewhat larger than the present restaurant and it seems less vulnerable to being shaped by Kenny's personality. Another has the appropriate funkiness but also has what everyone, Kenny included, believes is "the world's worst location." That tempts Kenny, of course. He is someone whose contrariness is so ingrained that he can begin a description of one cooking experiment like this: "At the time I was interested in baba ghanouj, I was reading a James Beard article about eggplants and he said never put eggplants in a microwave. So I went and put an eggplant in a microwave. . . ."

When Kenny mentioned that the second place was on such an awful block that my daughters and I would probably come only once, I assured him of their loyalty, assuming he continued to turn out "tomato soup the way Sarah likes it" and "Abigail's chow fun." They confirmed this when I phoned them to bring them up to date on the latest Shopsin's developments. They also expressed some concern about the possibility that writing about Shopsin's even now carried the risk of causing overcrowding or inadvertently saying something that could lead to the banishment of the author—and, presumably, his progeny.

"Don't worry," I told one of them. "Kenny says it's O.K."

"Just be careful," she said.

Dining Around

Food Fight

by Amanda Hesser
from *The New York Times Magazine*

This past year, Sunday magazine readers of *The Times* were hooked on Hesser's revealing series of columns spinning out the life and loves of a food editor—which naturally center around where she ate, with whom, what she cooked, and who she was cooking for.

I t had been a while since I'd been out with foodies, and I let my guard down.

We were convening at Craft, a new restaurant near Gramercy Park. It was the place all foodies were talking about. "Can you believe how expensive it is?" one shrieked. "I had the worst service ever!" Another griped: "Those leather walls are horrid. And the menu—preposterous!" That's how foodies talk. No one is ever optimistic about a restaurant for fear of looking silly if the place tanks. Better to predict doom and then be smugly triumphant.

There's a reason for this. Foodies are competitive. It's not enough to just eat well and enjoy it. You must be able to whip off commentary about the *amuse-bouche* at Daniel, know the bodega in Red Hook that makes the best churros and be able to recite the last five restaurants Wylie Dufresne has worked at.

Foodies are also overfed, which makes them cranky and jaded. Eat out too often, and you find yourself saying things like, "That foie gras was so flabby and bland!" and pooh-poohing meals that are fewer than three courses.

Normally I don't like to go to restaurants until they've been open for a few months. It takes a restaurant time to figure out what it's doing, how to define itself and how to deal with that fickle beast otherwise known as the New York diner. But my friend, and new foodie, A., insisted we go to Craft. He invited Ms. Foodie. Mr. Latte came as well.

When I arrived late, two Scotches and a pear Champagne cocktail were being delivered to the table. I ordered a glass of Manzanilla. There was a quick group evaluation of the room. We liked the Mission-style wood tables. The overhead lighting was unflattering to the face, we agreed, casting that Bermuda triangle over the nose.

When the menus arrived, a foodie ritual took place. Everyone stopped talking and attacked the page with their eyes. This is done to stock up ammunition for future conversations ("You won't believe it: there's NO tuna tartare!"). But also to get dibs on what you want to eat. Foodies do *not* allow order overlap. If you want the lobster, you'd better claim it quickly. A. was scratching his head furiously as his eyes flickered down the page.

With Craft's menu, you get to assemble your meal. You could have, for instance, raw oysters, roasted cod or braised red snapper. And with it, you could order arugula salad, roasted Jerusalem artichokes or lamb chops. It seems perfectly suited to New Yorkers, who love nothing more than calling the shots.

"This menu is stupid," chirped Ms. Foodie. A. squinted hard. "It's like an I.Q. test, for God's sake," he mumbled. "I like it," I said, indignantly. They looked up, expressionless. "What is up with the food at Town?" Ms. Foodie said. "Haven't had it," I replied. "But we've been to Beppe. You?" I could feel Mr. Latte tensing up. He suffers it politely, but foodie chat makes his skin crawl.

I plotted out a meal of oxtail terrine followed by roasted langoustines, braised ramps and roasted beets. But then the waiter suggested that rather than having just the oxtail terrine, we could have an assortment of charcuterie for the table. That meant less oxtail, and what promised to be every part of the pig turned into some form of rich, salted meat.

I do not like feeling as if I'm at a buffet when I go out to a restaurant. I like to construct my meal thoughtfully and then eat it. I don't want to pass plates and I don't want someone plopping a slab of her skate in my subtly seasoned lamb *jus*. It's disrespectful to the chef, who tries to create dishes that entertain your palate from the first bite to the last. And it's greedy. If you must taste other things on the menu, come back another time. But I lost on the charcuterie. Foodies always want the selection. A. ordered as if it were his last meal. Ms. Foodie took care of the wine, a 1999 Domaine Tempier rosé.

A conversation about film abruptly ended when the first course arrived. It was set out family style. Plump, wet Belon oysters. Prosciutto, duck ham and dried sausage stretched across a platter. Two slices of foie-gras terrine were set next to thick, airy toasts nestled in a linen napkin. A rectangle of oxtail terrine sprinkled with salt loomed over a coin-size sliver of aspic. Fat spears of white asparagus were stacked like logs. A tangled mound of marinated octopus was placed next to a strange and fragrant mushroom called the hen-of-the-woods. I could feel doom coming on. I searched for my sherry and took a sip before beginning.

"The asparagus needs salt, don't you think?" carped Ms. Foodie. "Can you *believe* these carrots?" She held up a slice cut into a flower shape for all to see. Soon, I had a circus going on at my place setting. I took a little oxtail terrine and a piece of sausage. A. wanted me to try his octopus, and then he wailed with pleasure about the mushrooms, pushing one my way. I resisted the foie gras, but Ms. Foodie dropped an asparagus spear on my plate. Mr. Latte gave me an oyster. It was cool and tender with a marvelous, sweet, iodine flavor. I don't remember a thing about the terrine.

Mr. Latte caught on to what was happening and stayed his

course. He ate all of his oysters, quietly moaning with delight. When the entrees arrived, he pulled his plates close, barricading himself with his food. He lifted the best, crispest pieces of chicken onto his plate, spooned on the cranberry beans and roasted cipollini onions and got to work. He sampled my firm, sweet, roasted beets and nothing else.

Meanwhile, I was caught up in a terrible gastronomic eddy. A. turned to me. "Taste this!" he demanded, raving at his roasted lobster. "What's the herb in there?" he then asked. Without fail, if you dine with foodies, this will happen. Someone will ask what it is they're tasting in a dish. Sometimes it is genuine curiosity. Sometimes it is to test you. Sometimes it is to give him an opportunity to display his superior palate. You rarely know which. A. is still far too new and innocent for such trickery. "Tarragon," said Ms. Foodie, doing me a favor. I wanted to get back to my langoustines. And I wanted to talk about something else besides food. Even a conversation about "The Sopranos" ended up being about how Tony eats. Out of desperation, I brought up golf.

Things sped up. A. passed his potatoes and skewered one of my langoustines. My ramps traveled out of reach. Ms. Foodie insisted I try her lamb. The rosé was suffering under the cloud of flavors. By the time dessert came, I had tasted 18 dishes, and we had discussed every new restaurant—Beppe, Town and Virot—in detail. I bet that Tom Colicchio, Craft's chef, never anticipated such a calamity.

I ordered a grappa in the vague hope that it would settle my stomach, and my annoyance. I could no longer speak. "So what do we think of this place?" A. asked. Everyone shrugged. Mr. Latte, well fed and content, got back to chatting about golf and sailed out of the room ahead of me.

As I staggered out, I was flagged down by Jeffrey Steingarten. "What's good?" he asked. I fantasized for a moment about the idea of getting to start over, then clicked into foodie mode and delivered a short list.

A few days later I sat next to a veteran foodie at a dinner. He explained that he doesn't like eating with foodies. "It's so uninteresting," he said, dragging a piece of bread through the sauce on his plate. "It's just this obsession with ingredients, this obsession with restaurants. There's a lot of one-up-manship." He said he was going to a place called Craft this Thursday. I told him I had been there.

"What is it?" he asked.

"It's Tom Colicchio's new restaurant," I said.

"Ugh!" he groaned. "Not him! I liked the tavern at Gramercy but I never had good food in the dining room." He paused. "So," he continued, rolling his eyes, "what's *this* one? What's the *concept?*"

Really Expensive "Drinks and a Bite" Followed by Thai Food at Blimpies

by Jim Leff
from chowhound.com

Among the omnivorous crew who visit or contribute to chowhound.com, the site's founder and guiding spirit, Jim Leff, is truly the Alpha Dog. As you'd expect from the author of *The Eclectic Gourmet's Guide to Greater New York City*, Jim will eat just about anything—and write about it at entertaining length.

A group of friends took Pat Hammond to have her first Western Hemisphere perceves at Ilo (40 W 40th Street, Manhattan; 212-642-2255). We tried their "tidal pool," an appetizer that's essentially miso [woops, hold on, I've been informed that I may be wrong about that; chowhound HLing says it's made with mirin, not miso] soup with perceves, sea urchin, oyster, and seaweed. It tasted . . . well . . . like good miso soup with a scant handful of pretty good shellfish mixed in. We split orders of tidal pools (the waiters kindly divided them for us) and ordered one drink each, and this ran us over $25 per person.

Perhaps if we'd sat at a table and taken our time, we'd have been placed in the proper frame of mind to read into this dish a lot more deliciousness than really existed (the luxe restaurant experience is, after all, intrinsically designed to hypnotize diners into finding their bites exquisite). But we ate in the noisy bar, chatting convivially, and it felt like we were eating some pretty good soup in a bar, nothing more. Aside from terrific service (and very skillful mixed drinks plus nicely selected wine list), there was nothing special about the experience.

What would it be like to visit all the NY Times' three and four star restaurants, sit at their bars with a big gang of friends, and eat the way we *normally* eat (offhandedly, if not unmindfully)? Which of these places could stand up to such treatment, without the psy-ops of cushy seats, starchy tablecloths, hushed sacramental presentations, slow, stately pacing, etc? Union Square Cafe and Gramercy Tavern come immediately to mind as places which would pass this test. It's hard to think of many others. This doesn't exactly *prove* anything, of course. Some styles of cooking absolutely do require and deserve undivided, contemplative attention (and there's nothing wrong per se, with cushy seats and starchy tablecloths). But the tidal pool wasn't refined. It was just some pretty good soup.

So we left in search of antidote, an unpretentious and warm place to actually eat dinner. After a detour through Koreatown to buy weirdly delicious canned grape drink and I.V. bags of green apple juice, we headed toward a would-be meal at Waterfront Ale House (540 2nd Ave @30 St, Manhattan; 212-696-4104). But we were stopped dead in our tracks by a fast food joint whose sign announced the grand opening of Blimpie Subs & Salads, AKA Joey Thai: Thai Fast Food Restaurant (17 E31 Street, Manhattan; 212-213-3773).

It was the sort of non sequitur which makes the mind race to find order in chaos. Were *all* Blimpies also Thai restaurants on the side? Why hadn't I heard anything about that? I knew that Kennedy Fried Chicken places are usually Afghan-owned, and very rarely one might find under-the-counter aushak and such, but I hadn't remembered Blimpies being a particularly Thaicentric operation. Of course, I don't eat at Blimpies much.

We went in, as we of course *had* to, and found the standard plastic, bleakly corporate, disgusting interior. But the mom-'n'-pop staff were sweet and seemed just as anachronistic in the setting as we were. Thai folks trapped in corporate amber. And they were glad indeed that, finally, someone wanted Thai food rather than tuna subs or "Bluffins" (egg, ham, and cheese on an english muffin).

The menu was dullsville ... ten of the most standard gringo-friendly Thai dishes (pad thai, tom kha gai, sate, fried rice, masaman curry, etc). But we didn't flinch for a second; determined to take the plunge, come what may, we used the smart aleck approach, challenging them to prepare off-menu stuff (crispy pork with Chinese broccoli, larb, and banana sticky rice). I begged for spicy. As we negotiated and enthused, the chef/owner's eyes flashed with the manic edge of a resourceful fellow desperately determined to overcome unknowable adversities. You could see him mentally planning his attack as he agreed to bring us everything we'd asked for.

The place was deserted, and the steam tables were empty. There is every reason to suspect that in the three weeks they've been in business, we were the first human beings ever to order Thai food. They not only didn't want to let us down, but were eager to stretch beyond Giant Value Choice Cheese Trio Subs.

Results were uneven but promising. The guy was obviously working under rigorous impediments, making a bunch of things from scratch which he didn't really have provisions to do right. Nonetheless, everything had the unmistakable flavor of real Thai food in spite of five gazillion shortcuts, compromises, and substitutions. It was the sort of meal you'd expect to eat if you'd met a Thai chef cooking spaghetti and steaks in a Peruvian railroad dining car, and got him stoked to extemporize some back-home dishes. It was wrong right Thai food rather than the standard right wrong Thai food.

The larb was amazingly good in some ways. It sported a nice balance of lime and red onion, the pork chunklets appropriately marinated and properly textured. It was even, by some miracle, adequately hot. Who'd have suspected serious larb on 31st Street (not to mention in a—may I say it once again?—Blimpie)! One problem, though: it was salty enough to make one retain Lake Huron. Tongue-scraping salty. Gargle-with-this-sweetie-you'll-feel-much-better salty.

As he did throughout the meal, the chef/owner apologized profusely for "all the mistakes". He had the nervous smile and flop sweat of Basil Fawlty genteelly handling customers while all hell breaks loose, unseen, in the next room. I felt for the guy. He obviously knows his stuff, but was up against untold challenges (man, he'd be horrified if he knew I was a writer). So he kept trying to compensate by bringing free food; dishes he knew he'd only be forced to screw up a little bit. Truly delicious sour shrimp soup with unfortunate shrimp (more on them in a sec), merely-slightly-rubbery chicken sate, and, for dessert, some very nice grapes which I suspect were from his private stash (we were too full for banana sticky rice, though we were assured those goods could have been delivered).

To regress back to the entrees: pad Thai was very good; the ingredients were on hand, it's on the normal menu, and I'd gladly return for another helping anytime. I did not, however, eat the shrimp, which seem to have gone through several cycles of de- and re-frosting. And shrimp were everywhere, festooning practically every dish. I suspect they came in on the Blimpie truck.

Crispy pork and Chinese broccoli was good but wrong. I couldn't put my finger on the reason, since all remnants of the heroic resourcefulness which had gone into its preparation were deftly erased. It wasn't a real crispy pork and Chinese broccoli, but it was Thai and was satisfying in its way. This is a man who could produce Thai-tasting food armed only with Triskets, Lipton onion soup mix, and Bac-o's.

Iced coffee came without the usual contraption, and without condensed milk, yet it still somehow managed to taste at least somewhat Thai. It was a morph of Thai ice coffee and American ice coffee—sort of an in-the-middle, Bikini Islands take on the drink.

Joey Thai: Thai Fast Food Restaurant (AKA Blimpie) is the diametrical opposite to Thai places which pander to gringos (that is, every NYC Thai restaurant except Sripraphai, 64-13 39 Ave, Woodside, Queens; 718-899-9599). Rather than evoke American flavors from Thai ingredients and recipes, they improvise and jury-rig to wrench Thai flavors from . . . well, from the kitchen of a *Blimpie*, for crying out loud.

I regret if this all reads like a put-down. Nearly all the food was good, and as for the mistakes, I admit, the problems may have largely been the result of my wise guy ordering. I violated one of my own rules, a counter-intuitive unchowhoundish dictum I'd picked up from long experience: unless you have good reason to suspect hidden grandeur, it's always best to let the kitchen simply do what it does. Otherwise, the meal will likely turn into a Dje-laloo. One day I'll explain about Djelaloos (it's a long, long—but very funny—story).

These guys are clearly panicking at the failure of their unique and innovative business plan. Since customers are probably not going for the Thai half of the menu, they're not fully prepared to cook those things at this point. But I'm sure of one thing: if there were demand for the Thai stuff, they'd stock up, prep, and gener-ally be ready to cook serious dishes without having to pray for miracles whenever errant chowhounds appeared. So let's all stop by, and help grow this place to its full potential. It's a worthy cause; when was the last time you found a Thai restaurant even *interested* in giving you a taste of Thailand, rather than pandering to what they presume to be gringo taste (dumbed down, toned down, and peanut buttered and sugared up)? As the hostess (yes, this is a Blimpie with a hostess) told us—in broken English offset by a wonderful smile—their aim is to serve the real homestyle cooking, which you can't usually find in restaurants. And, amid the surre-alism and bleak frontier circumstances, it tastes like it.

Also, these are the nicest people in the world. You may have to leave shrimp on your plate (better: tell them you're allergic), but by meal's end, return visits will be planned. You'll feel sad upon leaving. I have rarely felt as at home and as graciously, sincerely, warmly taken care of as I did tonight at my white plastic table—built into the floor—on my white plastic seat—also built into the floor—under the glaring florescent lights and huge flashy corpo-rate posters at the midtown Blimpie.

Porcus Troianu

by Stewart Lee Allen

from *In the Devil's Garden*

> Allen's book *In the Devil's Garden* has a
> clever culinary hook: each of its seven eru-
> dite, witty essays explores one of the
> seven deadly sins through the foods asso-
> ciated with it. This one is, as you could
> guess, from the section on Gluttony.

The first thing the waiter does is trim your toenails. Then a glass of Falernian wine from a century-old Opimian vintage is served. A servant singing a poem written by your host, Trimalchio, brings out a heaping platter of cold cuts: spiced sow udders, rooster combs, winged rabbits, testicles, flamingo tongues, and ostrich brains. Finally dinner begins. Milk-fed snails the size of tennis balls served in a sweet-and-sour sauce gets things rolling, followed by an *amuse-gueule* of dormice, eaten whole after being dipped in honey and poppy seeds. Fish are killed *à table* by pouring scalding hot sauce onto them. They're still moving as you dig in. The fowl course begins with a pastry "egg" containing a minuscule bird called *beccafio*, or fig-pecker, covered in raw yolk and pepper. You eat it in one mouthful, bones and all. Whole roast geese and swans are brought out, but when you take a bite, surprise! They're made of pork. Finally, the main course: cow-stuffed-with-lamb-stuffed-with-pig-stuffed-with-rooster-stuffed-with-chicken-stuffed-with-thrush. Dessert comes in the form of cakes that descend from the ceiling and squirt saffron-scented juice in your face. For those guests still peckish, there are pickled rabbit fetuses to nibble while Trimalchio stages his own funeral and has his obituary, praising his good taste and generosity, read out loud.

Trimalchio was the kind of arriviste that caused the Roman Senate to ban hundreds of dishes around the first century B.C., a former slave turned multimillionaire who blew his fortune on the most obscene luxuries money could buy. Almost everything he served at that famous dinner—described in the anonymous first-century book *The Satyricon*—was criminal contraband at one point or another. During one course, a whole roast pig is carried triumphantly into the dining room, only to have Trimalchio go berserk when he "realizes" that his chef has neglected to gut the beast. The cook is about to be strangled in front of the guests for his incompetence, but Trimalchio decides that his last act on Earth should be to gut the animal with everyone watching. When the chef, weeping, begging for his life, plunges a knife into the carcass, a sea of sausages gushes out. Ha! Ha! It was all a joke. The cook receives a gold crown, and the guests all make a quick visit to the vomitorium to empty their stomachs before digging in. This kind of dish was called *porcus Troianu*, or Trojan pork, because like its namesake, the Trojan Horse, it was stuffed with piquant surprises. It was banned so often that the dish must have figured on the Top Ten Most Wanted list of the Roman police.

Equally illegal were those poppy seed–crusted dormice. The dormouse was a long-tailed rodent that Romans kept from birth in ventilated clay jars called *dolia*, where their inability to move, combined with intensive force-feeding, ensured they would become a ball of butter-soft flesh. These potbellied rats were apparently so delicious, the government feared it would turn their army into a bunch of spineless, rat-eating gluttons. Guards were posted at the markets with orders to seize any specimens offered for sale. When dormice grew scarce, the elite simply "crammed" (force-fed) chickens and pigs until they reached unnatural size and tenderness. Clerks recorded the animals' weight at the dinner table, before oohing guests. Moralists like Cato the Elder then required that people dine with their doors open so everyone could see exactly what was being eaten. He then limited the number of dinner parties per week. He punished guests as well as hosts. Cato was such a prude, he even campaigned against the civilized fad of building statues to chefs instead of generals.

Roman excess eventually ate the empire alive by making it overreliant on foreign imports. (Unless you subscribe to the theory that their lead-lined wine flagons caused their downfall via brain damage, in which case they drank their empire to death.) During the ensuing Dark Ages, when there was nothing to eat, much less overeat, laws restricting gluttony disappeared, only to pop up again in sixteenth-century Florence, which sternly restricted cardinals to a mere nine dishes per meal. Japan's nineteenth-century royal family allowed only certain produce to be sold in designated seasons, thus ensuring no merchant ever got a better *matsutake* mushroom than the Emperor. Wild fowl was banned for similar reasons, as were new cake designs and, of course, "thick green tea." The number of courses served at dinner was determined by one's social class. Peasant farmers were allowed only one plate per course, as compared to the Samurai's nine, and were not allowed to drink sake. Peasant parties also had to end by sunset. The message was clear—farmers were meant to grow food for the emperor's dinner, not enjoy it.

All these laws were in vain, thank God, for what is civilization if not an eternal quest for a new sensation? Some call it moral rot, but, of course, one man's rot is another man's wine. So the eleventh-century Indian king Shrenika threw vegetarian orgies whose courses were defined not by the dish served, but how it was consumed; the first course consisted of fruits that were chewed, then a course of the sucked, then the licked, and so forth. Turn-of-the-century American millionaire Diamond Jim Brady would put away twelve dozen oysters in a sitting and hired naked girls to feed them to him by hand. England's King James I threw a memorable party in 1606, at which noble ladies playing the Seven Virtues ended up so sodden with food and drink they were unable to play their parts. "Faith was left sick and spewing in the lower hall," wrote one correspondent describing the scene, "and Victory slept off the ill effects." The most notable modern effort was a series of secret meals in the 1990s that featured endangered species like the *ortolan,* woodcock, and, presumably, dolphin and whale (all denied by the participants, of course).

But it's the normally abstentious Greeks who have the last word. Literally, because the longest single word in their language was a dish recorded by Aristophanes in his work *Ecclesutzusae.*

> *Now must the spindleshanks, lanky and lean,*
> *trip to the banquet, for soon will, I wean,*
> *high on the table be smoking a dish,*
> *Brimming with game and with fowl and with fish.*
> *(called)*
> *Plattero-filleto-mulelto-turboto-cranio-morselo-pickleo-*
>   *acido-silphio-honeyo-poureontehtopo-ouzelo-thrusheo-*
>   *cushatao-culvero-cutleto-roastingo-marrowo-dippero-lever*
>   *et-syrupo-gibleto-wings*
> *So now ye have heard these tidings true,*
> *get hold of a plate and an omelet too!*

Rating Zagat

by Mimi Sheraton
from *Food & Wine*

> Former restaurant critic for the *New York Times* and author of 14 books, Mimi Sheraton knows what it means to be able to make or break a restaurant—which makes her the perfect person to write this skeptical and well-informed critique of the Zagat restaurant ratings.

W here shall we eat tonight? If that's not *the* burning question of our time, it is surely one that torments those who want to win at the restaurant game. Where, then, can one turn for reliable, independent and authoritative advice? Where else, one might ask, but the nation's most popular guides, the Zagat surveys?

Between iconic wine-dark covers emblazoned with bold white type, each Zagat survey lists hundreds of restaurants, all rated on food, decor and service by a supposedly impartial and knowing public rather than by professional critics. The guides are nothing if not handy, with concise codes telling readers everything they need to know about a restaurant, except what to order. As the publishers do not reimburse their respondents for meals (although they do compensate each one with a copy of the final work), they can review more establishments than would be humanly or financially feasible for one person, or even one periodical. In last year's survey of New York City, 20,424 people rated nearly 2,000 places.

That unrivaled scope, and the democratic voting system, have earned the Zagat surveys many encomiums. According to its back-cover blurbs, the guide has been dubbed "the gastronomic bible" by the *Wall Street Journal,* "indispensable" by the *Los Angeles Times* and "the single best source of accurate dining information" by the *Washington Post,* which apparently doesn't mind undercutting its own critics. In this culture of celebrity, it is no surprise to find additional endorsements from Bill Cosby ("I love good food. That's why I love Zagat") and Andrew Lloyd Webber ("Obliter-ates the need for any other guide").

In fact, with their huge sales, the Zagat surveys have just about obliterated all other guides. Last year, true believers bought about 650,000 copies of the New York City volume alone. Tim and Nina Zagat, the founders and cochairs of Zagat Survey LLC, currently publish 45 city and regional guides covering the U.S., Toronto, Vancouver, London, Paris and Tokyo, plus separate reports on shops, hotels and nightspots. Now, backed by $31 million from assorted investors, the Zagats are preparing a major expansion of their Internet services and possibly even an initial public offering. That's a long way from the hobby that began in 1979 when the Zagats, as young lawyers living in Paris, mimeographed sheets of their friends' restaurant suggestions.

But what's missing from all these thousands of ratings is the most crucial evaluation of all: How well do the guides really work? If you took their advice, trusting that high scores for food at a given restaurant would translate into great meals, how would you fare? To find out, I recently toured eight cities, eating at the restau-rant singled out by Zagat as having the best food in town. These top-rated establishments were Le Bernardin in New York; L'Espalier in Boston; the French Laundry in the Napa Valley (first place in the San Francisco guide); the French Room in Dallas; the Inn at Little Washington in Virginia (the winner in Washington, D.C., and the only restaurant at which I felt I had been recog-nized); Matsuhisa in Beverly Hills; André's in Las Vegas; and

Norman's in Coral Gables, Florida (the Miami champion)—the last two being the only ones I had never covered before in my 35 years of restaurant reviewing. To gain perspective on the local food scenes, I also ate at many of the runners-up.

In a couple of instances, the survey's top choice was on the money, nowhere more so than at THE FRENCH LAUNDRY In Yountville, California. That's fortunate, considering the maddening obstacles to making a reservation, a feat so difficult that had this not been a work project, I would have given up, thinking no meal quite worth it. But if any were, this would be it. Although Thomas Keller, the celebrated chef and owner, was away, the kitchen turned out his inventive dishes exquisitely.

Keller's food is surprising but never unnervingly over-the-top. His soigné inventions seemed predestined: a gratin of oysters with sweet-sour Meyer lemon and caviar; toasted brioche sandwiching soft-shell crab and tomato confit; roasted saddle of lamb with a polenta cake and artichokes; and seared duck breast with a counterpoint of bittersweet endive marmalade. A plate of cheese that included strong and runny Époisses with brandied prunes led to Keller dessert classics such as "coffee and doughnuts"—cinnamon-and-sugar-dusted mini-doughnuts with silky cappuccino semifreddo—and a refreshing Alsatian rhubarb tart with creamy mascarpone sorbet.

I was curious to visit the top-rated NORMAN'S in Coral Gables, where Norman Van Aken is the chef; much as I admired Van Aken when he was cooking at A Mano in South Beach a decade ago, I feared that his florid inventiveness might by now have gone too far. But magically, even improbable-sounding combinations seemed harmonious. The food was lusty but subtle, from lightly fried shrimp with mashed yucca, habanero tartar sauce and Van Aken's famous mojo verde—tomatillo mayonnaise—to Vietnamese vegetarian spring rolls with crunchy jicama and fine noodle filaments. A lemongrass soy sauce perfectly complemented rose-red tuna carpaccio, as did a cumin coating on a succulent rare lamb porterhouse. And cool, satiny café con leche panna cotta with tiny, cinnamon-scented churros was an inspired Latin-Italian fusion.

Because one can quibble endlessly about the relative excellence of New York's best restaurants (and because it is the city I know best), I used a slightly different approach here, visiting the survey's top five picks in an attempt to determine only whether each deserved to be among the elite. I would not, for instance, rank **LE BERNARDIN, CHANTERELLE** and **NOBU** first, second and third, as Zagat does, awarding each 28 points out of a possible 30. Still, all three are remarkable enough that the choices are understandable. But when I scanned Zagat's list of the runners-up, plausibility flew out the window.

The really incredible designations are the fourth-rank status of **SUGIYAMA**, with its esoteric Japanese cuisine, and the fifth-rank showing of **PETER LUGER** Steak house. This places both restaurants above the consistently excellent and far more ambitious Jean Georges and Daniel, both with 28 points, and Lespinasse, La Grenouille, Union Square Cafe and Gramercy Tavern, all with 27. Sugiyama, which serves a formalized progression of courses that can include steak on a hot stone, sushi and creative small dishes, does all of them very well but excels at nothing. And at Peter Luger, I had very good lamb chops and steak, but also encountered unripe tomatoes, tasteless shrimp left too long on ice, burned German-fried potatoes, a brassy steak sauce, and creamed spinach that would make even Gerber wince. One can only surmise that the 28 rating applies to the meat alone.

The appearance of a French restaurant at the head of the New York list is repeated in Zagat guides across the country. Of the top-rated restaurants I visited, five are French, and a sixth—the Inn at Little Washington—is certainly French informed. Apparently, reports of the demise of haute cuisine are greatly exaggerated. Also surprising is that despite all we hear about Italian cuisine and its regional splendors, only four Italian places are ranked first for food in the 40 areas covered in the 2001 edition of Zagat's nationwide guide, *America's Top Restaurants*. Perhaps an unsure public still feels more confident in declaring for the French kitchen.

Because almost all of the restaurants with the highest ratings for food are extremely fancy looking and expensive, I had to wonder if amateur critics are capable of separating the cooking from the surroundings. Would they rate the same dishes as highly if they were served in a simpler setting? And do they perhaps feel the need to reassure themselves, as they're paying a check that tops $200, that the meal they've just eaten was superb?

A perfect case in point is **THE FRENCH ROOM** in Dallas, a gilded Versailles wanna-be with green marble floors, goldleaf trim, murals of flying cherubs and trompe l'oeil clouds. The overly ambitious kitchen sends forth such misguided creations as quail filled with roasted red peppers and Parmesan cheese wrapped in bacon and served with caramelized endive polenta on a balsamic red-currant sauce. I have heard postmodernism in architecture described as the illiterate application of symbols, and so it is with this dish. Inventions require more artistry than this kitchen exhibited with a tough lobster tail that was not helped by wild mushrooms or soupy, "sorrel-infused" risotto. Nor did a metallic lemongrass sauce do much for a badly overcooked crab cake. Zagat's capsule review describing the menu as "classic" is simply bizarre, although the best offering, a delicious rare-roasted rack of lamb, hints that traditional efforts might be better rewarded.

The French Room's top ranking raises other questions. For one, how valid is local opinion for the visitor? A Dallas native might consider French food more suitable for a special occasion than the regional cuisine. But a visitor would (or should) prefer the stunning Southwestern specialties at the third-ranked Mansion on Turtle Creek. I would rather dine there four nights in a week

than at either the French Room or the Riviera, whose
innocuous French food is Zagat's second choice. But then, I'm a
stranger here myself.

Like the kitsch-laden interior at the French Room, the dining
rooms of **L'ESPALIER** in Boston, laid out on two floors of a
Victorian-Edwardian town house, provide the kind of grandiose
setting that Zagat respondents seem to crave. About 10 years ago,
I considered the food here to be as excellent as it was diverting,
but now the kitchen seems to be overreaching. Most dishes were
disappointingly bland, including a giveaway appetizer of shrimp
in a seaweed gel with overly chilled cucumbers, a technically
correct game-bird pâté, overcooked day-boat halibut sautéed
under a mush of crushed sunflower seeds, and a nicely juicy
squab obscured by a heavy sauce and a starchy taro-and-parsnip
cake. As for lavender-perfumed mashed potatoes, think of eating
potpourri. Among better choices were the assiette of lamb and
the black sesame–flecked fried soft-shell crabs.

As I made my rounds, I began to wonder what role sentiment
plays in the Zagat ratings of restaurants that have been the scene
of so many family milestone dinners over the years. Can it be that
the food is highly seasoned with nostalgia? That, plus a certain
local resentment toward celebrated interlopers, must be at work in
Las Vegas. The level of cooking in the city has risen dramatically
over the past few years, but the people's choice is still **ANDRÉ'S**, for
21 years a fixture in the deserted old downtown residential neighborhood. This local icon is a funky anachronism with an "old
auberge" look—dark wood beams, china bric-a-brac and lace curtains and tablecloths. The more traditional French food is pleasant
in a gentle way, as with a sautéed fillet of sole véronique complete
with green grapes (itself something of an anachronism, albeit well
prepared), a nicely garlicked rack of lamb, a honey-roasted breast
of duck and a Grand Marnier soufflé. But everything else failed,
including a canapé of some duckish mousse on crumbly, dry croutons and a dreadful version of the old-time banquet cliché of

sweetbreads in a patty shell, here with pea-size chicken quenelles in a soggy bouchée.

One might suppose that the opinions in the guides would be reasonably up-to-date since the first instruction on the survey form is "Please rate the restaurants you've visited in the past year." But compliance with this request relies strictly on the honor system. Perhaps the weakest link in the Zagat method is that respondents are not asked to supply any proof as to when—if ever—they visited the restaurants they voted on. Zagat could request photocopies of receipts; even requiring those surveyed to write in the approximate date of their last visit would dampen the impulse to fill out the form willy-nilly, whether the responses are based on recent experience, fond memories or, perhaps, imaginings. Any such tactic, though, might discourage people from taking part in the survey. (Tim and Nina Zagat were not interviewed for this article, but they did respond in writing to several issues, including this one. They said they believe the "overwhelming majority" of those surveyed follow the questionnaire's instructions, and added, "In any event, with thousands of surveyors, we always have people visiting each restaurant up to the last minute. And our local editors, who are active food writers, have current knowledge of the restaurants surveyed.")

THE INN AT LITTLE WASHINGTON, in the Washington, D.C., area, has won the top Zagat rating for food every year since 1995; if, as I believe, the kitchen's performance has slipped a few notches in that time, the survey doesn't reflect it. I find the gussied-up Victorian-Edwardian decor stifling but had always felt it was more than made up for by the subtlety of the food. Not so on this latest visit. In his magnificently outfitted kitchen, Patrick O'Connell relies too heavily on fruit, whether in the apple coulis that overly sweetens bland boudin blanc, or the tropical fruit mix compromising lovely crabmeat, or the hot pineapple with duck that is said to be cooked "thrice," meaning overcooked to a fare-thee-well.

Apple cider sauce ruined the flavor of braised rabbit, but tart pickled cranberries perfectly complemented delicious, pepper-encrusted venison. O'Connell's obvious sweet tooth serves him well with desserts, judging by the luscious liquid Valrhona chocolate cake and the crunchy marjolaine with its hints of hazelnuts and chocolate. The cookies were good too.

Another restaurant that seems to be sliding is the number one choice in Los Angeles, **MATSUHISA**. When it opened in 1987, it was indeed a stunner, as Nobuyuki Matsuhisa, the affable Japanese sushi chef, who has spent time in Peru, Argentina and elsewhere in South America, created his own brand of fusion cuisine. But as he now divides his attention among his seven Nobu outposts around the world (including the one in New York), Matsuhisa has suffered. Baby eggplants with miso, cold soba noodles and the marinated yellowtail with slivers of jalapeños were all delicious. But many of the fusion specialties were oversalted and obscured by heavy brown sauces, especially overpowering when pitted against delicate tuna in a sashimi salad. Others, such as the Kobe beef with vegetables and the squid "pasta," suggested stir-fried Chinese takeout. Even the usually silken, signature black cod with miso arrived dry and shriveled, and the tempura was third-rate, soggy and floury. The colorful crowd, the helpful staff and the more inviting dishes would draw me back, but the indifferent preparations hardly justify the top rating.

Other writers have said that Zagat scores are self-fulfilling prophecies, a phenomenon William Grimes of the *New York Times* has called "the Zagat Effect." Grimes suggests that diners who go to highly rated restaurants, "convinced that they are eating at a top-flight establishment, cannot bring themselves to believe otherwise."

Because stories abound of restaurateurs trembling when Tim and Nina Zagat appear at the door, one has to ask whether they or their editors exert undue influence on their books. What does it mean, for example, when a humble score of 19 for food at Guastavino in the 2001 New York City guide prompts the editors to point out that the restaurant complex includes a more formal dining room "whose high quality is not adequately reflected by our ratings"? Says who? The Zagats reply that the editors made this statement because it was clear from survey comments that some people "had confused Guastavino's informal downstairs brasserie with its upstairs fine-dining restaurant." Then there is the matter of which places get into the guide. Last fall, publication of the Boston survey had to be delayed after a local critic noticed that one restaurant was described in the galleys as if it were already open when, in fact, it wasn't.

All of which says nothing about two phenomena that would seem to be beyond the publisher's control. Several restaurateurs have told me about visits from rogue respondents who announce themselves as survey participants in hopes of getting special food and service, if not a free meal. (The Zagats respond, "If anyone should be so crass as to act that way, we hope the restaurant would ignore him or her, just as they would any other patron who . . . drops a name in hopes of getting a good table.") Some restaurateurs, for their part, have enlisted friends, relatives, staff and clientele to stuff the ballot box. Although Tim Zagat says he has a system for detecting such a ploy, doing so seems virtually impossible. Such engineered responses obviously could result in huge profits for the restaurateurs and a disappointing waste of money for the customer.

These glitches aside, the Zagat surveys stand or fall on their central premise: that thousands of separate opinions add up to something like the truth. Asked about the reliability of their guides, the Zagats answered, "We argue . . . that our numerical ratings and our consumer-based reviews are more reliable than any individual critic because they draw on the shared experiences of a large cross-section of savvy customers (200,000 this year alone) rather than the personal biases of one, frequently recognized, professional critic. . . . [T]he enormous sales success of our books and the steady increase in the number of our participating surveyors year after year suggest that restaurant-goers do find our method to be a reliable basis for rating restaurants, which is a good enough measure for us."

Having always distrusted consensus, I feel the system of relying on a vast public rather than professional critics has no more validity in assessing restaurants than it would if applied to art or theater. The majority can be wrong, and one well-informed opinion is worth more than those of a thousand amateurs. Popular success is not a measure of excellence. If it were, it would mean that McDonald's serves the world's best hamburgers, KFC makes perfect fried chicken, Pizza Hut is the envy of Naples and, come to think of it, that the Zagat Survey is our best restaurant guide.

Adventures with a Frisco Kid

by Michael Lewis
from *Gourmet*

> Known for business best-sellers like *Liars'*
> *Poker* and *Next*, Michael Lewis can be just
> as irreverent when writing about his own
> culinary experiences—in this case, a foray
> into fine dining with a child in tow.

O ne night after we had been driven nearly mad by one too many visits to The Oakland Zoo, my wife and I decided to take another approach to our two-and-a-half-year-old daughter. We would conduct an experiment. We would travel around the Bay Area and see how hard it was to do the things with her that we assumed we could only do without her. How bad could it be? Perhaps we would learn something about the Bay Area; perhaps we'd learn something about two-and-a-half-year-old children; perhaps we'd learn something about ourselves. On this mad note, we set out for a very fancy San Francisco restaurant called Masa's.

"Fine dining" and "small children" do not typically wind up in the same sentence. That was the point. This was Tallulah's first $100 meal. And from the moment the lady at Masa's front door handed her the lollipop, she seemed willing to approach it in a different spirit than the one in which she approaches her usual slop. She followed the lollipop lady straight to a table, where she marveled at the array of silver and china spread out before her. Bread and water arrived with a pomp and circumstance she had never before witnessed. She looked around in stunned silence. This wasn't dinner; this was a parade. When the bread man handed her a second slice she took it and said, "Where's more?"—whereupon he handed her two slices more, and she went silent again in awe. The hushed tones, the formality, the reverence that attends people spending huge sums on food, made her think at least once about making her usual ruckus. Then the waiter arrived to take our orders, and my wife, Tabitha, pressed our luck.

"I'll have the six-course tasting menu," she said.

Now, no restaurant simply serves a six-course tasting menu. What with the tidbits and gewgaws that go with such a meal in such a place, six means nine. We were committing to clearing nine plates. You can't do that without sitting still for several hours. Tallulah's personal best was 20 minutes. Already she was clutching two giant silver forks in her little fists in the manner of an impatient Viking king. *Bam, bam, bam,* they went on the table. I turned to the waiter.

"Any chance we could have those courses faster than usual?"

"How fast would you like them?" he asked.

"How fast can you run?"

He saw what I meant. Off he ran and returned with the obligatory unrecognizable trifle on its munchkin plate, compliments of the chef. We'd ordered only a salad for our daughter, but they brought her the chef's compliment anyway. It was a surf clam, the waiter said, though of course it could have been anything. He went on to describe for Tallulah how the surf clam was prepared but before he could finish, hers was gone.

"Chicken!" she said. *"Bawk, bawk!"*

Out went the munchkin plate; in came doll-size cups of soup. Tallulah picked hers up, eyed it, and said, in a knowing tone, "Dippin' sauce!" When she'd finished she shouted out, "All done!" and then promptly suffered a change of heart. She dropped her head into her hands and rolled her eyes skyward, bored as a Raphael putto. "I'm crying," she said. The meal had still not even officially begun.

Out went the doll-size cups and in came our first course (*ahi tuna*) and her navel orange salad with avocado and assorted so-called microgreens. The avocado was, as always, intended by her mother as bait for the honest greens. Tallulah picked out the avocado and left the rest untouched. But before the usual nutritional debate with her mother could begin, a waiter whisked her plate away. Tallulah smiled her approval. She looked around. At the far end of the restaurant she spotted the cheese cart.

"Cheese! I want cheese!" The waiter was in the kitchen. The maître d' rushed over. "Did you say cheese?"

"Yes."

"White or yellow?"

Tallulah thought about this. "Both."

Assorted cheeses appeared. On these she nibbled while the remains of the tuna vanished and the oven-roasted Maine lobster appeared.

"I want ice cream," she said in her testing-the-waters tone.

I scanned the menu: sorbet but no ice cream.

"They don't have ice cream," said her mother.

"I want ice cream!" she hollered.

Almost before the words were out of her mouth, a waiter was at our side. "Vanilla or chocolate?"

"Both!"

After he rushed off she said, "I'm just going to hide a little bit," then slid under the table. We ate in peace for the next ten minutes. My child poked out her head only once, to howl "Fee fi fo fum, I smell the blood of an Englishman!" loudly enough that the people across the room turned, and the maître d' came over to say how delightful she was—and hand her a cookie to shut her up. At length, the ice cream arrived and lured her back up into her chair. When she finished she slid back under the table, where, for the next 20 minutes, she received like royalty many handsome young waiters.

As she vanished behind the tablecloth, I realized that in the previous 90 minutes the staff of Masa's had pacified my child. She realized that she could make no request so outlandish that they would not grant it, instantly. That knowledge alone tamed her: What was the point of making these mad demands on grownups when all of them were so easily met? Four courses into the feast, between the squab breast and the veal tenderloin with chestnut ravioli, I began, for the first time in my experience with Tallulah in a public place, to feel as relaxed as if she was not there.

That is the irony of the places rich people frequent. First-class airplane cabins, Ian Schrager hotels, fancy restaurants all are designed to insulate rich people from life's little annoyances. But rich people have committed a tactical blunder: Enough of them behave like small children that their habitats must be designed to accommodate the worst childish behavior. It's only a matter of time before people with actual small children discover this and ruin it for rich people.

By the time a cart full of something called "artisanal cheeses" arrived, I realized that life with a toddler was a lot like life with a billionaire. Only the billionaire combines the toddler's will with its absence of conscience to get what he wants, when he wants it, all the time. Only the billionaire and the toddler believe that not getting exactly what they want, exactly when they want it, is a violation of their natural rights.

The next morning we're back in the car, game for more. I'm driving. Tabitha is next to me. Tallulah is strapped in her car seat in the back.

"We had fun last night at Masa's, right?"

"Uh-huh." In the rearview mirror I can see her thinking.

"So today we go to another fun place."

A pitiful wail: She knows I'm lying. "I want to go to the ball pit!" she says. The ball pit at the local YMCA is not merely her favorite place but the only place she allows herself to be taken without making a stink.

"But this is like the ball pit!"

"Where we going?" she wails.

"SFMOMA!"

"A museum!" says her mother, with the false enthusiasm that has become our natural tone. "With art!"

Tallulah thinks about this. "Can I climb on it?"

"Some art is just to look at," says her mother.

She wails the wail that must have inspired whoever invented the earplug.

I am sure that there exist parents who take a hard line and hold it, never succumbing to the temptation to negotiate, never meeting their toddler's extravagant demands. These people no doubt wind up with beautifully disciplined children. But I am incapable of discipline, and, sooner or later, my conversation with my child turns into one long negotiation. You do this for me and I'll do this for you. You don't do this for me, I won't do this for you. And, as anyone who has negotiated with a terrorist knows, once you've done it once, you can never plausibly decline to do it again. The best you can do, I have found, is to exploit a curious hole in toddler logic.

"We can do one of two things," I holler. "We can either go to SFMOMA or we can go back home and eat broccoli."

For some reason it always works: It never occurs to her to say she doesn't want to do either. She considers my proposal most of the way to SFMOMA. SFMOMA is closed. We stand on the sidewalk and peer through the glass doors, wondering who decided museums should be closed on Wednesdays. With a logic recognizable only to parents of toddlers, our child begins to whine about not being able to go to SFMOMA. It's possible she's thinking about the broccoli.

• • •

Then, by some miracle, our luck turns. Tallulah notices, across the street from SFMOMA, the giant colorful Keith Haring sculpture *(Untitled, Three Dancing Figures)*. Art she can climb on—and does, for a full 20 minutes, which, in toddler time, counts as two days. Dangling from one side of the thing, she spies a carousel. I have never before noticed that there is a carousel in downtown San Francisco because (a) until very recently, there wasn't; (b) until recently, I couldn't have cared less; and (c) it is hidden to all but toddler eyes behind a giant convention center.

To the carousel we walk. I confess that many of the things my child loves to do leave me slightly cold. It would please me to know that I have seen my last zoo, or that I would never again have to ride on a merry-go-round. But this merry-go-round is different. It is part of a complex called the Yerba Buena Gardens, in which there are so many things for my child to do that the merry-go-round is soon forgotten. A bowling alley with balls light enough that a two-and-a-half-year-old can roll them and lanes with metal guards to prevent all gutter balls. A museum—called the ZEUM, and free for kids under five years old—with spinart Frisbees, a claymation studio, a Slinky racetrack, a wall of Legos, and on and on. A park with giant inflated animals to climb on. An ice skating rink with skates for toddlers. And maybe the best toy store I've ever seen. In this miraculous place, the distinction between what I like to do and what Tallulah insists on doing vanishes.

Half-Shell Boogie

by John T. Edge
from *Gourmet*

Chronicler par excellence of Southern cooking (he is the founder of the Southern Foodways Alliance), Edge knows the South's food traditions inside and out. A special gift for detailing the personalities behind the food makes his stories leap off the page.

The oysters tasted of the salt and the sea, soft waves crashing over my tongue and down my gullet. By all rights, this should have been a culinary epiphany in the making. But I couldn't take my eyes off the shuckers long enough to truly concentrate on the gustatory experience itself. I was enthralled by the glint of their knives flashing in the gilt-edged mirror hung behind the bar, by the ease with which they pried open the rough shells and extracted the sweet, silvery morsels.

I was, of course, in New Orleans, where the art of shucking is celebrated as a sacrament. In this city, rife with buskers and grifters, hustlers and hawkers, the accomplished opener of oysters is held in particularly high regard, recognized as the inheritor of a storied tradition that began with eastern European immigrants and 19th-century Creoles of color who operated jury-rigged stands along the river levee near Picayune Pier. These pioneers peddled bivalves by the gunnysack, cracking open a dozen at a time for anyone with a few coins jingling in their pocket.

There's always been some debate as to what constitutes a shucker. Old-school oystermen will tell you that a shucker is the man or woman who plies their trade at one of the city's wholesale houses, like Captain Pete's or P & J. Their yield goes into quart jars bound for grocery stores and, eventually, gumbos and po' boys.

An opener, on the other hand, is the man—rarely, if ever, do you see a woman—who works a raw bar in a restaurant or tavern, serving oysters on the half shell to be slurped up then and there. Today, however, the distinctions are blurred, and *shucker* is the almost universal appellation of choice.

Such quibbling aside, few would deny that the littoral of New Orleans is where the art of oyster opening can be observed at its zenith, where quicksilver speed, surgical precision, and randy banter converge and complement. For it is here, in dank French Quarter barrooms and dowdy Uptown emporiums, that the two great traditions of shucking and jiving fuse and reach fullest flower.

First, the shuck:

Michael Broadway, age 42 and a veteran of more than 25 years behind the bar, is the senior opener at the boisterous, neon-gilded Acme Oyster House on Iberville Street in the French Quarter. His friends and customers know him as Hollywood. Acme, in business since 1910, is the highest-volume oyster house in the city, the spot where oyster-eating contests are decided, where generation after generation of locals and tourists alike were first introduced to the bracing taste of these briny mollusks. And make no mistake: Hollywood is king of the middens.

"They call me Slow But Good Hollywood," he says, a shy smile spreading across his thin face. True to his moniker, he is a student of technique and yield, unconcerned for the most part with speed. "It's as important to cut a clean oyster as it is to cut it quick," Hollywood says. "I can go fast if I want to, but I'd rather go steady and clean."

He snags a mottled gray shell from one of the white tile bins piled high with chipped ice. In his right hand is a short knife with a plastic handle. If it weren't so dull, it would resemble a dagger. He taps once with the knife to "wake that oyster up, let him know I'm coming in to get him." He also listens for a telltale hollow report, which would mean the creature within is dead and shriveled.

Failing that, Hollywood tucks the shell against the lip of the bar, wedging it firmly in place with his gloved left hand. Others steady the oyster with a lead pallet shaped like a truncated trough, but Hollywood prefers the sure grip of his hand.

He leans into the oyster, ratcheting his body weight down like a vise. The knife comes in from the top right, aimed not for the narrow hinge but for the wide end of the shell, seeking purchase in a crook or cranny. "That's how you tell the boys from the men," says Hollywood. "The men take it in through the front door." With a grating screech, the knife skips along the seam of the shell, and then slips in the side.

Hollywood pulls the knife back toward his body, twisting as he goes. The shell pops open with a gurgle that is at once mechanical and nautical, something akin to what it must sound like to open a submerged treasure chest.

For the briefest of moments, the oyster is suspended between the two halves of the shell, tethered by the bone-white adductor muscle near the center. Two quick chops of the knife and the quivering gray mass is free of its mooring. Not a trace of the meat remains attached to the shell.

"One last thing—you got to clean that oyster up before you're done," says Hollywood, as he draws his knife alongside the meat, pushing aside a thin effluvium of silt. Maybe 7 seconds after he began he slides the oyster onto the marble bar, taking care to tip the wide end of the shell up, reserving the precious liquor.

On a good night, Hollywood and his band of fellow shuckers open 1,000 oysters apiece, maybe a few more. Come New Year's Eve or Mardi Gras, the number reaches 2,000. But after all these years—and all those oysters—the mechanics are rote, the shell count unimportant.

Even among shuckers who consider themselves to be as good

or better, Hollywood has earned a grudging respect. He's the shucker that other restaurant owners turn to when they're scouting for new talent. He's the man to call when you want to hire a crew for a private party. And this past fall, in concert with the Louisiana Department of Wildlife and Fisheries, he began teaching shucker certification classes at Nicholls State University, in nearby Thibodaux. Hollywood's coworkers were quick to dub the enterprise Shuck U, eliding the first syllable in a blatant effort to exploit the double entendre.

And now, the jive:

"When I was little, my mama used to tell me that I talked too much," says Thomas Stewart, the opener at Pascal's Manale, a 1913-vintage, Italian-Creole restaurant set on an Uptown side street. "She was right. I do like to talk. The thing is, I found a way to make a living at it."

Thomas works alone at a sloping, white marble bar in the front room, just inside the door. The wall behind him is plastered with black-and-white photographs of prizefighters. Above hang wagon-wheel chandeliers.

Twelve years into his tenure, Thomas has worked his way up from dishwasher to chief shucker. "When I started out, there was no one to show me how," he says, scooping a pail of cubed iced into the bar bin. "So I just snatched a few oysters and a butter knife and sat down on a slop bucket to teach myself. Now I'm the man. The 'I-Pop-'Em-Until-You-Drop-'Em Man.'" A violent swivel and bump of the hips accent this last linguistic flourish.

If Hollywood is, at heart, a steely-eyed technician, then Thomas is his alter ego, with a style best described as an amalgam of the flamboyance of Little Richard and the zealotry of Ron Popeil. He is also handy with a knife. "I don't believe in serving chippies," says the 39-year-old. "No chipped shells. My hustle is my hands. Without a good set of hands, I'm nobody." But that's not what keeps his regulars coming back.

On a recent Friday night, as the cocktail hour gives way to

dinner, the crowd at Pascal's Manale turns as thick and boisterous as a rugby scrum. Orders for oysters pour in, dozen upon dozen upon dozen. Just when Thomas is on the verge of losing it, he hits a groove. His knife work slows, his voice drops a register. And he goes skittering back and forth across the duckboards, trading jibes here, slinging shucked platters there. When he catches sight of a regular leaning in close, waving a ten-spot, Thomas stops dead in his tracks, tosses a imaginary cape across his shoulders, and leaps for the bill, calling out in his best imitation of Mighty Mouse, "Here I come to save the day!" His voice rings clarion, a basso profundo worthy of an opera star weaned on cartoons.

At a little before eight, a young couple walks in. The boy makes a beeline for the bar, but the girl hangs back. She looks anxious. The boy orders a dozen. "I got big ole good-uns and good ole big-uns," says Thomas. "Which you gonna have?" The girl cracks the barest of smiles and sidles up alongside her date. The boy introduces himself. "Howdy, chief," replies Thomas. "What's slappin', captain?" And then he attempts to answer his own question in a singsong rap: "Ain't nothing shakin' but the eggs and the bacon and the beans on the grill. Ain't nothing shakin' but the peas in the pot till the water get hot."

"Better make that two dozen," allows the boy. Thomas fishes the first oyster from the bin and plunges his knife in to the hilt. "If I can get 'em smiling," he says to no one in particular, "I can get 'em swallowing."

Kings of the Hill

by Rich Lang

from *Saveur*

> As a native Rhode Islander (he now lives in Newport), Rich Lang comfortably navigates the old Italian neighborhoods of Providence, making its colorful characters and garlicky aromas come to life.

On Atwells Avenue, when people talk of "the old country", they can mean only one place. Up and down this street, the main thoroughfare of the area called Federal Hill in Providence, Rhode Island, the shop signs offer clues: Gasbarro's wine store, Garbolino's dress shop, Rialto furniture, even Passaretti's karate school. The cheese shop, the butcher shop, the grocery stores, the cafés, and the dozens of restaurants crowding the avenue—most of them are Italian, and they are the living legacy of a neighborhood that was once one of the great crucibles of Italian life in America.

Today, Federal Hill, a tangle of angled streets and triple-decker wooden row houses above downtown Providence, includes Latinos, Cambodians, and West Africans in its population—but in the early 1900s, it was home mainly to thousands of Italian immigrants, drawn by dreams of liberty and the promise of work in the city's giant textile mills and factories. In the years that followed, the Italians redefined Rhode Island's sense of itself as names like Brown,

Green, and Francis gave way to Antonelli, Carlucci, and Pastore. The Italian population, just 25 in 1850, had swelled to 9,000 by 1900 and, including children born on American soil, to a whopping 92,000 by 1930. The state's spirit—and especially its dinner table—would never be the same. By the 1970s, when I was growing up in Warwick, a suburb of Providence, most Chinese restaurants were serving Italian bread with dinner and spumoni for dessert, and eggplant parmesan and pizza strips could be had in just about any sandwich shop or convenience store. By 1980, tiny Rhode Island, with 20 percent of all the Italian-Americans in the country, had arguably become the most Italian place in America.

And the state's vibrant Italian heart was—and remains—Atwells Avenue. All along this street, you'll find warm smiles, passion in both alliances and disputes, and the conviction that simple pleasures are what make life worth living—especially when they take place around a food-laden table where wine flows and friendship prevails.

"Hey, pal, you're looking good," says Joe Marzilli, patting me on the back of the neck. Dapper and portly, with a trimmed mustache and a sparkle in his eye, Marzilli has charmed the crowd at his Old Canteen restaurant nightly for nearly 50 years. He winks at my girlfriend sweetly and moves on to the next table. "How are you, folks? Nice to see you."

The "folks", like the menu, have changed little since Marzilli bought the place in 1956. That's how he likes it, and obviously he's not alone. A friend of mine who kept calling the Old Canteen, pushing for a Saturday-night reservation after being told that no tables were free, was finally dismissed—kindly but firmly—with the truth: "As I said, sir, we have a regular Saturday-evening clientele. So unless there's a death in the family, there is no availability on Saturday night." If the rose pink walls and campy gilded mirrors in Marzilli's dining room could talk, they'd recount some choice anecdotes (it's said that John F. Kennedy Jr. was once tossed out for wearing jeans). And if they went much beyond that, they'd probably have to enter the witness protection program. Federal Hill is a pretty tame place today, but there was a time when the *Sopranos* writing staff could have found enough inspiration there for a trunkful of scripts. My favorite late-1970s headline from the *Providence Journal* was "Man Found in Trunk Riddled with Bullet Holes. Police Suspect Murder."

Veteran waiter Andy Fackos, who has worked this room since 1969, arrives with my beef braciola, prepared by Marzilli's son Sal, the chef. Stuffed with raisins, pine nuts, and boiled egg, the rolled steak crumbles under my knife into a pool of thick, rich marinara (here on the Hill, adding the word *sauce* would be redundant). Marinara is about much more than tomato, olive oil, and garlic. I'm not even Italian, and yet its smell, tangy taste, and velvety texture are simmered into my sense of being a Rhode Islander. Marinara ushers me straight back to childhood excursions to the cozy restaurants of Atwells Avenue, where dinner seemed like a sensuous pageant of huge, celebratory family meals and men with carefully blow-dried hair and gold chains wooing dark, dolled-up women.

"Try the snail salad. It's delicious tonight." Marzilli is welcoming two couples from out of town, who are unaware that the snail salad—made with meaty mollusks from Narragansett Bay, first explored by the Italian Giovanni da Verrazano—is always delicious. "Geez, you guys lucked out," he continues, gently placing a hand on each of the men's shoulders. "Look at these two beautiful ladies."

While good cooks abound on Atwells Avenue, one in particular carries the gastronomic torch: Walter Pocenza, the chef-owner of Aquaviva. A man brimming with charm and enthusiasm, Potenza arrived from Abruzzi at 19 and has been a vital part of the food scene here for three decades. Early on, he cooked at Camille's, the most renowned restaurant on the Hill until it closed last year, and has had seven of his own restaurants since. He is an avid student of Italian-Jewish cuisine (part of his menu is devoted to dishes like Sephardic semolina-coated tuna from Sicily) as well as the terra-cotta cookery of the ancient Etruscans (dishes baked in his own line of terra-cotta pots also appear on the menu). He gives cooking classes in Providence and in Italy and has even written a cookbook about the Hill (*Federal Hill: Flavors and Knowledge,* which he published himself two years ago).

I stop by Aquaviva one afternoon for some polenta with gorgonzola sauce and a Roman-Jewish specialty: simple yet exquisite sautéed spinach with lemon, garlic, pine nuts, and raisins. Potenza starts telling me about the local classics, the dishes that perfume the air along Atwells Avenue. Some, like saltimbocca and osso buco, come relatively unchanged from Italy, and others, like snail salad, were invented or adapted here. I ask Potenza whether he ever makes shrimp fra diavolo (brother devil)—shrimp in a spicy tomato sauce, often served with linguine. It's based on Italy's black pepper–laden alla diavola (devil's style) dishes, and it's a pasta I love. "I haven't made it in 20 years," Potenza says, laughing, "but hang on." Within minutes, he reappears with a steaming plate. With its pink-tailed shrimp fanning out from a thick, scarlet sauce over a tangle of white noodles, the dish is an archetypal picture of Italy in America's eye.

Potenza lifts an eyebrow. "Good?" My expression says everything. He beams and slaps me on the back. "Enjoy, enjoy. Wait, let me get you a glass of wine. You can't just eat it alone like this!"

Recently I strolled through some of the food shops on the Hill with a friend visiting from Washington, D.C. "My God," he marveled as we wandered past olives and oils, cases of cheeses, hams, and peasant breads at Tony's Colonial Food Store. "If Washington had just one place like this I'd feel like I'd died and gone to heaven."

We picked up a couple of Wimpy Skippys—thin-crusted pizza

dough turnovers filled with spinach, mozzarella, and pepperoni—at Caserta Pizzeria and ate them on the way to one of my favorite places on the Hill: Providence Cheese. As a teenager I distributed posters around the city for a local theater, and I'd always stop by the store to say hi to Francesco Basso, a sweet old man with a black beret and a rolling Neapolitan accent who would hang a poster and give me a piece of homemade mozzarella in exchange.

"He loved this place," says Wayne Wheatley, Basso's grandson, offering me a slice of provolone. "Try this. It's the sharpest you'll find on the avenue." That's an understatement—the cheese practically sizzles on my tongue.

At age 5, Wheatley was already grating parmigiano-reggiano at his grandfather's side. After he grew up and moved west, Wheatley flew back most Christmases to help out at the shop, and after Basso passed away, in 1986, Wheatley took over the store. In 1991, Wheatley married Patrizia, from Rome. Now she makes the shop's fresh ravioli to order, and her mother, Carmina Conti, occasionally sets out peerless eggplant rollatini on the counter for sale.

Nearly every business on the avenue is likewise infused with family tradition. At Fed-Rick's House of Veal, Gennaro "Jerry" Balzano Jr. and his brother, Carmine, learned the butcher's trade from their father, who learned it from *his* father. Says Jerry, "My grandfather Carmine was so amazing with a cleaver that people used to get off the bus right there"—he points to the street—"to stare in the windows and watch him cut. I swear to you."

At Scialo Bros. Bakery, Carol Scialo Gaeta shows me around. "My father, Luigi, got started in 1916," she recalls. "He stayed in the business 70 years, right up until he passed away at 103." (The other Scialo brother left for Italy in the mid-1920s, and Luigi became the sole owner.) Today, Gaeta, who married the son of one of her father's bakers, runs the store with her sister Lois. But Luigi Scialo's soul still seems to reside in the cavernous brick ovens in the back flanked by stone lion heads and worked with long wooden peels.

"People look for shortcuts today," Gaeta says, offering me a pignoli cookie just out of the oven. "My father taught us otherwise." She won't sully her cookies by using a mix of cheap nut pastes. I take a bite, and my teeth sink into sweet, nutty tenderness. Gaeta chuckles. "That's pure almond paste. You taste the difference, don't you?"

You taste the difference everywhere on the Hill. It's something that survives from the world our grandparents bequeathed us, something that all the progress of a century has not been able to improve.

When my family moved to Rhode Island in 1972, the Hill was suffering from urban decay, and most of its residents had fled to the suburbs. In a neighborhood once packed with hundreds of shops and restaurants, a handful of businesses remained, and Atwells Avenue had become most famous as the seat of the powerful local mafia.

"But look at it today," says Camille Parolisi, peeling a potato in her kitchen at home, a white house on the bay with a Roman-statue-studded garden about 20 miles southeast of Providence. "It's wonderful up there again." Many Rhode Islanders credit the mayor of Providence, Buddy Cianci (who strode into city hall in 1975 and began resuscitating the downtown area, including the Hill—with the turnaround. Parolisi has certainly been around long enough to see Federal Hill rise, fall, and rise again. For 35 years, she and her late husband, Jack, owned Camille's restaurant, which was founded by Jack's father in 1914 and was, until it closed last year, Rhode Island's first (and best-known) fine dining establishment, patronized by everyone from Old Blue Eyes to the King.

Parolisi prefers not to reveal her age but moves with the grace and energy of someone decades younger. "When my husband was still here, there were never fewer than 12 people in this house for Sunday dinner. This was a party house," she says. Today, as she helps her great-nephew, Gary Mantoosh—Camille's last chef and owner—prepare Sunday dinner for the family, not much seems to have changed.

A few hours later, we sit down to eat at a table crowded with food: fried eel with onions, oranges with prosciutto, and an eye-popping antipasto display. "Eat!" Mantoosh says as the second courses begin to flow from the kitchen. "I'm not comfortable unless you're eating!" I help myself to spaghetti, stuffed peppers, and potatoes filled with bread crumbs, chopped olives, garlic, and onions, baked in marinara—his grandmother's specialty. Mantoosh serves me a massive veal chop, pounded thin: "This was one of our signature dishes at the restaurant." The meat melts in my mouth, enrobed in the warm, citrusy tang of its piccata sauce—lemon, butter, and caper berries on the stem. I take another bite. "Careful," Mantoosh teases, urging me to save room. "You're not allowed to leave until after the spumoni." When that dessert comes, it is a tower of banded colors—chocolate brown, pistachio green, and strawberry pink—crowned with a froth of meringue, dried fruit, and a drizzle of balsamic vinegar syrup. As we dig in, conversation gives way to moans of approval.

"You want to know why everybody loves Federal Hill so much? I'll tell you in one word," says Walter Potenza on a buzzing Saturday night at Aquaviva, ladling lamb stew with gnocchi from a terra-cotta crock onto our bread plates as my friends and I wait for our entrées. "People. There are plenty of good restaurants around. But you come up here for something more, to feel connected to something bigger than the food on the plates. The people, the human connection, is what this place is all about." I nod in agreement but am entranced by precisely what is on our plates: the gnocchi are plump, the chunks of lamb succulent, the pecorino cheese melting into buttery pools in the rich, smoky sauce.

The diners next to us crane their heads for a better look. "Excuse me, what is that?" one of them asks Potenza. "C'mere, give me your plates!" he replies, spinning around and ladling out

gnocchi. "Try this. You're gonna love it!" Their faces light up.
Potenza starts to tell them tales of the Hill, and soon they're
laughing with delight—enjoying something bigger than the food
on the plates, indeed.

Braciole alla Marinara
(Rolled Stuffed Meat with Tomato Sauce)

Serves 4

Sal Marzilli, the chef at Joe Marzilli's Old Canteen (and
Joe's son), makes this dish with either veal or beef. Veal
is lower in fat and tenderer, he points out—but he adds
that beef is cheaper and has a heartier, meatier flavor.
Marinara often contains oregano or basil, but Sal's version omits herbs. Save the leftover meat-enriched sauce
for pasta.

For the sauce:
2 14-oz. cans crushed tomatoes
2 cloves garlic, peeled and finely chopped
3 tbsp, extra-virgin olive oil
Salt and freshly ground black pepper

For the meat:
6 sprigs fresh basil
4 8-oz. pieces veal or beef top round, pounded to ¼"
   thickness
1 tsp. garlic powder
Salt and freshly ground black pepper
4 tbsp. toasted pine nuts, finely chopped
2 hard-cooked eggs, peeled and finely chopped
2 tbsp. raisins
4 cloves garlic, peeled and finely chopped
4 tbsp. freshly grated parmigiano-reggiano

¼ cup vegetable oil
Leaves from 2 sprigs parsley, chopped

1. For the sauce: Put tomatoes, garlic, oil, and 1 cup water into a large saucepan and simmer over medium heat, stirring occasionally, until sauce thickens slightly, about 15 minutes. Season to taste with salt and pepper and set aside.

2. For the meat: Chop leaves from 2 of the sprigs of basil and set aside. Working with 1 piece at a time, put meat on a clean surface with one of the narrow ends facing you. Season with some of the granulated garlic and salt and pepper to taste. Scatter one-quarter of the pine nuts, eggs, raisins, chopped garlic, chopped basil, and parmigiano-reggiano along edge of meat closest to you, leaving about a ½" border on either side. Fold long sides of meat over filling by about ½" on either side, roll up snugly, and tie securely with kitchen twine.

3. Heat oil in a medium heavy-bottomed pot with a tight-fitting lid over medium-high heat. Add braciole and brown all over, about 5 minutes. Add reserved sauce, scraping browned bits stuck to bottom of pot with a wooden spoon. Season to taste with salt and pepper and bring to a simmer. Cover pot, reduce heat to medium-low, and gently simmer, turning braciole occasionally, until very tender, about 1 ½ hours for the veal or about 3 hours for the beef.

4. Transfer braciole to a cutting board; cut off and discard twine. Slice braciole crosswise and transfer to 4 warm plates. Spoon sauce on and around braciole and garnish with parsley and the remaining 4 sprigs basil.

Home of the Squealer

by Robb Walsh

from *The Houston Press*

As both restaurant reviewer and food reporter, Walsh has a penchant for the ethnic storefront, the corner diner, the taqueria, and the down-home roadhouse. Reading his articles is the next best thing to pulling up a chair beside him for dinner.

Bet you a beer the biker is going to get the Squealer. The guy with the Fu Manchu mustache and a blue bandanna on his head is sitting at a table near mine at a roadhouse called Tookie's. He's wearing a Harley-Davidson sweatshirt with the sleeves torn off to showcase his tattoos. His blond girlfriend keeps her sunglasses on as she props her chin up with her hand. Every detail of this man's meticulously selected accoutrements—from his transportation to his choice of companion—is working hard toward a fashion statement. That's why I'm betting he's not going to ruin the whole thing by ordering a fish fillet sandwich.

Tookie's Squealer is the hamburger that goes with this look. It exudes attitude. Instead of sporting a pile of bacon that's been fried separately and drained of its grease, this extreme bacon cheeseburger has bacon ground up *with* the beef. The thick, hand-formed, bacon-slick patty is fried crisp on the griddle, covered with cheese and served on a bun. The genius of this concept is that the bacon grease bastes the patty while it cooks. The result is a very salty, very greasy, crisp-edged burger that is exceptionally juicy, even when well done.

Tookie's is in Seabrook, a scenic half-hour drive down State Highway 146. All along the route, bayside refineries shimmer in the afternoon sun; the smokestacks stand as straight and tall as palm trees. The aroma of petroleum permeates the air in Pasadena and La Porte. As they say in these parts: "That's the smell of money." Here, in the toxic heart of the oil industry's urban jungle, you forget about alfalfa sprouts and textured tofu. Instead, you long to be a part of all that awe-inspiring machinery and industrial might—and Tookie's Squealer takes you there.

But if you were thinking that this must be the most artery-clogging, cholesterol-elevating, life-threatening hamburger ever devised, you would be wrong. After I got my Squealer, five people sat down at the table beside mine, and one of them ordered a double Squealer. This sent me back to the menu with a furrowed brow. And there I found it: Officially known as the Piggyback, this is the double-patty version of the Squealer; it takes the original's excess and squares it. When it was delivered, I admired the double-decker burger with some amazement. It seemed as tall as a cracking tower, and it was dripping grease down both sides. It's a good thing I didn't see it on the menu.

After a solid month of eating healthy, I was craving a wicked overdose of greasy meat—"moderation in all things, including moderation," as the saying goes. But I offset my cholesterol fix by ordering the Squealer "with everything," which includes a healthy portion of lettuce and tomatoes. I got the famous onion rings, too. And onion rings are a vegetable; ask any vegan.

There's a large painting of a sprightly, middle-aged woman in a purple dress behind the cash register. They tell me that this is Miss Tookie, the founder of the place. She used to come in early every morning to make the onion rings by hand. Frankly, I'm not all that impressed with the rings. They're kind of chewy, and the batter falls off too easily. But the people at the next table are really in a huff about them. Actually, it's not the rings they're making a scene about; it's the lack of ranch dressing.

"We don't serve salad, so we don't have any dressings," the waitress tries to explain, but the customers don't accept her excuse. Ranch dressing has nothing to do with salad in Texas. Several Texas chefs have told me they've been astonished by the rise in requests for ranch dressing in their restaurants in the last ten years. It's now used as a dip and a sauce more often than as a salad topping. (In West Texas, some restaurant patrons seem to regard it as a beverage.) I suspect it long ago surpassed ketchup *and* salsa as the No. 1 condiment in the state. For a major segment of the dining public, onion rings without ranch dressing are unthinkable—so are pizza, biscuits and canned peaches. They ask the waitress for it again every time she checks on them. "Why don't you go down to the convenience store and buy a bottle?" she finally chides.

The waitresses at Tookie's are no shrinking violets. This one wears dirty blue jeans, a green Tookie's T-shirt and sneakers. She got straight to the point when I asked her which burger she recommended. "The Champion burger is our biggest seller," she said. "The meat is marinated with Chablis wine and mixed with cheddar cheese and onions. The Squealer is made with bacon. Get the Squealer," she advised. The burger choices also include a bean burger, a barbecue burger and a chili cheeseburger, along with a pepper-infused burger called Stomp's Ice House Special, which carries the disclaimer "very hot."

I wonder if there really was a Stomp's Ice House around here somewhere, and what happened to it. If it once existed, odds are there's some memorabilia from the place hanging in the rafters at Tookie's. The ramshackle premises are decorated with loads of cast-off junk. From my table, I can see a pair of hockey skates, several old traffic signals, a Shell station sign and the feet of a mannequin wearing white high heels and red stockings.

As I get up to leave, the biker's burger is delivered. It's a double Squealer. I'm only half right. So you can buy me half a beer.

My second visit to Tookie's is at night. I'm expecting a Hell's Angels convention, but oddly the place has been transformed into a family hangout. Small children scamper back and forth between their parents' tables and the bathrooms. Moony high school kids on dates occupy several other tables.

I consider the double Squealer for a minute, but then decide to sample another extreme and order the "very hot" burger. The young waitress has trouble discerning the difference between Miller and Miller Lite, but several minutes of remedial menu-reading finally gets me a cold draft in an icy mug. This frosted fire extinguisher proves crucial to the enjoyment of the food.

According to the menu, the Stomp's Ice House Special features "beef topped with Pace picante sauce, chopped jalapeño peppers and chopped grilled onions with mayonnaise, lettuce and sliced tomatoes." All of those ingredients are indeed present when the burger arrives. But how many of them will make it into your mouth is something of a crapshoot. A sloppy avalanche slides off the sandwich and onto the plate every time you take a bite. They give you a fork, if you want to eat the excess hot sauce and jalapeños that way.

The heat level isn't excessive for the average Texan. But the jalapeños do add a little fire, and beer is necessary for keeping occasional flare-ups from getting out of hand. But all in all the hot sauce burger isn't nearly as exciting as the Squealer.

It's the ratio of wet stuff to ground meat on this bun that leads me to ponder the logic of Tookie's burger creations. Clearly, what they're doing is coming up with ways to keep well-done hamburger meat tasting moist. And for that they deserve our undying gratitude. Ever since the Jack in the Box hamburger scandal of 1993 and the subsequent changes in FDA cooking temperatures, the liability department of the food service industry has insisted that we eat our ground meat well done. For those of us who like it juicy and medium-rare, this change in the American institution of the hamburger has led to a lot of disappointment.

I have always attempted to get around the rules by cooking my own rare burgers at home or begging some patty flipper to take a walk on the wild side. But Tookie's has come up with several innovative ways to raise the moisture level of the sandwich while working within the confines of the new restaurant reality: mixing the ground meat with bacon, marinating the beef with wine and then combining it with cheese, topping the patty with lubricants like beans or hot sauce.

We've come to expect this kind of clever culinary engineering down here in the land of a thousand refineries. After all, this is where used oil pipe was first transformed into that icon of Texas barbecue, the double-chambered steel smoker pit on wheels. So when the modern-day burger is hampered by a soluble grease diffusion problem, it should come as no surprise that Texas oil field ingenuity shines through once again. In Tookie's Squealer, they've got a gusher.

The Hungry Traveler

by Lydia Itoi

from *The San Jose Mercury News*

Writing for a sophisticated Silicon Valley readership, Itoi kicks local food writing up a notch. Raised Japanese-American in the Deep South, now married to an Italian, she approaches culinary subjects with a culture-bridging outsider's whimsical wit and sense of the absurd.

E veryone eats while traveling. But there are those who will travel, sometimes many, many miles out of their way, in order to eat. For the hungry traveler, sightseeing is what happens on the way to the next fabulous meal. Some people book plane tickets and hotels first, then place themselves at the mercy of a poorly tipped concierge for dinner. The hungry traveler might leave hotels and other trivia to the last moment, but critical restaurants are always researched and booked months in advance.

You hungry travelers know who you are. You're the one jumping out of the ticket line to scan one more menu, the one interrogating every local you meet about their favorite restaurant, peeking into their grocery carts to guess what unseen delights they're having at home. For you, eating *is* the adventure.

Hungry travelers, in hot pursuit of an interesting meal, often find themselves in unusual situations that would discourage all but the most determined gastronomic tourist. Hunger is one reason

—perhaps the only sane one—to make a trip to Sylt in the dead of winter. In the summer, this slender wisp of an island suspended off the northwestern coast of Germany at the Danish border is a tony beach resort, often called "The St. Tropez of the North" by sun-starved Germans. In winter, it is a bleak land of outer darkness, blasted by wild North Sea storms.

I was in Hamburg visiting Rudi Bubert, older brother of Dittmer, my esteemed German butcher in Mountain View, when I heard about *Biikebrennen*, a bonfire festival held on Sylt every February 21. The festival is of ancient origin, and each village tries to outdo the others in building the biggest bonfire. The idea is to burn a hole through winter, bring luck and fertility, and send warm greetings to lonely sailors out at sea. The highlight of the feast is *grünkohl*, a North German specialty of frost-kissed kale with pork and sausages. Dittmer will tell you that I like a good sausage, and Germans are so crazy about frostbitten kale that they organize field trips to gather it, hanging shot glasses around their necks to keep up their strength. Next thing I knew, I was breaking every speed record on the Autobahn and streaking north in my rented BMW, trying to make it to Niebüll in time to catch the car train to Sylt.

Hamburg is 3 hours from Sylt by train. I'm not sure how long it would take by car if you aren't willing to exceed 110 mph in the rain. But even in the best weather, Sylt is remote. There is a small airport in Westerland, the well-heeled main town on the island, but the car train is the only way to reach it by land. I somehow managed to maneuver the car onto the roof of the double-decker transport, and in a few minutes we were bumping and swaying out into the North Sea on a waterlogged ribbon of land barely wide enough for a single track.

Despite freezing wind strong enough to lift the thatch right off the quaint village cottages, the entire island was packed for the festival, and there was not a room to be had. We would have to leave on the last car train at 7:30 p.m., too early for the bonfires. Never mind, I told my hungry companion. We still had time to eat.

Grünkohl was on just about every menu, so eventually we sheltered in the cheerful, cozy bistro in the Hotel Stadt Hamburg in Westerland. Exposing the kale to frost, it turns out, turns the starches to sugar. The *grünkohl* was mellow without a trace of bitter green. I realized that in the context of surviving a north German winter, a big platter of *grünkohl* with *Pinkelwurst* sausages and smoked pork chops, washed down with stiff shots of icy *Lütten Klaren* (rye whiskey), is health food. Not so the overcooked, gluey seafood pasta with sodden Provencal vegetables and tomato pesto. The lesson here is that clinging to Californian eating habits abroad can be dangerous, if not deadly.

By the time we rolled up to the car train platform, it was sheeting rain. We consoled ourselves that we had sampled *grünkohl* and the wild beauty of Sylt, and that there wouldn't be any bonfires to miss. We braced ourselves for the bone-rattling, 45-minute return journey to the mainland. At that moment, the miracle happened. As the train slowly pulled away from the island, one by one the fires sprang into view, the high flames leaping through the darkness. We moved over the water like a ship leaving a friendly port, and the flickering lights on the shore wished us goodbye and godspeed.

Something Very Special

by Anthony Bourdain
from *A Cook's Tour*

Riding on the coattails of his best-selling restaurant exposé *Kitchen Confidential*, Bourdain's new book doubled as a Food Channel travelogue series—but the reigning Bad Boy of the Kitchen put a gonzo spin on things at every turn.

I had come to Risani to find *meshwi*, the whole roasted lamb so integral to my delusions of desert adventure. It had been arranged in advance over the phone with a group of Tuaregs who guided people around the Merzouga dunes as a business concern. But after a conversation on his battered cell phone, Abdul was telling me that the next night's dinner in the desert would be 'something very special.' I knew what that meant: The bastards were planning a big meal of couscous, brochette, and tagine. I was furious. I had not come all this way to eat couscous again. I could eat that in the lobby with the Japanese and German tourists. I'd come for whole roasted lamb, Berber-style, tearing at fat and testicles with my bare hands around a bonfire with the Blue Dudes, the whole beast, crispy and delicious, laid out in front of me. 'But, but . . .' I stammered, 'I wanted *meshwi*! I was getting *meshwi*!' Abdul shook his head, whipped out his cell phone, made a call, and spoke for a few minutes in Arabic. 'They don't have whole lamb,' said Abdul. 'If you want, we must bring ourselfs.'

'Fine,' I barked, irritated. 'Call them back. Tell them tomorrow morning we'll go to the market, buy a whole lamb, dressed and cleaned, and anything else they'll need. We'll throw it in the back of the car and take it on out. All they've gotta do is the voodoo that they do—cook the damn thing.' The plan was to get up early, swing by the market, buy lamb and supplies, load it all into the back of a hired Land Rover and rush out to the desert before the food began to rot.

Abdul looked dubious.

The next morning, we arrived as planned. The ground meat, vegetables and dry ingredients were no problem. The lamb, however, was proving to be difficult. At a butcher counter down an alleyway to the rear of a flyblown souk, a gold-toothed butcher considered our request and opened his ancient nonfunctioning stand-up fifties-era Frigidaire, revealing one hapless-looking leg of lamb, cut rudely through the hip and leeching blood.

'He has only the leg,' said Abdul.

'I see that,' I said irritably. 'Tell him I want the whole thing. What do I have to do to get the whole thing?'

'It is bad day,' said Abdul. 'The sheeps, they come to the market Monday. Today is Wednesday. No lamb comes today.'

'Ask him . . . maybe he's got a friend,' I suggested. 'Tell him I'll pay. I'm not looking for a bargain here. I need a whole fucking lamb. Legs, body, neck, and balls. The whole animal.'

Abdul embarked on a long and contentious new tack—one that was of clear interest to the butcher, who raised an eyebrow. I imagine Abdul was saying something like 'You see this stupid American next to me? He has no sense at all! He'll pay a lot of money for his whole lamb. It'll be worth both our whiles, my friend, if you can hook us up.'

The conversation became more animated, with multiple rounds of negotiation. Others joined us, materializing from dusty, trash-strewn alleyways, getting involved in the discussion, offering suggestions and strategies—as well as debating, it appeared, their respective cuts of the action. 'He say one hundred dollars,' said Abdul, uncertain that I'd go for such a figure.

'Done,' I replied without hesitation. Not too terribly far from New York prices, and how often would I get to eat fresh whole lamb in the Sahara?

The butcher abandoned his stall and led us down the sun-streaked streets, deep into a maze of buildings that seemed to go on forever. People came to upstairs windows to look at the strange procession of Americans, Moroccans, and TV cameras below. Children and dogs joined us as we walked, kicking up dust, begging and barking. I looked to my left and noticed a smiling man holding a large, menacing knife. He grinned, gave me the thumbs-up sign. I was beginning to get an idea of what it means when you say you want fresh lamb in Risani.

We arrived at a low-ceilinged manger, surrounded by worried- and unkempt-looking sheep. Our party had shrunk to four people and a TV crew. The butcher, an assistant, Abdul, and I crowded into a tiny mud and straw structure, sheep jostling us as they tried to look inconspicuous. A particularly plump beast was grabbed by the scruff of the neck. Abdul pinched his thigh and then rib sections; a new round of argument and negotiation began. Finally, consensus, and the poor animal was dragged, protesting, out into the sunny street. Another man was waiting for us with a bucket of water and a length of rope. I watched queasily as the intended victim was brusquely pointed toward Mecca. The man with the knife leaned over and without ceremony quickly cut the sheep's throat.

It was a deep, fast, and efficient movement. Were I, for one of many good reasons, condemned to die in the same fashion, I doubt I could have found a more capable executioner. The animal fell on its side, blood gurgling into the alley. There had been no cries of pain. I could readily see the animal's open windpipe; the head appeared to have been damn near cut off. But it continued to breathe, to twitch. While the executioner chatted with his cohorts, he held his victim down with a foot on its head.

I watched the poor sheep's eyes—a look I'd see again and again in the dying—as the animal registered its imminent death, that terrible unforgettable second when, either from exhaustion or disgust, it seemed to decide finally to give up and die. It was a haunting look, a look that says, You were—all of you—a terrible disappointment. The eyes closed slowly, as if the animal were going to sleep, almost willfully.

I had my fresh lamb.

My new pals strung up the body by the ankles, letting the blood drain into a pail. They cut the woolly pelt at one ankle and the butcher pressed his mouth to the opening and blew, inflating the skin away from the meat and muscle. A few more quick cuts and the skin was peeled off like a dancer's leotard. Stray dogs looked on from the rooftops as blood continued to drip, more slowly now. The assistant poured water constantly as the carcass was worked over, the entrails removed and sorted. The head was removed, heart put aside for the butcher, intestines and *crépine* (stomach-membrane) saved for merguez and sausage. Soon, the sheep looked comfortably enough like meat, save for two mango-sized testicles that hung upside down from the inverted carcass in distinctly separate blue-veined scrota. The butcher winked at me—indicating, I gathered, that this part was indeed very good and should be protected during the long ride out to our camp in the dunes—and made two slashes in the animal's belly, tucking a testicle in each.

There was more washing, a fidgety moment during the de rigueur postmortem enema, and then more washing. They were fast. The whole procedure, from 'Baa-baa' to meat, took maybe twenty minutes. I walked back to our Land Rover, retracing my steps with my new buddies in tow. With my hundred-dollar bill in the butcher's pocket, and the eerily bonding experience we'd just shared, they seemed to like me a lot more. The carcass was wrapped in a clear plastic tarpaulin, like a dead wise guy. I got a strangely pleasurable thrill hearing the thump as the body's dead weight flopped into the back of the Rover.

We filled in a few holes in our *mise-en-place* at the souk, gassed up, and headed for the Merzouga dunes. I was looking forward to seeing clean white sand, free of the smells of sheep and fear, far from the sounds of dying animals.

For a while it was more hard-packed lunarscape, until suddenly I felt the tires sink into softer ground, and soon it was sand, sand, and more sand, the vehicle gliding through the frosting of a giant cake. On the horizon were the mammoth red peaks and dips of the Merzouga dunes—the real Sahara of my *Boys' Own* adventure fantasies. I felt exhilarated and relieved, considering, for the first time in a while, the possibility of happiness.

A small sandstone hut with blue-clad Berbers sitting on couches awaited us. A camel train had been assembled nearby, the big animals kneeling and ready. We mounted up and set out across the dunes, single file, a lone Tuareg in head-to-toe blue leading on foot, another to the rear. Global Alan rode on the lead camel, just ahead of me, Abdul, still in his orange-and-green tweed jacket, behind me. Matt and the assistant producer rode farther back.

Riding a camel, particularly if you're comfortable on horse-back, is not hard. I was real comfortable, cradled behind the animal's hump on a thick layer of blankets, my beast gently lurching forward. My legs rested in front of me. It was a long ride and I had—in an unusually lucid moment—made proper prior preparations: briefs instead of boxers.

Global Alan, however, had not chosen his undergarments with comfort and security in mind. Already in the awkward position of having to ride half-turned with a camera pointed back at me—for those all-important Tony of the Desert shots—he was not having an easy time of it. Whenever his camel would descend at a steep angle into the deep hollows between dunes, I could hear him grunting and whimpering with pain as his balls were pinched by the saddle. Alan hated Morocco. He'd hated it before we'd arrived, having been there before on assignment. Whenever I'd complained—in France or Spain or Portugal—about crummy bathrooms, uncomfortable rooms, rude waiters, or cold climate, Alan had just smiled, shaken his head, and said, 'Wait till Morocco. You're gonna hate it. Just wait. Buncha guys who look like Saddam Hussein, sitting around holding hands. Drinking tea. You're gonna hate it. Just wait.'

In fact, I was really beginning to enjoy myself. This was exactly the sort of scenario I'd envisioned when I'd dreamed up this scheme. *This* was what I was here for! To ride across desert sands with blue-clad Berbers, to sleep under the stars, surrounded by nothing, to eat lamb testicles in the middle of nowhere. Not to sit stiffly at a dinner table like a pinned moth, yapping at the camera.

After a few hours, we made camp at the foot of a huge dune. The sun was setting and long shadows appeared, growing in the hollows and swells of sand as far as the eye could see. The Blue Men got busy working on a late snack, something to keep us going until we hit the main encampment, where we'd spend the night. One of them built a fire out of a few sticks of wood and dried grass. While the flames burned down to coals and tea was made, the other Berber made bread dough in a small bowl, mixing and working it by hand. He covered it for a while, allowing it to rise under a cloth, then wrapped it around a filling of meat, onion, garlic, cumin, and herbs. Judging the fire to be ready, he brushed aside the coals, dug into the hot sand beneath, and dropped the fat disk of meat directly into the hole, covering it back up immediately. Time to wait, said Abdul.

Warm enough for the moment to remove shoes and socks, to strip down to a single layer of shirt, I climbed the big dune, dragging my tired, wheezing, and hideously out-of-shape carcass up the most gradual incline I could see, feeling every cigarette and mouthful of food I'd had in the last six months. It took me a long time. I had to rest every fifty yards or so, gasping, trying to summon the strength for the next fifty. I picked my way slowly along the soft but dramatic edge of a sharply defined ridge, then fell onto my back at the highest point. Rising after a few moments onto my elbows, I looked, for the first—and probably last—time in my life, at something I'd never seriously imagined I'd cast eyes upon: a hundred miles of sand in every direction, a hundred miles of absolutely gorgeous, unspoiled nothingness. I wiggled my bare toes in the sand and lay there for a long time, watching the sun drop slowly into the dunes like a deflating beach ball, the color of the desert quickly transforming from red to gold to yellow ocher to white, the sky changing, too. I was wondering how a miserable, manic-depressive, overage, undeserving hustler like myself—a utility chef from New York City with no particular distinction to be found in his long and egregiously checkered career—on the strength of one inexplicably large score, could find himself here, seeing this, living the dream.

I am the luckiest son of a bitch in the world, I thought, contentedly staring out at all that silence and stillness, feeling, for the first time in awhile, able to relax, to draw a breath unencumbered by scheming and calculating and worrying. I was happy just sitting there enjoying all that harsh and beautiful space out there. I felt comfortable in my skin, reassured that the world was indeed a big and marvelous place.

I was eventually disturbed from my maharishi-style meditations by the familiar sound of bread being scraped. I took that to mean my snack was ready, so I loped down the dune and returned to camp, to find my Tuareg buddies brushing the last grains of sand off a fat cooked loaf of meat-filled bread. Not a grain of sand or grit remained when one cut me off a thick wedge, a waft of spicy aromatic vapor escaping from inside. We crowded around a small blanket, eating and drinking tea as the sun finally disappeared completely, leaving us in blackness.

The camels picked their way across the desert in the pitch-dark, moving slowly up and down the steep rises and dips. At one point, I could see the dark shape of poor Global Alan, asleep on his camel, nodding off, then nearly falling off his animal. He woke with a start and a cry, frightening the whole formation. We traveled for about two more hours in near-total absence of light, the only discernible sight the off-black surface of the sand sea. Then I began to glimpse a few winking lights in the distance. As the camels trudged on, the lights grew larger. I could make out a bonfire, sparks rising from the flames, the outlines of what looked to be tents, moving bodies. There was the sound of drums, and singing or chanting in a language I'd never heard. The spectral apparition disappeared as our camels descended into another hollow, where I could see nothing, the only sound—once again—the breathing and snorting of our camels. After a long, tedious climb over a last rise, suddenly we were there.

A vast floor of ornate carpets stretched out for fifty or sixty yards, surrounded by tents. A covered table, fabric-wrapped stools, and pillows waited under an open canopy. A mud and straw oven, like a giant cistern, or the muzzle end of a sixteenth-century cannon, glowed to the left, away from the tents. Musicians beat drums and sang by a huge pile of burning logs, everyone dressed in the same blue or black head-to-toe robes of our escorts. And wonder of wonders: A full bar, nearly ten yards long, stocked with iced bins of beer and a row of liquor bottles, shone under a string of electric bulbs next to a humming generator.

It was a good old time: the Blue Men whacking drums with hands stained blue from the vegetable dyes they use on their clothes, singing and dancing by the fire, a capable and friendly French-speaking bartender in full headdress. In no time, I was fully in the spirit of things, banging on the drums with my blue pals, rolling a fat blunt, watching as one of the tribe rubbed my whole lamb with onion, pepper, and salt, then wired it to a long pole. Assisted by two others, they hoisted my dinner onto their shoulders and walked to the smoldering, volcanolike mud oven.

'See?' said Abdul, nursing a Heineken in one hand while sticking the other hand into the glowing opening atop the oven. 'Something very special. Very hot.' The Tuaregs leaned down to the base of the oven, to another, smaller opening, and removed with a stick every

ember of coal and stick of burning wood. Then they quickly sealed
the opening with fresh, wet mud. My *meshwi* went in the top,
straight down, securely held to the pole by wire, placed vertically
into the wide, still-nuclear-hot oven, a round meat lid placed on
top. The lid was sealed in place with more mud, the Tuaregs carefully examining the oven from every angle to see that it was completely sealed, pausing now and again to patch or reinforce any
holes or weak spots, any flaw that might allow all that residual heat
to escape. Abdul and I retired to the bar.

We were brought water and soap on a silver tray, as in Moulay
Idriss, washed our hands, and were soon being fed with the usual
array of tasty olives, salads, and bread. A thicker, lambier version of
harira soup arrived in a tureen, very welcome on what was
becoming an extremely cold night. Abdul had loosened up considerably after many beers, entertaining us with a high-spirited
round of joke telling—most of which, sadly, led me to believe that
jokes about Jews are very big in Morocco. I found that Polish and
hillbilly jokes work just as well in the desert, if you substitute
Libyans. Finally, after about an hour and a half of eating and
drinking, the *meshwi* arrived, stretched out on a long, flat board, a
Blue Man with a long and sharp-looking dagger right behind. Still
sizzling-hot, the lamb had been roasted crispy and straight
through—far more cooked than I would have done in the world
of knives and forks. The skin was black in places, the rib bones
poking through shrunken muscle. It did, however, smell amazing,
and I found that well done, while almost never my preferred temperature, although, unfortunately, the chosen level of doneness for
most of the unrefrigerated world, was in this case absolutely necessary to the kind of hacking, tearing, peeling, clawing, and
sucking the meal required. There were no steak knives, after all, to
be cutting tidy pink loin chops off the lamb.

The chef broke the lamb into primal sections, then broke those
down into smaller pieces, small enough to wield with a fist. I
invited the chef and my new Tuareg buddies to join me at the

table, and after a few *bismillahs*, everyone was poised to dig in. The chef made a quick motion with his dagger and lifted free a dismayingly large testicle from the lamb's crotch. With some ceremony, and a few appreciative smiles from around the table, he deposited the crispy, veiny object in front of me, then sat down and helped himself to a thick slab off the other nut. Abdul contented himself with ripping steaming-hot chunks of shoulder and leg with his fingers while I, God help me, tore off a sizable piece of gonad and popped it in my mouth.

It was sensational. Tender, even fluffy, with a subtle lamb flavor less intense than shoulder or leg; the whole experience, the chewing and swallowing, was reminiscent of sweetbreads. It was certainly the best testicle I'd ever had in my mouth. Also the first, I should hasten to say. I enjoyed every bite. It was delicious. Delightful. I'd do it again in a hot second. If I served it to you at a restaurant, as long as you didn't know what it was, if I called it, say, '*Pavé d'agneau maroc*,' you'd love it. You'd come back for more. I felt proud of myself. I'll try almost anything once, but I often feel let down when I fail to enjoy myself as much as I'd hoped. Telling people about the cobra bile you drank when you were in Vietnam makes a great story, but it's dismaying when the experience was just as unpleasant as it sounds. Sheep's balls, however, are great. I would recommend them unhesitatingly and without reservation.

Abdul, the crew, the Blue Men, and I made short work of the lamb, getting serious with our hands, until the thing was only well-picked-over fragments, looking like an autopsied burn victim. When the fire began to die down, as the musicians, servers, and camel drivers melted away to their tents, I was left with Global Alan and Matthew, and a big hunk of hash—and that classic emergency smoking device of sixties legend: the toilet paper roll and tin foil pipe.

As it was near freezing now, we wrapped ourselves in heavy camel blankets and staggered aimlessly into the desert, heading in the general direction of a waxing moon. With the blankets covering us from heads to shins, we looked like lepers, stumbling on uncertain feet into the dark. When we finally agreed on the right distance and the right dune—still reasonably certain we could find our way back to camp—we sat down on the cold sand and smoked ourselves into a state that once, many years ago, might have been mistaken for enlightenment, our coughs and giggles swallowed up by the dunes. I lifted the description 'a bewildering array of stars' once from a far better writer—I can't remember who now, only that I stole it—and that expression came to mind as I stared up at an awe-inspiring sky over the Sahara, the bright, penetrating lights, the quick drop of comets, a cold moon, which made the rippling patterns of sand look like a frozen sea. The universe was large all right, but no larger, it appeared, than the whole wide world ahead of me.

Personal Tastes

The Joy Of Cooking

by Lucian K. Truscott IV

from *Saveur*

> Every cook, every eater, remembers certain pivotal people or periods in their lives that defined their sense of taste. This is novelist/screenwriter Lucian Truscott's personal culinary biography.

I started cooking 31 years ago. It was 1971, and I was living on a retired Pennsylvania Railroad barge that had been used for nearly a century to ship bags of coffee beans and flour up the Hudson River. The barge was parked at the end of a deteriorated dock on River Road, on the New Jersey side of the Hudson, across from the 79th Street Boat Basin in Manhattan. An out-of-work actor friend and I had bought the barge for $500 and divided it into two huge lofts, each with its own kitchen and bathroom. I don't want to make it sound more elegant than it was: the place was heated by a potbellied stove, a couple of vicious nor'easters revealed numerous leaks in the roof, and the pipes froze for 22 days that winter. But you could stand at the stove in the brick-floored kitchen and look out the big French windows I had built and see the entire west side of Manhattan—and, on a clear day, all the way down to the Statue of Liberty.

I spent many hours at the stove that year because I had made the startling discovery upon moving to New York and going to work at the *Village Voice* that you couldn't eat out at restaurants very often on $80 a week. David Vaught, a friend from college, was rooming with me on the barge while he went to law school at NYU, and he had even less money than I did. Hamburger Helper had just hit the markets and was being heavily promoted on TV, so one day Vaught and I drove down the Palisades to the Pathmark in Jersey City, bought a box and some ground round, and mixed up a batch. It was so awful that we immediately decided we would have to learn to cook. The next afternoon, I went to Brentano's and shelled out $1.75 for a paperback French cookbook, which I have sadly lost and the title of which I cannot remember. But I do recall our experiments in the kitchen that year.

Unlike Vaught, I wasn't a complete kitchen novice. But while I'd been raised to appreciate good food, I was far more comfortable wielding a fork than a skillet. Given the circumstances, the two of us agreed to work our way through the book recipe by recipe, pledging we would cook each dish until we got it right. We spent a month and a half on chicken, and I'll never forget the week we had duck with peas seven nights in a row. We didn't finish the meat section, however; we stopped when we hit pork chops piquant, a dish of sautéed chops smothered in onions and sliced pickles and finished with a little dijon mustard and red wine vinegar. It was so extraordinary that we had it at least twice a week for the rest of the year—and recently Vaught's daughter, a graduate student in New York, called him for the recipe so that she could make it for her new boyfriend.

There were line drawings of village streets and stone barns and boulangeries scattered throughout our cookbook, and it included a short history of French cooking, the main point of which seemed to be that a lack of refrigeration in the provinces encouraged a heavy hand with spices and strong flavorings to obscure the musky sourness of slightly spoiled meat. So that's what made everything taste so good!

But the book did more than just provide me with recipes.

While something bubbled away on the stove, I would often gaze at the drawings and imagine the food-centered life of the French: shopping for fresh bread every day, visiting the cheese store, buying farm butter and live chickens at the market.

After two icy winters I moved off the barge into a 2,500-square-foot loft on Houston Street in the largely Italian south Village and was able to shop daily myself. I'd tuck a net bag in my back pocket every morning, and on my way home from the *Voice* on University Place, I'd stop at Florence Prime Meat Market on Jones Street and Zito's bakery on Bleecker, pick up lettuce and onions at the greengrocer on Sixth Avenue, and buy fresh mozzarella at Joe's Dairy on Sullivan Street, which was directly across from my home.

The guys at the meat market taught me how to bone game hens, chickens, and legs of lamb, and I fell in love with their popular Newport steaks, softball-size cuts from the bottom butt. I liked to sear the steaks in a skillet, finish them in the oven, and serve them with a snappy tarragon mustard butter. (Old habits die hard: since moving to California in 1992, I've had the shop ship me a box of Newports, which I've never seen anywhere else, once or twice a year.) There were also two fish stores in the neighborhood, and they waged a stiff competition for business. Whole bluefish ran about 15 cents a pound, and softshell crabs were a quarter each. I boycotted both stores when they simultaneously raised the price of the latter to 75 cents, but after a long crabless year, I went crawling back.

I was surrounded by wonderful restaurants in the south Village, too. In the early evening I used to wander around the corner to Rocco on Thompson Street and hang out in the kitchen, where I learned their recipe for roasted bluefish and how to whip up a simple yet impressive zabaglione. Raoul's opened on Prince just after I moved to Houston, and a few years later Thomas Keller was stunning taste buds at Rakel down the street on Varick. I also acquired more cookbooks—*The New York Times Cookbook* was a favorite, as was *The New Orleans Cookbook,* a gift from a former classmate from that food-mad town—and quickly became a fan of Pierre Franey's new 60-Minute Gourmet column, which ran on Wednesdays in the *Times.*

I imagined that I was living like the people described in the cookbook, a life where the acquisition and preparation of food was rich and interesting, not a chore. And I was.

At some point early on I discovered that cooking was far more than the process by which one got fed. For me, the gentle prodding of a recipe and the skills it demanded were like the discipline of my other lifelong passion—fishing for trout in a difficult stream—and just as rewarding. But not only did I love to cook; I even liked doing the dishes. While watching people rush about on the busy streets below my loft, I'd scrub plates and pots in hot soapy water, carefully rinse each piece under the tap, then put them in my wooden dish rack. I felt so completely at peace that it got me thinking: What was going on, that I ended up making my home in the kitchen?

The routine of the kitchen explained it in part. Cooking and cleaning up every day felt good because it was something I could count on, during years when I could count on very, very little. And for me, I think, the physicality of cooking provided an outlet to a life that was lived largely in the mind. You can't cook without touching and feeling and smelling and looking for the crust or the sheen or the blackened edge that says something is just right. I loved it all. God, how I loved it!

I inherited a great deal of my love of the kitchen from my grandfather General Lucian K. Truscott Jr. When we were growing up, my brother, Frank, and I spent the summers with our grandparents in Washington, D.C., where my grandfather was a special adviser on intelligence to Eisenhower and then deputy director of the CIA. Our grandparents had a large vegetable garden, which Frank and I tended as part of our chores, and every night after work, my grandfather would put on a set of khakis and we'd go into the backyard with him to pick vegetables for our dinner. Grandpa was the cook in the family, and by the time I was 12, he had taught Frank and me to carve a turkey, a roast beef, a ham, and a leg of lamb. I can still recall my apron-clad grandfather serving platters of food to guests like Allen Dulles and Richard Helms. It must have been quite a sight to them, but to me, seeing my grandfather in an apron with greasy hands and a wide grin made perfect sense because he was so happy in the kitchen and everything he grew and cooked tasted so good.

That first year on the barge I inaugurated what became my customary "lonely, left behind, no place else to go" Thanksgiving dinner. I invited everyone I knew who would otherwise be sentenced to a table for one, including my friend Maurice, a grizzled old man who sold the *Voice* on the street. Maurice (I never knew his last name) wore a long overcoat even in the summer and appeared to be homeless, though I knew he had a place up on 26th Street that had been bequeathed to him by no less a personage than the screen and stage star Zero Mostel. Every Thanksgiving, Maurice was the last to arrive. Once he turned up with a grimy friend who really was homeless. Another time he brought a young Japanese tourist he had met that day. Then there was the year a smiling Maurice walked in with the folksinger Odetta on his arm.

The pair joined the typical gaggle of retired seamen, former card-carrying Communist party members, struggling writers, surly bartenders, part-time waitresses, and pretty girls with no money. Many of them had heard Maurice late at night in the Lion's Head—a legendary bar on Christopher Street—talking about the famous authors and actors and musicians he had known, but no one paid him much notice. I knew that at least some of his stories were true; nevertheless, even I marveled that he had pulled off showing up at my odd-lot, leftover Thanksgiving feast with Odetta.

I remember stirring a big pot of gravy that night and thinking to myself, *This* is why I've spent all those hours at the stove. This is why I bought all those cookbooks. This is why I used money I didn't really have on a big Le Creuset casserole and a set of Sabatier knives. It was a rather sappy epiphany, a perfect kitchen moment.

The Filicudi Effect

by Laura Fraser

from *Bon Appetit*

It's a chicken-and-egg situation: Does a happy event make food taste delicious, or does delicious food make the event happy? Laura Fraser's essay may not solve the conundrum, but it sweeps the reader along through her experience.

There's something about being in the Mediterranean, and particularly its islands, that reduces life to its simple essentials. There's the sun and the sea, the stars and the night, the terraced vineyards and the wooden fishing boats. Lying on a rocky beach, it's possible to imagine that the world hasn't changed that much since Odysseus sailed by

Mediterranean food, likewise, is simple—grown and cooked as it has been for centuries. The dishes are made with few ingredients, those that are hardy enough to survive on dry and craggy islands, like the capers that flourish everywhere in the cracks of old stone walls and the cherry tomatoes that seem oblivious to sea air and drought. The fish are plentiful in the clear, blue waters, and show up on plates in the most straightforward fashion—as swordfish skewers with lemon leaves, or scorpion fish grilled with olive oil. But the food, like the islands, has a hidden history, and an ancient alchemy of sensuality. Its simplicity lures you in to its deeper delights.

I was lured in when I came to Filicudi, one of the most remote of the Aeolian Islands. I was with a friend I had met two years before on another Italian island, Ischia. He had chosen Filicudi for our trip because—I realized too late—it was the island where there was absolutely nothing to do.

That is certainly not true of the other Aeolian Islands: On Stromboli there is an active volcano you can climb; Panarea has a flashy nightlife; Lipari has a castle and a spectacular archaeology museum; Vulcano has mud baths and volcano-warmed beaches; and Salina, where the movie *Il Postino* was filmed, is full of art galleries, churches, and vineyards that have been producing wine grapes since the Hellenistic period.

But on tiny Filicudi, where the introduction of electricity was a recent event and cars have yet to disturb the donkeys, there is little to attract tourists—which was precisely what appealed to my friend. The boat from Naples stopped at the other islands, and one by one, the honeymooners, backpackers and German photographers departed. We were left alone with the fishermen, the locals, and the man bringing the weekly post. As we approached the island, there was nothing to see but craggy rocks, a sprinkling of white houses, and an endless view of the sea.

On our first day on the island—we were staying for ten days—we had coffee, wandered down for a swim, ate lunch, and sat around the pebble beach again until sundown. The second day, we did the same thing, only in a different order. By the third day, I had become restless.

I walked along the beach, swam a bit, opened my book. Little by little, I was lulled into the rhythm of the waves and the slow-motion days. In the midst of stark nothingness, I began to watch the changes in the sky, the vegetation, and the clouds around the volcanoes in the distance. And I began really to taste—as I never had before—everything that I ate.

Against the lolling dullness of the days, the food became clear and sharp and exciting. The flavors were as moody as the weather, by turns bright and shadowy, as fragrant as the caper bushes after a rain.

It seemed that everywhere on this small island there was wonderful food. We'd hike up the trail from the beach to our little rented house and pluck ripe figs off a tree. If we wanted a picnic, we bought fresh ricotta, prosciutto, grapes, crusty bread and wine at the island's one store. And for dinner, we could choose from a surprising number of restaurants.

After two days, we had already settled on our favorites. There was Da Nino Sul Mare, a spot near the tiny port, with a deck overlooking the fishing boats. Its motto, *dove fermarsi diventa un piacere*—"where to stop and do nothing for a while becomes a pleasure"—summed up the Filicudi experience.

We were regulars by the time we arrived for our third meal. The waiter insisted that there was nothing, really, to eat that day but the stuffed *totani* (squid) caught that morning by Peppe, a fisherman now sitting at the bar. We tried the totani—stuffed with mint, garlic, capers, breadcrumbs and green olives and simmered in tomato sauce—and sent Peppe another of whatever he was drinking.

Then there was Villa la Rosa, a rose-colored stucco restaurant and pensione up on the hill. The pizza was extraordinary, with strong oregano and a thin but determined crust. And the pasta was unlike any I'd ever had. My friend preferred the *spaghetti alla filicudara,* with anchovies, capers, olives and rosemary. But my favorite was the *pasta con le sarde,* with fresh sardines, wild fennel and pine nuts. I asked the cook to show me how to make it. A little bemused—wasn't everyone born knowing how to make *pasta con le sarde?*—she gave me the recipe.

Our days, despite their languid pace, came shortly to an end. The late-summer season was over, there were storms in the afternoons, and all but a few restaurants were shuttering their windows. Over dinner at Villa la Rosa, I told my friend that I thought I could live on Filicudi forever.

"Just ten days ago, you couldn't stand to be here for even an afternoon; there was nothing to do," he reminded me.

I twirled some homemade *spaghetti allo scoglio*—with fresh shellfish and parsley—on my fork. That, I thought, was before my senses had been awakened, before I had the time to really stop and taste several centuries' worth of cookery. I had no desire to return to the city, to do anything but lie by the sea and anticipate my next meal.

The next time I saw my friend was in San Francisco, where I live. I surprised him with dinner. I'd found salted capers and made a salad with ripe cherry tomatoes. I went to great lengths to find fresh sardines and fennel to make pasta the way the cook in the rose-colored restaurant had showed me.

He ate the meal with pleasure, and gave me compliments. But I knew some ingredient was missing. "It's like a postcard," was all he could say.

He was right. The pasta may have had the same ingredients, but it could never taste like the pasta we ate on Filicudi. It was good—good enough to fool someone who had never been to the islands. But the water, air, sunlight and soil—even the history and the sense of time—were simply not the same.

For the truest, deepest flavor, the only thing you can really do is go back and do nothing for a while again.

On Board the Bombay Express

by Shoba Narayan
from the *New York Times*

Born in India but now based in New York, Narayan is an essayist with a gift for tracing the fine connections between cultures. Sensory details splendidly recreate the exotic setting of this memory piece.

The most important thing when traveling by train in India is not whether you have a seat in first class (more comfortable) or second class (more congenial), not whether you have confirmed tickets or even your destination. The most important thing is the size of your neighbor's tiffin carrier, the Indian lunchbox. If you are lucky, you will be seated near a generous Marwari matron whose way of making your acquaintance is to hand you a hot roti stuffed with potato saag.

I was 14 when this happened to me, and I still remember biting into the soft, ghee-stained roti bread and feeling the explosion of spices in my mouth as I encountered cumin, cilantro, ginger, green chilies, pungent onions and finally—like a sigh—a comfortingly soft potato. It was dawn. The train whistled mournfully as it click-clacked its way through the misty countryside. A cool breeze wafted through the open window and teased the curls behind my ear. Fragrant turmeric-yellow saag dribbled from the corner of my mouth. A perfect symphony for the senses.

It was 1981, and my family and I were taking the Bombay Express from Madras to Bombay (now officially called Chennai and Mumbai) for our annual summer vacation, a trip of about 30 hours. Across from me, my parents, still faint and groggy from the effort of packing and bundling us onto the train, were nodding off. Beside me, my 13-year-old pest of a brother was elbowing for the window seat, which I had no intention of relinquishing. I turned toward the Marwari matron hopefully. She smiled as she opened another container. In a trance, I went to her.

Marwaris are from the desert state of Rajasthan, and Marwari women are known to be fantastic cooks. They are also known to be generous to a fault, which makes them dream companions for a long train journey. Enterprising Gujaratis, on the other hand, were more businesslike, which meant that I had to ingratiate myself to gain access to their divine kadi (sweet-and-sour butter-milk soup). A boisterous Punjabi family was always good for card games interspersed with hearty rajma (spiced kidney beans). Intellectual Bengalis from Calcutta, now called Kolkata, were a challenge. I had to match wits with them before they would share their luscious rosogollas (sweet cheese balls) and sandesh (milk and sugar squares) with me. I didn't bother with the South Indians, being one myself.

It was this glorious home-cooked food that made the train journeys of my childhood memorable. My uncle in Bangalore was a few hours away by the Lal Bagh (Red Garden) Express; my grandparents were an overnight journey away on the Blue Mountain Express. We got on the train in the evening and later climbed into the sleeper berths. We woke up to the smiling faces of my grandparents, who met the train with flasks of hot coffee and crisp vadas (lentil doughnuts) fried right on the platform.

Unlike these short overnight journeys, the trip from Madras to Bombay was satisfyingly long. The train left Madras at dawn and reached Bombay the following morning. My brother and I had all day and all night in the train to stake out corners, play card games, make friends with the other children, run riot through the compartment, annoy ticket inspectors by singing to the rhythm of the train, and most important, partake of our neighbors' tiffin carriers.

The tiffin carrier is a simple, yet wonderful Indian invention. Several cylindrical stainless-steel containers are stacked and held together with a metal fastener that serves as a handle. Although the word tiffin means light food, the tiffin carrier can hold anything. The one I took daily to school had two containers—the bottom one for a hearty rice dish and the top one, a vegetable.

If my school lunchbox with its measly two containers was a Manhattan town house, the Marwari matron's tiffin carrier was the Empire State Building, with more than a dozen stainless-steel containers. She opened each container at a strategic point in our journey. At dawn, we had the roti and potato saag. At 10 a.m., a snack of crisp kakda wafers speckled with pepper. For lunch, a bounty of stuffed parathas (flatbreads filled with mashed potatoes, spinach, radishes, paneer-cheese and other such goodies).

My mother had brought lunch in a tiffin carrier, too—petal-soft idlis wrapped in banana leaves and slathered with coconut chutney. Idlis are steamed dumplings made from a rice and lentil batter that is allowed to ferment for a day. American idlis are hard and don't possess a tangy sourdough taste. To eat the authentic spongy idli in all its glory, you have to go to Madras and get invited to someone's home for breakfast.

My mother always made idlis for train travel because, among their other virtues, they keep well. The Marwari boys scooped hers up with gusto and wolfed them down with gentle, satisfied grunts.

As the sun climbed high in the sky, the train rolled into the arid plains of Andhra Pradesh. I began salivating for mangoes. The moment the train stopped at Renigunta Station, passengers jumped off on an urgent errand. My father and I disdained the train-side hawkers who carried baskets of high-priced, inferior mangoes, and sprinted toward the stalls on either side of the platform. About a dozen different types of mangoes were piled high:

custardy Mulgoas, robust sweet-sour Alphonsos, ultrajuicy Banganapallis, parrot-beaked Bangaloras, and finally, the Rasalu, the king of mangoes in terms of sweetness.

A few minutes of intense bargaining followed, fueled by the fact that the train would leave the station at any minute. Just as the whistle blew and the guard waved his green flag, my father and I jumped back on the train carrying armloads of juicy mangoes, which tasted even better for the adrenaline and tension that surrounded their purchase. My brother and I sat at the open door of the train as it rumbled slowly through the Deccan Plateau, slurping mangoes and waving at villagers. I threw the mango seeds into opportune clearings and imagined entire mango orchards rising behind me.

Almost every station in India sells a regional specialty that causes passengers to dart on and off of trains. My parents have awakened me at 3 a.m. just to taste the hot milk at Erode Station in Tamil Nadu. Anyone passing by Nagpur Station is entreated to buy its glorious oranges. Allahabad, home to Hinduism and the river Ganges, is famous for its guavas; Agra, where the Taj Mahal stands, has wonderful pedas (chewy squares of candy made with milk). Shimla, called queen of the hill stations by the British, was known for its apples. Kerala, where my father spent his childhood and still leaves his heart, has the best plantain fritters, fried in coconut oil on the platform.

As if the stations weren't distraction enough, a steady stream of vendors brought food onto the train. Our midafternoon card games were almost always interrupted by teenage boys in khaki shorts selling coffee. "Kapi, kapi, kapi," they would call, pausing to check out who had the best hand of cards. Frequently, the person with the best hand ordered a round of coffee for the group, inadvertently giving away his advantage.

If we were lucky enough to stop at Andhra Pradesh at dinnertime, my parents would buy us aromatic biriyanis. Andhra cooks make the best biriyanis in the world. They combine Basmati rice, succulent meats marinated in a yogurt-mint sauce with ginger, garlic, green chilies and a long list of ground roasted spices. These ingredients are slow-cooked in a vessel with a lid sealed on with dough so that the flavors don't escape. Being Brahmins and therefore vegetarians, my parents encouraged us to eat vegetable biriyanis. The only times I almost strayed are when I encountered the mouth-watering smell of lamb biriyanis on trains.

Having lived in the United States for 15 years, I made my most recent annual visit to India a few months ago. My father considerately booked us on the Shatabdi (Century) Express from Madras to Bangalore. My parents were thrilled to be showing off the Shatabdi Express. "It is just like your U.S. airplanes," my mother exclaimed. Indeed it was. Fully air-conditioned with reclining seats, this super-fast train is frequented by business people and foreigners. It leaves on time and doesn't make random stops. The sealed windows and air-conditioning keep away heat, dust and stray vendors. As soon as we got on, two plastic-gloved attendants gave us bottled water, newspapers and a hot breakfast served from a trolley. In a scant four hours, we had reached Bangalore.

Yes, the train was clean, punctual and efficient, an entirely new concept for India, which was why my parents loved it. But I didn't want convenient and efficient. Although I appreciated the air-conditioning, I wanted color, characters and memories. For that, I should have taken my daughter, who accompanied me to India this year, on the Bombay Express. Second class.

Pride and Prejudice

by Yvonne Durant

from *Gourmet*

> The cultural baggage attached to certain foods varies from region to region, gender to gender, race to race. A writer pretty much has to go first-person to explore this honestly, as veteran magazine writer Yvonne Durant does here.

Most people probably can't tell you where they were the first time they ate watermelon in public. I can.

I was 35 years old, in the south of France. I was living in Milan at the time, but I'd gone to Cannes for an advertising festival (one of the wonderful perks that came with my job). In between looking at hours of commercials from all over the world, I had some time to explore the beaches and sample the food at the many shorefront restaurants.

So there I am one sizzling afternoon, lunching with my friend Antonio. It is so hot you can hear the heat. The meal is going swimmingly until the waiter rattles off the dessert selections. I understand all but the last—*pastèque.* "It's that, over there," Antonio says, pointing. I follow his eyes, and there it is, juicy red and refreshing-looking—a great big slice of watermelon.

Suddenly I am ten years old, sitting in our old Brooklyn kitchen listening to a conversation between my mother and her cousin

Bobby. "June," he says, "You know why I don't eat watermelon? Because years ago, whenever summer rolled around, they'd find the darkest kid in town, give him a pair of new overalls and a big ole slice of watermelon, and tell him to bite into it and grin. They'd hang that poster everywhere."

My mother nods.

Negative images of happy, lip-smacking blacks eating generous portions of watermelon date back to the 19th century. You can still find old fruit-crate labels with pictures like that. There were even movies with titles like *The Pickaninnies and the Watermelons.*

Okay. I'm thinking too much. I'm annoyed. I want dessert. I want some watermelon. But first I have to dig through a few hundred years of ignorance—back to that first fool with a capacity to draw who saw a couple of slaves enjoying a piece of watermelon. It wasn't a crime; the fruit was plentiful and cheap. But it became something to ridicule, something that would keep the workers in their place by turning them into caricatures. He drew their lips huge and red. Splashed silly wide grins across their faces and made it so the whites of their eyes practically glowed in the dark. He gave the boys short, kinky hair; the girls, dozens of tiny braids. And he showed them all slurping up the luscious fruit and spitting out those seeds like it was nothing.

My taste buds are screaming, *"Waah-tee-mel-lon!"*—recalling the obbligato of the guys on the horse-drawn wagons that used to lumber though our Bedford-Stuyvesant neighborhood laden with watermelons. There would always be one sliced open so you could see its brilliant reds and deep pinks, its glistening jet-black seeds.

We used to eat a lot of watermelon. In fact, there was probably a piece on the table the day my cousin told us how he really felt about the fruit. But that was years ago. Right now I'm in the south of France, and all I want to do is order my dessert. It's not the watermelon that's the enemy, but the image that goes with it. If I eat it, will I be transformed from a well-dressed career woman with slicked back hair into—*quelle horreur!*—a grinning pickaninny?

I throw the politics of being black into my shopping cart, too. A fancy market in my Manhattan neighborhood offers two types of watermelon—classic red and contemporary yellow. I've bought the yellow kind several times: It takes the stigma off the black woman making her way through the aisles pushing an enormous wedge of watermelon. But I buy classic red at the big, affordable supermarket, where the environment is less pretentious and so am I.

Blacks aren't the only people who have watermelon moments. A white acquaintance confessed that he'd decided against serving watermelon at a dinner party because he was worried about insulting his one black guest. Another white friend remarked, "That's not very PC" when I ordered a watermelon Martini at a bar one night.

The waiter turns from Antonio to me. "And what can I get you, *mademoiselle?*"

I give the beach a once-over. I don't spot anybody I know. And everyone looks European. I assume the entire beach won't turn around pointing their fingers and laughing at me. "I'll take the watermelon, please."

There's no reaction from Antonio, from the waiter, from anybody on the beach. My fruit arrives, accompanied by a silver knife and fork. I smile at Antonio. He smiles back. And then, at the age of 35, I dig into my watermelon with the whole world looking on. And it tastes fantastic.

Include Me Out

by Fred Chappell
from *Gastronomica*

North Carolina's poet laureate, Fred Chappell, is a good example of *Gastronomica*'s quirky range of contributors—writers of all stripes who happen to have something new to say about food. Chappell's message may be downright heresy to many Southerners.

There are people who eat cold pasta salad. They enjoy despoiling their greenery with gummy, tasteless squiggles of tough, damp bread dough that are usually made palatable only when heavily disguised with hot tomato sauce and a stiff mask of Parmesan cheese. This salad does have the virtue of economy. Wednesday leftovers can be marketed to Thursday customers of perverse taste.

It is probably perversity also that accounts for the prevalence of ice tea in our American south. It was Edgar Allan Poe who first diagnosed this immitigable contrariness of human nature in his short story "The Imp of the Perverse," and he undoubtedly saw it as a normal trait of Dixie character. But please include me out. I am one southerner who detests that dirty water the color of oak-leaf tannin and its insipid banality. When I am offered ice tea by one of our charming southern hostesses I know I'm in for a long afternoon of hearing about Cousin Mary Alice's new babe and its genius antics in the playpen.

Hot tea makes sense. It can relax as well as stimulate and in fact may be sipped as a soporific. It can offer a bouquet pungent or delicate and causes us to understand why the Chinese designated certain strains of flowers as "tea roses." It can be a topic of conversation too, as southerners revive the traditional English debate as to whether the boiling water should be brought to the pot or the pot fetched to the water. Such palaver reassures us that all traces of civilization have not disappeared under the onslaughts of video games and e-mail.

But if you ice the stuff down it cannot matter in the least whether the water or the pot has journeyed. Any trace of the tea's bouquet is slaughtered and only additives can give this tarnished liquid any aroma at all. There is, of course, plenty of discussion about these added condiments. Even the mildest of southern ladies may bristle and lapse into demotic speech when they consider that a glass of ice tea has been improperly prepared.

Notice that we say "ice tea." Anyone who pronounces the successive dentals of "iced tea" is regarded as pretentious. And if you say "Coca-Cola" you will be seen as putting on airs, just as obviously as if you employed "you" as a collective pronoun. Down here we say "you-all," "CoCola," and "ice tea" and collect monetary fines from strangers who misspeak. Ignorance before the law is no excuse.

In recent years some enterprising women have seen the futility of the pot/water controversy and have begun making "sun tea," a beverage that is never acquainted with either stove or teapot. They simply fill a gallon jug with water, drop in a flock of tea bags, and set the collocation out on the back porch to brew in the broiling August sunshine. If this method does not make the kitchen more cheerful, it does at least lessen the hypocritical chatter about proper procedure. Ice cannot harm sun tea; it is created beyond the reach of harm or help.

Now as to the recipe for ice tea:

Lemons are essential and should be of the big thick-skinned variety, cut into sixths. They are never—repeat: *never*—squeezed but only plumped into the pitcher, four or five slices. Extra slices are offered on a cut-glass plate six inches in diameter. Mint may be added, but it is always submerged in the pitcher and never put into a glass where it would glue to the interior side like a Harley-Davidson decal.

And sweetening is the soul of this potation. The sugar bowl passes from hand to hand at a pace so dizzying it is like watching the rotating label on an old 78-rpm record. Southerners demand sweetness. The truly thoughtful hostess shall have already sweetened the tea for her guests with a simple sugar syrup that excludes the possibility of unpleasant graininess from bowl sugar. Sugar syrup for ice tea is concocted by adding one pound of Dixie Crystal sugar to a tablespoon of water.

In the south sweetened ice tea is taken for granted, like the idea that stock car racing is our national pastime and that the Southern Baptist church is a legitimate arm of the Republican Party. If you order ice tea in a restaurant it will arrive pre-sweetened. If you want it unsweetened you must ask for it. Actually, you must demand it with pistol drawn and cocked. And you will have to repeat your demand several times because tea unsweetened is as abstruse a proposition to most servers as a theorem of Boolean algebra. Even then you can't be sure. My wife Susan once ordered unsweetened but it arrived as sweet as honey. The waitress pleaded for understanding. "We couldn't figure how to get the sugar *out*," she said.

Why southerners are so sugar-fixated may be a mystery, but it is an indisputable fact. We are a breed who makes marmalades of zucchini, tomatoes, onions, and even watermelon rinds. Our famous pecan pie ("puhKAWN pah") is a stiff but sticky paste of boiled Karo corn syrup studded with nuts. Since this is not sweet enough, it will likely be served with a gob of bourbon whipped cream dusted with cocoa powder and decorated with vegetable-peeler curls of milk chocolate.

"Do you want ice tea with that?"

"Oh yes. Sweetened, please."

Well, I'll confess that, though born in North Carolina, I make a poor example of a southerner. I don't even capitalize the name of the region. I'm a Democrat, a non-Baptist, and don't care what kind of car I drive. To me, adding broiled marshmallows to yams is like putting raspberry jam on porterhouse. I once spotted a recipe in the magazine *Southern Living* for CoCola cake and had to fight down a surge of nausea. I flee as if pursued from fatback, spoon bread, barbecue, grits, and—ice tea.

Susan tells me I need sweetening.

In My Mother's Kitchen

by Christina Eng

from *The Oakland Tribune*

> "Literary nonfiction" is how writer Christina Eng defines her genre—novelistic in style, but determinedly wed to fact.

H ave you eaten yet?

My mother picks up the phone. It's a friend, a woman in Milpitas. Or a brother-in-law, calling from Philadelphia. She says hello and asks if they've had dinner. She starts the discussion this way. Have you eaten yet? The question is synonymous with "How are you?" or "How was your day?" With these words, she asks if they're well. Are their appetites healthy? She asks about their work. Have they had a chance to unwind? She asks about their lives. Are they satisfied?

When I call my mother, I ask her whether she's had dinner before jumping into the rest of my conversation. It's a habit I have no doubt learned from her. I want to make sure that I'm not inter-rupting her meal, that she's at a point in her evening when she can sit and talk. I use the question to gauge her mood. I show that I care without actually telling her so.

Have you eaten yet? It is shorthand for many other concerns, the way that food, I have also learned, is shorthand for things like love and affection, kindness and consideration.

The cabinets in my mother's kitchen are filled with cans of baby corn and bamboo shoots. They contain jars of preserved bean curd and dried black mushrooms. The drawers are crammed with bags of rice flour and rock sugar. Condiments and cooking oils cover the countertops.

In her refrigerator, my mother keeps bunches of leafy Chinese broccoli or fresh Napa cabbage, vegetables she'll cook later that evening. She stores leftovers in plastic containers—the steamed chicken she made last night, the watercress soup she made last week. She waits for us to visit, to help her finish the food, to take some with us when we leave. "Otherwise," she says, "everything will spoil."

The cabinets in my kitchen are stocked with cans of tuna and sliced olives. They're filled with jars of sun-dried tomatoes and artichoke hearts, things my mother never uses. The drawers contain packages of split peas and kidney beans.

In my refrigerator, I have Parmesan cheese and sour cream, jars of salsa and relish. I have five-pound bags of carrots and potatoes, items that will keep for weeks. I have lots of food but nothing I can really eat. To curb my hunger, I snack on chips or crackers. Fifteen minutes later, I pour myself a bowl of cereal for dinner.

My mother shops every day. She steps into fish, poultry and produce markets in Oakland Chinatown, a few blocks from her house, unfazed by the odd smells or narrow aisles in those small spaces. She picks up sea bass one afternoon, a whole chicken the next, checking off items on a mental list. Three or four stores later, she heads home, weighed down with plastic bags. The handles leave creases across her palms.

When she cooks, my mother watches several pots at a time—fish steams in one, soup simmers in a second, rice boils in a third. The wok sizzles over high heat; in a moment she'll stir-fry vegetables.

My mother cooks what my father craves, what she thinks we'll like. She cooks instinctively, without books. She knows the recipes by heart.

I shop every other week, when I've run out of milk or need a loaf of bread. I write down the things I want before heading to the supermarket 15 minutes from my house. I roam the wide aisles, pushing a clean cart, gathering packages of ground beef or frozen fish fillets. Half an hour later, I wheel my purchases to the car.

When I cook, I focus on one or two dishes—stew, for instance, or stroganoff. I can't multi-task like my mother; I get easily distracted. I cook what I crave, thinking mostly of myself. I consult recipes clipped or copied from magazines and books. I haven't memorized a thing. I follow carefully the directions in front of me; I don't trust my instincts. For my mother, cooking is a dynamic and eclectic art. For me, it is an imperfect science.

At the table in the center of my mother's kitchen, my brothers, sisters and I ate.

In the mornings, before my father got up at 10 for work, my mother cooked congee, or rice porridge, for us. Sometimes she made it with pork and pieces of preserved duck eggs. Other times she tossed in slivers of fish and chopped green onion. The steam rising from our bowls warmed our faces. With each spoonful, we steeled ourselves for the rest of the day.

"You could never concentrate in class," my mother said, "if your stomach wasn't full."

In the evenings, when my father was still at work, my mother served us dinner. In between bites of chicken steamed with Chinese sausage and mushroom or bean-thread noodles mixed with egg and barbecued pork, we told her about our friends and teachers, assignments and field trips.

Inevitably we started talking among ourselves—in English—about baseball or football, music or television. My mother didn't understand the phrases that came out of our mouths then.

"Jee jee, jah jah," she mimicked the chatter she heard. "What's there to talk about anyway?" she asked a few minutes later. "Stop talking," she said, picking up a piece of food with her chopsticks. "Stop talking. Finish eating."

As we got older, my brothers, sisters and I spent less time in the kitchen.

In high school, we left the house at a quarter past seven to catch a bus that took us across the city, away from Chinatown, into the Oakland hills. The ride lasted 45 minutes. We had to forsake our mother's congee for dry toast or Eggo, things we could eat quickly on our way to the bus stop.

When my older siblings were students at UC Berkeley, they lived at home but seldom made it home for dinner. They grabbed Blondie's pizza or Togo's sandwiches between classes. They began to rely on other people's cooking to get them through the day. The noise level at the table in the center of my mother's kitchen decreased.

Years later, when we'd long since moved out, my mother would tell me how much she missed having all of us together in one place to eat. We had lives of our own, she knew this, lives that went in different directions. Steven worked in Lafayette; Eric worked in Palo Alto. Linda had a job in San Francisco; Evelyn commuted to Santa Clara. We didn't have time to visit.

But my mother often insisted we go to dinner at her house anyway, telling us we wouldn't have to cook or clean or anything. She needed no special occasion.

Reunited in her kitchen, my brothers, sisters and I bumped elbows at the table. Had it gotten smaller when we weren't looking? In between spoonfuls of winter melon soup or braised pork spareribs, we yammered away. My mother told us about her morning walks around Lake Merritt and the conversations she had with women in Chinatown. My father, who had retired when we were in our mid to late teens, talked about things he read in the newspaper or saw on television. Through the commotion, we ate.

My first time away from home, at a college in New England, I longed for the foods my mother made. I'd convinced my parents months earlier to let me go to school across the country. I'd talked about adventure, growth and independence. Did I have any idea then what I would leave behind?

When I wasn't in class or at the library, I hung out in the dining halls with my friends. Over veal cutlets or baked ziti, we gossiped about the people we liked, laughed at the weird things we did and talked about the foods we craved.

I told them I hungered for my mother's Chinese cooking: egg-and-bacon fried rice, oxtail soup, preserved mustard greens stir-fried with diced salted pork. I could never get these dishes on campus, I said. And I'd searched in vain for restaurants in Providence that served them.

In the tiny kitchen of the place I shared senior year with my best friends, I tried to replicate a few of my mother's dishes. In a $10 skillet from Woolworth's, with a nonstick coating that began to peel after a couple of months, I stir-fried beef, carrots and broccoli. Although I followed a recipe clipped from a magazine, the meat and vegetables turned out tough, the seasonings bitter. I didn't know why.

No matter how often I tried or how many other entrees I attempted to make, the flavors would never be the same as the ones I remembered. My congee turned out soupy and bland, not hearty or comforting like my mother's. It did nothing to get me through an East Coast winter. My bean-thread noodles turned out sticky and plain. They clumped together in the pan. They disappointed me so.

I gave up eventually. If I craved home cooking, I told myself, I would just make rice. I'd learned to do that perfectly on my own. I would eat white rice with Salisbury steak and gravy. I would have rice with Snow's clam chowder or Campbell's cream of mushroom soup. I would improvise.

Over time I integrated into my repertoire things like meatloaf and lasagna, quiche and jambalaya, foods my mother never cooked, foods for which I had no prior comparisons. Three thousand miles away, I longed for a taste of home. I wanted soy sauce chicken, fish steamed with ginger and green onion, and braised stuffed bean curd. I had to settle for something else.

Returning to the Bay Area several years later, I asked my mother, now in her 50s, to teach me how to cook Chinese; in other words, to teach me how to make for myself the foods that are hers. I wanted to learn each and every dish she knew. I was determined to get specific directions for all of them.

Early one evening, when she was making pork with aubergine, or Chinese eggplant, I slipped into the kitchen to watch, to take notes, to pick up whatever I could. It was one of my favorites; my mother knew this. I hadn't been able to find the right recipe in a cookbook, I told her. And the eggplant dishes I'd ordered in restaurants had been swimming in grease. I begged her to show me how she made hers.

I followed my mother from the stove to the counter to the sink and back again, tripping over myself to catch her movements and measurements. I threw out questions every five seconds: Do you preheat the skillet? How high is your flame? What kind of oil do you use? How much? A teaspoon? A tablespoon? "I don't know," my mother replied, swirling some into the pan. "This much."

When the oil popped, she added the pork. Had it been marinated? With what? For how long? My mother listed ingredients I'd never heard of, then tossed the eggplant into the pan. She coated the meat and vegetables with a mixture of water, soy sauce, sugar and chili paste. My questions continued: How much water? How much soy sauce? "About this much," my mother said, pointing to the skillet. "A spoonful. Two spoonfuls. Up to you."

Before I knew it, she was done, having transferred the food onto a serving plate. Was that it? If my mother had finished cooking, why was I no closer to a recipe? I sat at the table and reviewed my notes. They were incomplete. The phrases I'd scribbled? Illegible. My mother moved around the kitchen faster than I could write. She handled the spatula like a wand. The magician in her had outperformed the lab-coat technician in me. I laughed. It was all I could do.

Did I really think I could learn in 15 minutes something my mother had spent a lifetime doing? Cooking, my mother had said when we were young, wasn't the kind of work she needed us to do. Instead, she needed us to get good grades, go to college and land well-paying jobs when we grew up. In her mind, she'd envisioned a future where her children would be educated, successful, American. We could be architects, engineers, lawyers or executives. We would wear suits; we would do better for ourselves.

When my mother was my age, she'd met and married my father, immigrated to the United States and given birth to my brothers, sisters and me. She'd made a home for her husband and family. Where had I gone in my life so far? What had I accomplished?

Perhaps I thought I could be more like my mother, more considerate, more Chinese, less self-indulgent, if I could cook as an adult the way she cooked, if I could make the dishes she made. Perhaps I thought I could learn a thing or two about love and commitment, sacrifice and gratitude if I mastered her recipes. Those values were embedded in my mother's foods.

In my mind, perhaps I'd envisioned a future for myself where I, too, would have a husband and a family, when the time was right. I'd be responsible for other people; I'd consider their needs ahead of mine. I would share with them dishes I'd grown up eating and ones I'd learned to cook on my own. I would shop for the freshest ingredients; I would want the best for them.

I would serve them bowls of hearty congee or oatmeal in the mornings and prepare winter melon soup or clam chowder in the evenings. We would sit together at the table for dinner. My children would yammer away among themselves, ignoring my pleas for them to stop talking and finish eating. Some nights we would have fish steamed with ginger and green onion. Other nights we would have meatloaf. Some nights we would have braised pork spareribs. Other nights we would have stroganoff. We would be Chinese and American. I would know all the recipes.

Making a Connection Via the Kitchen

by John Kessler

from the *Atlanta Journal-Constitution*

Former chef, now chief restaurant reviewer for the *Journal-Constitution*, Kessler is one of a handful of gifted local writers who are vital players in their regional dining scenes.

I came home from school and there was an acrid, alien smell in the house. Something burning, fleshy, sharp.

I was 14. I put my book bag down in the front hall and hurried into the TV room, where my mother was in her usual position, sprawled on the sofa, watching the last few minutes of "General Hospital."

"What's that smell?" I demanded.

"Maybe it's the hamburger," she answered wanly, not taking her eyes from the screen.

"Oh, Mom," I moaned and rushed to the stove. Inside was a severely warped package of shrink-wrapped hamburger meat. Fat was bubbling under the plastic surface and blackish, greasy drops dripped to the oven floor.

When Mom forgot to thaw dinner in time, she sometimes turned the oven on to "warm" to speed the process. But today she had made a mistake: The oven was set to 350.

"I'll take care of dinner," I yelled from the kitchen.

"Thank you, sweetie," she called back.

I transferred the hamburger to the sink with two spatulas. I gingerly peeled off the plastic wrap and the deformed Styrofoam pan underneath. The sizzling meat on the edges smelled and tasted horrible, so I cut it back to the center, where it was still red and (ta-da) thawed.

Mom came into the kitchen after her show was over and surveyed the damage with a smile hovering on her lips. She wore a sleeveless sundress that tented over her round form. (Her bust line had gotten so voluminous she sometimes referred to it as her "ledge.") She stood there with her left wrist pressed to her hip and her hand splayed backward. Her hair was flyaway gray, and her cheek was cool and clammy when I gave her the perfunctory son's peck I knew she wanted.

"What's for dinner?" I asked.

"Spaghetti," she said with a low laugh, eyeing the curled Styrofoam in the sink.

I began frying onions and garlic in the old cast-iron skillet. Mom, complaining of a headache, went to lie down on the sofa with a Harlequin Romance novel. She read one a day, sometimes two. They arrived by the box at our front door. I crumbled the meat, which still smelled foul, into the pan. I added the cans of tomato and as many spices as I could find on the beige Lazy Susan next to the stove. I added oregano. I added curry.

Dad came home at 6:30, as he did every night. "I'm home," he bellowed from the front hall.

"We're having spaghetti," Mom called back. With her first show of energy, she heaved up from the sofa and went to meet him in the hall. They kissed with pursed lips, making the "mmmmm" sound.

I brought the big orange spaghetti bowl to the table, and we ate. It was a Simpsonsesque snarf, over in 20 minutes. Mom loved to eat. The sauce tasted a little like curried plastic, but it wasn't awful.

Dad, who had an iron palate, told her it was delicious.

I know now there were several reasons for my mother's depression. She had nearly died during open-heart surgery two years before. The recovery was hell.

But I think in retrospect, the main problem was she was lonely. All of her kids except me were off in college. Her teaching career was over. Her husband worked constantly, ironically, as a psychiatrist taking care of depressed people. Most of her friends had given up on her because she had gotten just too weird.

I was there for her but didn't quite know what to do to show her my love.

Except cook.

Dinner with Moth

by Brett Anderson

from *The Times-Picayune*

A high-profile food city like New Orleans needs and deserves a perspicacious yet unpretentious dining critic like Brett Anderson, who recently relocated there from Washington, D.C.

My first taste of Galatoire's came in the form of soufflé potatoes. I'd never encountered the oblong beauties before, and as I dipped each one carefully into a small dish of Creole bearnaise, our waiter brought out the rest of our appetizers—crab maison, shrimp remoulade, fried eggplant—with each plate balanced expertly along his forearm.

It was early January, a Friday lunch, and I had lived in New Orleans for less than three weeks. I couldn't have hoped for a better introduction to the stately old restaurant. My dining companion, an old-line regular, was well-known by the staff, who treated us like senators.

My friend handled all of the ordering duties without ever looking at a menu. For our main course, he deferred to the waiter, who steered him to a veal chop and me to trout meuniere, dishes rendered with the sort of faith and precision that Ella Fitzgerald brought to Cole Porter.

The brabant potatoes were nearly as delicious as their soufflé cousins (Let's be honest: Are any potatoes really as delicious as those crispy poufs?), and we washed it all back with iced Sazeracs and brandy milk punches. Cocktails at lunch!

I've since learned to love New Orleans, but I've rarely felt the intense, amused appreciation that I felt that day.

A week later, I hosted my first visitor. Gordy Aamoth—or Moth, my personal favorite of his many nicknames—was a high school buddy with whom I remained close through and after college, our friendship fueled by shared pasts, interests and acquaintances, as well as by our close proximity to each other on the East Coast.

This was not someone with a strong interest in cutting-edge food; I'd seen him thrown off his game by a menu that didn't offer plain old steak. A banker by trade and, in some ways, disposition, Moth nonetheless appreciated the implication of power that typically accompanies fine dining. He was also one of the most joyfully conversational people I've ever met. He flat-out loved to, as he put it, "be involved"—code for being close to the fun.

So while we didn't eat there when he visited in January, I told Moth about my Galatoire's lunch partly because it helped illustrate what little I knew about New Orleans at that point—a side of New Orleans I wanted to share—and partly because I knew he'd like the place. We stopped in for a drink, just to check it out, and made plans for his return trip this fall, a trip that was to be centered around a Louisiana State University football game and a soup-to-nuts Galatoire's expedition: a Friday lunch followed by no plans, just in case we decided to order another Sazerac or three and stick around for dinner.

Moth could accurately be described as a "sharp dresser," a phrase few people would use to describe me. He wanted me to buy a new suit for our meal.

"Anderson!" he howled when I talked to him a few weeks back about trip logistics. "We need to do this right!"

From the beginning, my hope was that Moth and I would have

an experience roughly akin to my first. He'd told me several times about a restaurant he particularly enjoyed in New York. It was not a famous place (I forget its name), but he enjoyed the fact that the staff knew him, that he could simply tell the waiters to bring out whatever looked good—just as my friend did at Galatoire's.

Most of all, of course, my intention was for the meal to be entertaining, and at first blush I recognized the quality of entertainment that Galatoire's could provide us. One of the joys of riding into middle age with friends from the pimple years is that you see the kid in one another even after the visual evidence has faded. A restaurant critic in New Orleans? My source of pride was Moth's source of amusement, and that reality would be our centerpiece at Galatoire's.

Moth understood this when we stopped in to look at the classic room downstairs, with its heavy curtains, classic cuisine and uniformed waiters. Moth had a taste for these things, but he also had a taste for the absurd. Our dinner would be both fulfilling and funny. The waiters would never know that beneath our 30-something exteriors we were still just 17.

A lot ran through my head on Sept. 11 as I watched both towers of the World Trade Center crumble on live television, knowing somehow in my heart that Moth was not, as he often was, away on business but in fact at work on the 104th floor of Tower 2. In those first few hours, I couldn't help but personalize the catastrophe to make it more digestible.

I was specifically heartbroken that we'd never share a plate of those potatoes.

I was angry, too, angry at the monsters who did this terrible thing.

I went to Galatoire's, hell-bent on eating the meal that they tried to take away.

My girlfriend gamely stood in for Moth. I knew that creating something akin to my first experience would be hard, and it was.

But it was still an epic meal, and not just because it took a surprising amount of courage to stage it. Even when it's hitting just half of its cues, Galatoire's is a place where adults are given license to have corny fun.

While poking forks into cool, firm, remoulade-coated shrimp, we enjoyed the fruits of a strange irony: For the first time since the tragedy occurred, we talked about something else. It took trying to wish Moth back into existence to forget that he was gone.

But the oblivion didn't last, thankfully. As I unfurled the inevitable Moth tales for my girlfriend, his memory gained flesh, which was the goal. I was not going to let terrorists keep me from dinner with my friend.

Why We Dine

by John Mariani

from esquire.com

One of the deans of American restaurant reviewing, New York–based Mariani has sat through innumerable restaurant meals over the years. It took a national tragedy to make him understand why what he does matters.

L ast Tuesday, I had a difficult time deciding whether I should dine out at a restaurant I had been assigned to review. Psychologically, I had no desire to go out; professionally, I felt bound to do so. Then I remembered what Winston Churchill said when told that the Germans had completely destroyed the city of Coventry. Seeming flippant but deadly serious, the old lion thought for a moment, then said, "Well, let's have lunch. Everything looks better after lunch."

That sentiment has always carried weight with me. Sitting down to a meal forces the harried mind to focus on a familiar ritual—in the disorienting wake of tragedy, eating is as close to "normal" as you're going to get. The appetite may flag, eating may be the last thing on one's mind, and fine dining seems downright frivolous. On the other hand, to restore one's appetite is to restore one's strength.

A year and a half ago, when I heard that my mother had passed away, I was tying my tie in a room at the Crillon Hotel in Paris, ready to go down to dinner. The news brought me to my knees. But after commiserating with my wife, I decided that dining would be the very best thing we could do. We went to dinner, sure that my mother, who gave me life, nurtured me as an infant, and imbued me with a love of good food, a woman who was a great hostess and loved nothing more than going out to a fine restaurant, would have insisted I do so. And so we ate very well and drank a very fine wine, toasting my mother as she so richly deserved.

As a food and travel writer, what I do for a living may seem odd to you—sometimes it seems odd to even me—but whenever I think of it as ephemeral to the great issues of the day, I am reminded of a scene from the play based on "The Diary of Anne Frank" in which the family members, isolated for months in an attic but still believing they will soon be out, fantasize about the first thing they'll do when they return to the world outside. Anne says she yearns to go to a dance. The teenage boy wants to go to a movie, a Western movie! And the adults all dream of a wonderful pastry shop, a good stew, a romantic restaurant with thick linen and fine wines. None, not one, declared that priority number one was to change the political structure of Europe.

This scene made me understand that deprivation of this kind steals not only freedom of movement, but also access to the sights, sounds, and tastes of life. For when all goes well, when the doctor cuts out the cancer, when debt is retired, when the debris is cleared away, returning to normal means returning to those things that make life worth living.

So I carry on extolling and criticizing our world's food culture, sometimes whimsically, sometimes with vitriol. For the importance of dining out, and drinking good wine, and lingering at the dinner table with loved ones is to enjoy all that terrorists—especially those whose fanaticism seeks to deprive people of all such "Western" pleasures—would seek to destroy. By indulging in life's passions, we do much more than live out our lives. We gain strength in the belief that they are part of the goodness of man.

Eat well, be well.

acknowledgments

We gratefully acknowledge all those who gave permission for written material to appear in this book. We have made every effort to trace and contact copyright holders. If an error or omission is brought to our notice we will be pleased to remedy the situation in future editions of this book. For further information, please contact the publisher.

"Let Us Now Praise Bacon" by Scott Raab. Copyright © 2001 by Scott Raab. Originally appeared in *Esquire*. Reprinted by kind permission of the author. ✤ "Elegance" by Megan Wetherall. Copyright © 2001 by Megan Wetherall. Originally appeared in *Saveur* Magazine. Reprinted by permission of Saveur. ✤ "Tomato Lust" by Gerri Hirshey. Copyright © 2001 American Express Publishing. Reprinted with permission of *Food & Wine* Magazine, September 2001. All rights reserved. ✤ "Cheeses for All Seasons" from *The Cheese Room* by Patricia Michelson. Copyright © 2001 by Patricia Michelson. Reprinted by permission of The Penguin Group UK. ✤ "War Fare" by Patricia Sharpe. Copyright © 2002 by Patricia Sharpe. Reprinted with permission from the January 2002 issue of *Texas Monthly*. ✤ "Hidden Charms" by Patric Kuh. Copyright © 2002 by Patric Kuh. Originally appeared in *Gourmet*. Used by permission of the author. ✤ "The Reviewer and the Recipe" by John Thorne. Copyright © 2002 by John Thorne. Originally appeared in *Simple Cooking* Newsletter, No. 75. Reprinted by kind permission of the author. ✤ "When the Path to Serenity Wends Past the Stove" by Regina Schrambling. Copyright © 2001 by The New York Times Agency. Reprinted by permission of The New York Times Agency. ✤ "Searching for Lillian" by Jeanne McManus. Copyright © 2002 by *The Washington Post*. Reprinted with permission. ✤ "Brownies: A Memoir" by Lisa Yockelson. Copyright © 2002 by Lisa Yockelson. Originally

Holly Hughes is a writer, the former executive editor of Fodor's Travel Publications and author of *Frommer's New York City with Kids*.

Submissions for Best Food Writing 2003

Submissions and nominations for *Best Food Writing 2003* should be forwarded no later than June 1, 2003, to *Best Food Writing 2003*, c/o Avalon publishing Group, 161 William Street, 16th floor, New York, NY 10038, or e-mailed to will.balliett@avalonpub.com. We regret that, due to volume, we cannot acknowledge receipt of all submissions.